How Healthcare Data Privacy Is Almost Dead ... and What Can Be Done to Revive It!

How Healthcare Data Privacy Is Almost Dead ... and What Can Be Done to Revive It!

John J. Trinckes, Jr.

CRC Press
Taylor & Francis Group
Boca Raton London New York

CRC Press is an imprint of the
Taylor & Francis Group, an **informa** business

AN AUERBACH BOOK

CRC Press
Taylor & Francis Group
6000 Broken Sound Parkway NW, Suite 300
Boca Raton, FL 33487-2742

Printed on acid-free paper
Version Date: 20161115

International Standard Book Number-13: 978-1-138-19775-6 (Hardback), 978-1-4987-8395-8 (Paperback)

Library of Congress Cataloging-in-Publication Data

Names: Trinckes, John J., Jr., author.
Title: How healthcare data privacy is almost dead ... and what can be done to revive it! / John Trinckes, Jr.
Description: Boca Raton : Taylor & Francis, 2017.
Identifiers: LCCN 2016035054| ISBN 9781138197756 (hb : alk. paper) | ISBN 9781498783958 (pb : alk. paper)
Subjects: | MESH: Health Information Management--methods | Computer Security | Electronic Health Records--standards | Medical Errors--prevention & control | Privacy | United States
Classification: LCC R864 | NLM WX 175 | DDC 651.5/042610285--dc23
LC record available at https://lccn.loc.gov/2016035054

Visit the Taylor & Francis Web site at
http://www.taylorandfrancis.com

and the CRC Press Web site at
http://www.crcpress.com

Contents

Foreword

Before the turn of this century, Scott McNealy (then CEO of Sun Microsystems) was quoted as saying: "[P]rivacy issues are a 'red herring.' You have zero privacy anyway. Get over it." Fast forward more than 15 years, and his (then) inflammatory comments have become prophecy of how the world has evolved. From the Patriot Act and government surveillance to the type of data collected by Google, Facebook, and ad networks along with the type of daily surveillance networks that are blanketing cities like London, we find that the concepts of privacy that our parents and grandparents held are becoming obsolete.

Nowhere is this trend more significantly affecting the world than healthcare. The industry is collecting many petabytes of information that never existed before—from the immense amount of data collected by providers for quality of care measures to advanced data like genetic information (e.g., 23 and Me), we are collecting data on humans that have never been able to be assessed in a scalable and centralized way. This is causing significant privacy impacts—we've had more than 100,000,000 healthcare records breached in the past few years. This is also increasing spending within the healthcare industry, causing the entire industry to slow down and implement massive sets of security controls.

This complexity makes it hard for the security experts the industry relies on to fully engage the problems. When I moved from the normal security industry to working on healthcare security and privacy issues, I was surprised at the immense amount of learning I had to undertake: terms like HIPAA, FDA quality regulations, meaningful use, statistically significant anonymization/de-identification, etc., were terms that I had to learn on the fly. Consideration for what these terms meant and how to deal with them I had to learn as well and until I understood all of the interactions of the various considerations, it was hard for me to have impact on moving the ball forward on innovation within the healthcare industry.

If this book had existed years ago when I went to work in healthcare, I could have short-cut that process immensely. Jay's book goes deep on all of the various competing interests around the healthcare industry—from governments to payers and providers and to doctors and patients, Jay goes deep on all of the things you need to know to really understand what the difficulties within the healthcare industry are.

And, more than anything, he lays out a strong case that shows why, if we truly have zero privacy, we will significantly impact our ability to have strong healthcare outcomes. This is a serious consideration on our ability to create a healthcare industry that actually innovates and improves the quantity and quality of our lives. That's no *red herring*.

Mike Murray*

* Mike Murray is the vice president of Security Research & Response for Lookout, a San Francisco–based mobile security company. Mike has more than a decade of experience managing information security consulting practices within organizations such as GE Healthcare and Neohapsis and as a managing partner for MAD security and The Hacker Academy. Mike has built global information security programs and has a proven track record of implementing results-driven security organizations that balance risks against business rewards. Mike prides himself on producing appropriate security outcomes from a business focus perspective by surrounding himself with great talent. Mike is also a professional speaker, author, social engineer, and triathlete.

Preface

With great power, comes great responsibility.

—Stan Lee

After some discussion with one of my contributing authors (and friend), Ramon Balut, and reading *Lights Out: A Cyberattack, A Nation Unprepared, Surviving the Aftermath*, written by Ted Koppel, I was inspired to write my third book. Koppel's book on the risks that our power grid faces from a cyberattack compelled me to look at healthcare from the same perspective. Balut's experiences and confirmations of conclusions that I've drawn myself about the healthcare industry also provided the spark of interest. Although I've been working in information security in the healthcare industry for some time and have witnessed the lack of care that most healthcare organizations place over the information they maintain, performing research for this book has opened my eyes to so much more. Privacy isn't only about keeping secrets or ensuring that your personal information isn't told to the world, it goes deeper than that; it is rooted in our souls and is the one specific element that makes us individuals.

Being a former law enforcement officer, I swore to support and protect the Constitution of the United States. Of course I read and studied this document in school and throughout my time in the police academy, but as you get older, you forget or sometimes distort the details.

Let's take *privacy* for example. As many Americans may believe, we have the right to privacy; however, nowhere in the text of the Constitution is *privacy* explicitly written. Of course, this right of privacy has developed over time from whence former Justice Louis Brandeis in 1890 expressed "a right to be left alone." It is inferred in the Constitution through the right of free assembly (First Amendment), right to be free of unwarranted searches or seizures (Fourth Amendment), protection from self-incrimination (Fifth Amendment), and the right of due process (Fourteenth Amendment). Several of these amendments have been interpreted by the Supreme Court in creating this right to privacy.

I could only assume that our forefathers didn't specifically enter *privacy* into the text of the Constitution since they believe that it was a God-given right and they didn't need to "spell it out." Some states, however, felt that the right of privacy did need further explanation. From my home state here in Florida, our State Constitution expressly provides for the Right of Privacy under Article I, Section 23, and states: "Every natural person has the right to be let alone and free from governmental intrusion into the person's private life except as otherwise provided herein. This section shall not be construed to limit the public's right of access to public records and meetings as provided by law" (State of Florida, 2016). It is interesting to note that this right to privacy is from *government intrusion* but doesn't limit large corporations from treading on your privacy. We'll see how this works in just a bit.

Furthermore, The General Assembly of the United Nations adopted the *Universal Declaration of Human Rights* on December 10, 1948. Article 12 addresses the right to privacy: "No one shall be subjected to arbitrary interference with his privacy, family, home or correspondence, nor to attacks upon his honour [sic] and reputation. Everyone has the right to the protection of the law against such interference or attacks" (Claiming Human Rights, 2016).

We have seen a rise of privacy policies and statements that are put out by all types of companies. We have seen enforcement of our privacy rights by the Federal Trade Commission, but *are we really protected from invasion into our private lives? Is the world we live in all just a facade like the world portrayed in the movie* The Matrix?

I'm sure a lot of you were required to read the George Orwell novel *1984* while in school. In his book, Orwell referred to the term "double-think." This term is defined as "the acceptance of or mental capacity to accept contrary opinions or beliefs at the same time, especially as a result of political indoctrination" (Google, 2016). *So, what is the relevance of this term on privacy you ask?* The term *private* has many definitions. What information you consider to be *private* isn't necessarily what is considered to be private by many, including several well-known (and large) corporations.

From the attribution given to Sir Francis Bacon in 1597 from his book, *Meditationes Sacrae and Human Philosophy,* the phrase "Knowledge is Power" and people love power. Thus, these people must obtain *knowledge*. To get this knowledge they must obtain *information*. In our technologically advanced age, this information comes in the form of *data*. This is how many companies build their business model and make money, on the back of your data. They need this data to grow and to become more powerful, but *why?* As Aral Balkan explains in his *Camera Panopticon* theory, they get data about the world and data about all of us, "And that's probably a useful tool for manipulating behavior, for even, depending on how good your lens is, in predicting the future and creating it" (Balkan, 2016).

Well, at least this data isn't in the hands of our government, *right?* The Defense Advanced Research Projects Agency (DARPA) created the Information Awareness Office after the terrorist attacks on the United States on September 11, 2001. Their original logo is shown in Figure P.1.

Symbolic is the "All-Seeing Eye" at the top of the pyramid looking over the entire Earth. Included in the logo is the Latin phrase "SCIENTIA EST POTENTIA" often translated to mean "Knowledge is Power." *Coincidence?* I think not. Due to public scrutiny, the Information Awareness Office appeared to have been shut down, or *was it?* Edward Snowden, former U.S. government contractor, shed some light on the fact that the National Security Agency (NSA) was collecting large amounts of private information on citizens. *How was the government getting this information?* According to Bruce Schneier, a renowned security expert and chief technology officer of Resilient Systems, "NSA surveillance largely piggybacks on corporate capabilities—through cooperation, through bribery, through threats and through compulsion. Fundamentally, surveillance is the business model of the Internet. The NSA didn't wake up and say let's just spy

Figure P.1   The original Information Awareness Office logo. (From https://cseweb.ucsd.edu/~goguen/courses/tia.html.)

on everybody. They looked up and said, 'Wow, corporations are spying on everybody. Let's get ourselves a cut'" (Chickowski, 2016).

So, *what is the mindset of these corporations that are supposed to be trusted to protect the privacy of your information?* Founder of Facebook, Mark Zuckerberg, when he started Facebook while at Harvard, explained to his friend that he had access to information on Harvard students due to his control over Facebook. In the exchange, he indicated that he had more than 4000 e-mails, pictures, addresses, etc. The friend asked him how he was able to get this information and Zuckerberg replied, "people just submitted it…I don't know why…they 'trust me'…dumb f**** [expletive]" (Vargas, 2016).

Former CEO of Google, Eric Schmidt, in an interview with CNBC back in 2009 responding to a question about sharing information with Google, said, "If you have something that you don't want anyone to know, maybe you shouldn't be doing it in the first place" (Esguerra, 2016). Unfortunately for these mega-corporations, privacy is "a fundamental human right…because privacy is fundamentally incompatible with their business models…all they can offer you is the *illusion of privacy*" (Balkan, 2016) (emphasis added). Since a lot of these "data collection" corporations are backed by venture capital, Balkan contends that "you've already [been] sold out…it's more than a lie…more than a con…it's also a monopoly, and that's what makes it so dangerous" (Balkan, 2016).

As you'll see throughout this book, I'm very passionate about information security and privacy. If I hadn't scared you off from the information presented to this point, we are going to further explore other issues of privacy as it specifically relates to our healthcare information. From medical identity theft to the use of medical devices, from the state of our healthcare security to the overwhelming number of breaches that are occurring within the healthcare industry, we are going to be transported to a place where our healthcare data privacy is just barely hanging on to life. *How Healthcare Data Privacy Is Almost Dead…And What Can Be Done to Revive It!* is a hard-hitting, no-holds-bar, in-your-face perspective of the struggles healthcare organizations are facing in trying to uphold their patients' rights to privacy. This book is a must read for anyone that gets medical attention, shares medical information, and for those organizations that are responsible for this data. It focuses on solutions and provides recommendations in an effort to advance the security posture of the healthcare industry while attempting to revive the importance over patient privacy.

At its core, the problem is that "in order to share something with your friend, you shouldn't also have to share it with a stranger. You should be able to share it directly with them… This is the future that we must build. This is the future that humanity deserves" (Balkan, 2016). Thank you for being willing to take this trip with me, but please stand clear, we are going to need to shock the life back into humanity.

> If you drop a frog in a pot of boiling water, it will of course frantically try to clamber out. But if you place it gently in a pot of tepid water and turn the heat on low, it will float there quite placidly. As the water gradually heats up, the frog will sink into a tranquil stupor, exactly like one of us in a hot bath, and before long, with a smile on its face, it will unresistingly allow itself to be boiled to death.
>
> **—Version of the story from Daniel Quinn's The Story of B (Wikipedia, 2016a)**

Acknowledgments

To my lord and savior, Jesus Christ, thank you for your blessings, although I know I'm not worthy.

To my loving wife, thank you for believing in me and providing me your support. I'm not sure why I'm so driven, but I know that with you by my side, anything is possible. I love you so much and thank you for being my soulmate.

To my daughter and son, thank you for allowing me the time to pursue these extra projects. I know it doesn't permit me to spend as much time as I would like with you both, but the time we do have together is just all the more precious.

To my publisher and all the staff at CRC Press, thank you for believing in me and giving me another opportunity to share my inspirations.

To my contributing authors (Ray, Mike, and others), thank you. This book would not have been the same without your assistance, expertise, and, above all else, commitment to the cause.

In Remembrance of All the Untold Victims

From The Glider: A Universal Hacker Emblem, Retrieved from
http://www.catb.org/hackeremblem/, June 7, 2016.

Author

John "Jay" Trinckes, Jr. (CISSP, CISM, CRISC, CCSFP, CDA, NSA-IAM/IEM, MCSE-NT, A+) is a practice director of the Healthcare and Life Sciences Practice at Coalfire Systems, Inc. He is the author of *The Definitive Guide to Complying with the HIPAA/HITECH Privacy and Security Rules* and *The Executive MBA in Information Security*, both published by CRC Press. Trinckes leads efforts in developing standards and product/service offerings and performing highly technical compliance assessments for a wide variety of healthcare organizations across the country. Trinckes has been instrumental in developing audit plans, compliance assessments, business impact analyses, business continuity, and disaster recovery plans and has conducted security/privacy awareness training for several different clients. Trinckes has presented on the topics of HIPAA, privacy, and other related information security matters as a professional speaker across several leading nationally recognized healthcare industry associations.

Trinckes is a Certified Information Systems Security Professional (CISSP), a Certified Information Security Manager (CISM), Certified in Risk and Information Systems Control (CRISC), a HITRUST CSF Practitioner (CCSFP), and HITRUST Certified De-Identification Associate (CDA). He holds certifications in the National Security Agency (NSA) INFOSEC Assessment Methodology (IAM) and

INFOSEC Evaluation Methodology (IEM), along with Microsoft Certified Systems Engineer (MCSE-NT) and Comptia A+ Certifications. Trinckes provides a unique perspective to compliance as a result of his previous executive-level work experience as a chief information security officer for both a profit and nonprofit managed healthcare service provider along with his past experience as a business owner, healthcare security consultant, information security risk analyst, IT manager, system administrator, and law enforcement officer.

Trinckes graduated with a bachelor's degree in business administration/management information systems from the Union Institute and University with a 4.0 GPA and is always staying up to speed with new trends within the healthcare industry. Trinckes is a current member of the Information Systems Audit and Controls Association (ISACA®) and the International Information Systems Security Certification Consortium (ISC²).

When Trinckes isn't consulting or writing books, he likes to spend his spare time with his wife and kids, cruising on his CanAm Spyder RT motorcycle, cooking, and working out. Trinckes can be reached for comments related to this book at hitechpo@windstream.net.

Contributing Author

Ramon Balut, CISSP, has more than 20 years of experience in health-care information systems and security as well as with electronic medical record (EMR) development and deployment.

Ray has worked within several national, regional, and local not-for-profit and university environments, including Sutter Health in California, Adventist Health in Orlando, and the University of VA and MedStar Health in Washington, DC.

Ray received his BS in computer and information systems from King's College and his master's in information security and assurance from Western Governors University. He has had the opportunity to speak on the topic of information security at Georgetown University, Brown University, and Pennsylvania State University.

Ray's current certifications include

- CISM (Certified Information Security Manager)
- CISSP-ISSMP (Certified Information System Security Professional)
- CEH (Certified Ethical Hacker)
- CHFI (Certified Hacking Forensics Investigator)

1

CODE BLUE

Privacy is not about whether or not you have something to hide. It's about having the right to choose what you want to keep to yourself—and what you want to share with others.

—**Aral Balkan (Balkan, 2016)**

Erroneous Information

It was another beautiful day in Florida as Dr. Smith, a new physician intern, was preparing his rounds. Dr. Smith logged onto his computer and pulled up the record of his first patient in his hospital's electronic medical record software. Going through the patient's notes, he noted that the patient was a "status post BKA (below the knee amputation)." He read through other parts of the record to get a good understanding and medical background of his patient. Being a new doctor, Dr. Smith took special care in knowing his patients. He also tried very hard to impress his attending physician, Dr. Jones. Dr. Smith had already figured out a diagnosis for the symptoms his patient was complaining about as Dr. Jones met him at the patient's door.

Dr. Jones is an "old school" doctor and doesn't necessarily care for the new records' technology. He would rather talk to the patient to get to know them first as opposed to relying solely on the data in the electronic medical record.

"Good morning, Dr. Jones," Dr. Smith called out as he continued to type away on the computer.

"Good morning, Dr. Smith. Who do we have to see this morning?"

"This is Mr. Ford. He is complaining of flu-like symptoms and he is also a status post BKA," Dr. Smith responded.

1

The senior attending physician, Dr. Jones, asked, "Oh, *how do you know he is status post BKA?*"

Looking up from his keyboard, Dr. Smith explained, "Mr. Ford's several past discharge notes all indicated this status, and based on the symptoms he is currently presenting, I think I know his diagnosis."

"Okay," Dr. Jones replied, "let's go check the patient out."

As the doctors entered the room, they found the patient up on the exam bed with two perfectly working feet. With a surprise, Dr. Smith questioned, "*How is this possible?*"

Dr. Jones responded with a sigh, "Technology."

*****

Although the names in this story are fictional, the story was based on true events. As it turned out, the patient was seen in the hospital many times and on a prior visit, the voice recognition dictation system used to assist physicians with entering their notes into the electronic medical record solution misunderstood DKA (diabetic ketoacidosis) as "B"KA. The physicians that reviewed the medical record before didn't catch the error and it had become a permanent part of the patient's record (Hsleh, 2016).

No harm came to the patient and the error was easily fixed, but what about the horror stories we hear on the news of surgery mishaps where wrong organs or body parts are removed from patients? "Over a period of 6.5 years, doctors in Colorado alone operated on the wrong patient at least 25 times and on the wrong part of the body in another 107 patients, according to the study, which appears in the Archives of Surgery" (Gardner, 2016). When new physicians are only spending about eight (8) minutes of their time with patients, while in contrast they spend 40% of their time utilizing the information systems, one may see why we hear about stories of patients dying from allergic reactions to drugs that were incorrectly reported in their medical records. *Or how about people being wrongly diagnosed?* (Figure 1.1).

In 2004, Trisha Torrey, now a patient advocate, was diagnosed with an "aggressive, deadly cancer, and six months to live unless I got the necessary chemo to buy myself an extra year" (*Share Your Story— Medical Errors*, 2016). Trisha took it upon herself to learn all she

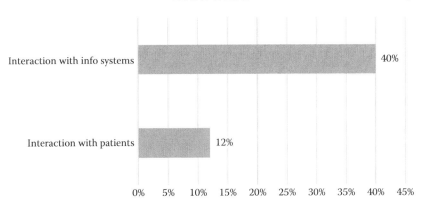

Figure 1.1 Comparison of hospital interns' time spent with patients versus interaction with information systems. (From Gunderman, R., The drawbacks of data-driven medicine, Retrieved from *The Atlantic*, http://www.theatlantic.com/health/archive/2013/06/the-drawbacks-of-data-driven-medicine/276558/, May 29, 2016.)

could about the diagnosis and the lab results that led up to it. After learning more and deciphering some of the results, Trisha was convinced she didn't have cancer, but the battle was on to prove it. After fighting a system that didn't want to admit that they were wrong, the final word came down upon a review of an expert from the National Institute of Health that finally put the issue to rest. Years later, Trisha never had a treatment and now speaks, performs broadcasting activities, and writes for About.com and Every Patient's Advocate (http://trishatorrey.com) to improve patients' outcomes.

A study "from doctors at Johns Hopkins, suggests medical errors may kill more people than lower respiratory diseases like emphysema and bronchitis do" (Christensen, 2016). If this is true, medical mistakes would be just behind heart disease and cancer as the third leading cause of death in the United States. Estimates indicate "there are at least 251,454 deaths due to medical errors annually in the United States" (Christensen, 2016). Most of these errors can be contributed by human or technology errors related to miscommunications substantiating the fact that we have a serious issue on our hands.

Not only can errors be propagated through an individual's own medical record, but with the number of individuals seeking healthcare services, we need to be concerned with records being mixed up. In another case, two individuals with the same first and last name were seen in a provider's office at the same time. Confusion occurred and procedures were performed on the wrong patient. According to Chief Executive Officer Lynn Thomas Gordon of the American Health Information Management Association (AHIMA), "Accurately matching the right information with the right patient is crucial to reducing potential patient safety risks. At the very foundation of patient care is the ability to accurately match a patient with his or her health information" (Davis, 2016a). In a survey conducted on eight hundred fifteen (815) AHIMA members using a dozen different electronic medical record solutions, less than half indicated they had a quality assurance process in place during or after the registration process to ensure patients are matched to their appropriate records along with minimizing or correcting duplicate records.

The survey indicated that fifty-five percent (55%) of the respondents had policies related to duplicate records, but no standards on how these duplication rates factored into their organization. Only forty-three percent (43%) indicated they utilize patient matching in metrics to measure data quality. The survey authors state, "Reliable and accurate calculation of the duplicate rate is foundational to developing trusted data, reducing potential patient safety risks and measuring return on investments for strategic healthcare initiatives" (Davis, 2016a).

Of course patient safety is the top concern for matching the appropriate medical records to the right patient, but it is also a financial burden. Marc Probst, the chief information officer for Intermountain Health, a healthcare system based in Utah, indicated his organization spends $4–$5 million annually on costs associated with administration and technology related to accurately matching records. Probst states, "As we digitize healthcare and patients move from one care setting to another, we need to ensure with 100 percent accuracy that we identify the right patient at the right time. Anything less than that increases the risk of a medical error and can add unnecessary costs to the healthcare system" (McGee, 2016a).

It sort of makes sense that we should have a primary "key" or identifier that could be utilized to ensure all medical records associated to you are accurately matched back to you, *right? Why didn't anyone think about this before?* Well, Congress did and called for the creation of a unique health identifier for individuals when it passed the Health Insurance Portability and Accountability Act (HIPAA) of 1996.

In response to privacy concerns, however, three years later, Congress prohibited the funding of this identifier.

Unfortunately, the failure to match records accurately and without a standard employed across the entire healthcare system has led to patient safety and privacy concerns. Accordingly to a RAND Corporation study, "providers on average incorrectly match records and patients about 8% of the time, costing the U.S. health care system about $8 billion annually" (The Advisory Board Company, 2016). Issues range from minor inconveniencies to all-out fatal results. A report published in the *Journal of Patient Safety* titled *Electronic Health Record-Related Events in Medical Malpractice Claims* provided a plethora of case examples where someone was harmed due to a related electronic medical record error and a lawsuit occurred. "Considerably over 80% of the reported errors involve horrific patient harm: many deaths, strikes, missed and significantly delayed cancer diagnoses, massive hemorrhage, 10-fold overdoses, ignored or lost critical lab results, etc." (Koppel, 2016). As seen in Figure 1.2, users are more commonly to blame than systems; however, in some cases,

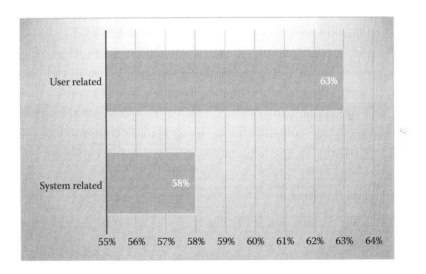

Figure 1.2 System-related versus user-related issues (total of 248 cases). (From Mark Graber, D.S., Electronic health record-related events in medical malpractice claims, Retrieved from *Journal of Patient Safety*, http://pdfs.journals.lww.com/journalpatientsafety/9000/00000/Electronic_Health_Record_Related_Events_in_Medical.99624.pdf?token=methodIExpireAbsolute;sourceIJournals;ttlI 1463323186055;payloadImY8D3u1TCCsNvP5E421JYK6N6XICDamxByyYpaNzk7FKjTaa1Yz22MivkHZ qjGP, May 15, 2016.)

there were multiple factors that led to harm. To be fair, most of these examples weren't directly related to a matching error, but these do demonstrate the extent and complexities of the issues as the healthcare industry was so quickly forced to turn over to technologies that may not have been thoroughly vetted.

For these reasons, organizations are calling for Congress to assist in the implementation of a national patient identifier and why the College of Healthcare Information Management Executives (CHIME) has launched a $1 million competition with HeroX, a crowdsourcing site, to encourage innovators in developing a national patient identifier solution. According to CHIME's CEO Russell Branzell, the identification system "could be a number, a complex software/algorithmic system, it could be biometric, using handprints or some other characteristic" (The Advisory Board Company, 2016).

This may sound like an easy task, but it is much more involved than one would think. Since there is no current standard in place for entering individuals' names or other demographic information, it becomes very difficult to ensure that individuals are appropriately identified. Most providers use algorithms that employ several pieces of personal information like a Social Security number, date of birth, and name to match these records. *What happens if a name is spelled wrong or a number is mistyped in a record? How does this record get matched to the appropriate individual?* This task becomes even more difficult when privacy and security concerns must be considered and built into the solution from the start. Some would argue that it makes the healthcare system more private since "a key step to securing private information is determining whom it belongs to" (The Advisory Board Company, 2016). Others believe that the issue with privacy really involves the lack of regulations over data brokers and not patient identification itself. The $1 million prize is planned to be awarded in February 2017 to an individual, group, or organization that can develop a working prototype.

Medical Identity Theft

Being an older gentleman, Mr. Johnson was in great health. It had been a windy fall and leaves were collecting in his rain gutters. It was a sunny Monday morning and Mr. Johnson felt the urge to clean out these gutters before the winter snow set in. Mr. Johnson secured his ladder to the roof and began the tedious task of removing the leaves. After an hour or two, Mr. Johnson's back started to hurt. Pain shot up from the middle of his back up through his arms. It got so bad that he had to stop cleaning and drive himself to the emergency room.

Dr. Clarke, the attending physician, walked into the exam room and said, "Good afternoon, Mr. Johnson. What brings you into the emergency room?"

"I was cleaning out my rain gutters and must have pulled something in my back. I've got a lot of pain that radiates into my arm," Mr. Johnson explained, holding tears back in his eyes.

"Let's order you an x-ray and see what we can find," responded Dr. Clarke.

The x-ray results came back and nothing was broken. "It appears you have a muscle sprain. I'm also a little concerned with your temperature; it is a little high. It looks like you may also have a mild infection. I'm going to prescribe a muscle relaxer for your pain and it looks like we've given you penicillin before when you came here last time," Dr. Clarke stated.

Mr. Johnson looked confused, "*Last time?* I've never been here before in my life! AND I'm allergic to penicillin. What are you trying to do doc, *kill me?*"

Come to find out, someone utilized Mr. Johnson's insurance card, after he had previously lost it and the insurance company replaced it with the same number, to obtain medication and other services at the hospital. Although the names and events were changed, this story was based on actual events (Shin, 2016).

In another example, Katrina Brooke was enjoying the time with her new baby boy when three weeks after having him, she received a bill from a local health clinic addressed to her baby. The bill was for a prescription painkiller related to a back injury. After calling the clinic, it was confirmed that someone used her baby's personal information to obtain services only a week after the baby was born. The clinic agreed to waive the charges (Rys, 2016).

In this case, it was easy to resolve the situation, but for other victims of medical identity theft it is more difficult. Anndorie Sachs, a mother of four, received a call from a social worker notifying her that her newborn tested positive to methamphetamines. The social worker notified Sachs her children were going to be taken into protective custody. Sachs hadn't given birth in more than two years, but did lose her driver's license that was utilized by Dorothy Bell Moran. Moran was on drugs and used Sachs's name to give birth to a newborn. Sachs was able to keep her kids after several calls and hired an attorney to assist in recovering from any damages caused by the theft of her identity.

Sachs thought her problems were solved, but months later after being seen for a kidney infection, even though she avoided going to the hospital where Moran gave birth, Sachs found errors in her medical record. Her emergency contact and blood type were wrong. Sachs notified the staff and the error was immediately corrected, but with a blood-clotting disorder, a mistake in any medication given could have been deadly (Rys, 2016).

In another example, a psychiatrist, in order to gain more money from submitting false claims, entered false diagnoses into medical records for different disorders such as drug addiction and depression. The issue was finally caught, but not before a victim discovered the false diagnosis when he applied for a job (U.S. v. Skodnek, 933 F.Supp. 1108; 1996 U.S. Dist. LEXIS 9788 [D. Mass. 1996]).

Medical identity theft can occur by multiple suspects for several different purposes. Family members who know personal information of their relatives may utilize this information to obtain costly medical services when they may not have insurance. Drug addicts or dealers could obtain prescription drugs by utilizing identities of individuals with insurance. Insiders may use information to commit billing fraud or sophisticated scams that may target Medicare, which could be perpetrated by organized criminal groups.

The Ponemon Institute conducts an annual survey on privacy and security of healthcare data. According to Ponemon, "When we first started doing this survey and asked about medical identity theft, people would shrug their shoulders and say what is that?" (Raths, 2016). Figure 1.3, according to the *Sixth Annual Benchmark Study on Privacy and Security of Healthcare Data* conducted by the Ponemon Institute issued May 2016, provides some interesting information.

"At least it is now on the radar screen, but that doesn't mean they [healthcare organizations/business associates] have a plan in place to help the victim. Medical ID theft seems to be an increasing issue, and someone has to be accountable for it," Ponemon states (Raths, 2016).

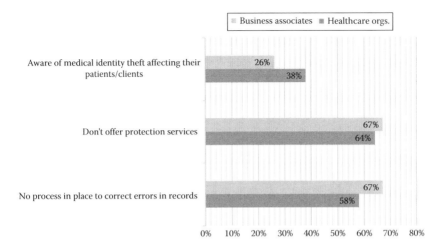

Figure 1.3 Responses to medical identity theft. (From Raths, D., Sixth annual ponemon survey: Criminal attacks cause 50% of breaches, Retrieved from Healthcare Informatics, http://www. healthcare-informatics.com/article/sixth-annual-ponemon-survey-criminal-attacks-cause-50-breaches?utm_source=feedburner&utm_medium=feed&utm_campaign=Feed%3A+healthcare-informatics+%28Healthcare+Informatics%29, May 27, 2016.)

Credit Troubles

Credit makes the world go around. Or should I say *debt* makes the world go around because that is actually what having credit is all about, *debt*. My wife has become very good at playing the "credit game." Yes folks, it is a game, or should I be more professional in calling it a "process." When my wife and I first got together, we didn't make a lot of money. We were getting by, but it was hard. Not to worry, the creditors swooped in for the rescue giving us credit cards, credit lines, car loans, and department store charge accounts. We were just starting out and neither of us was really taught how to manage our money. There was never any "credit" course taught in school or how not to get into trouble with these financial accounts. We only had to make a small monthly payment to keep them in good standing, *right*? After a few months of making these payments, the limits on the accounts automatically grew, allowing us to spend more, or should I say get into more debt. We thought we were doing pretty well when we had a high FICO score; this meant we could get even more credit. When people say they are "drowning in debt," literally, this is what it feels like.

Although not one of the proudest moments of our lives, we dismissed our mountain of debt through bankruptcy. We aren't bad people and we didn't take advantage of the situation. We were young and didn't know better. Lesson learned. For over a decade later, we pretty much had to live by cash only. Not a bad thing, but definitely more difficult than being showered with credit offers after credit offers. Our motto turned out to be that *if we couldn't pay for it with cash, we didn't need it.* This was a blessing and a curse. As we started to do better financially and moved up the career ladder, we still couldn't escape the fact that we needed credit. Credit determined where we could live, what we could drive, and of course what we could buy. I believe it also determined what potential jobs were available to us. *How many companies do a background check that includes a credit review?*

The answer: everything in moderation. We swore off credit for the longest time and still do, but we now understand that to live in this world, you need to have good credit. My wife, more so than me, learned the tips and tricks to improving the credit score. Through some trial and error, she learned specific times to make payments, what limits should be set, and how much should be charged. We never charge more than what we can pay, so our motto of buying things "You can pay with cash" is still valid, but the methods we actually pay for these items have changed. We may "charge" the item through one credit card as opposed to using our bank card, but pay this balance at the end of the month. Of course, we need to keep a little on the card to make it appear that the credit card company is making a little finance charge (i.e., a little money) off of us. If the financial company isn't making money, they won't give you the card. It is all perspective. Credit is a lot like a plant; you have to nurture it to grow.

I share this personal story only to emphasize how important credit has become and the damage that can be caused if someone runs amuck with your credit. It took us a long time to repair our credit and it cost us a lot more with additional finance charges. We now monitor our credit on a continuous basis to ensure that the information is accurate and is kept in good standing.

Of course during our times of financial trouble, the debt collectors were calling. Cell phones were gaining in popularity; however, they didn't replace the home phone like they do today. There was very little protection from the bombardment of calls received. Now, we have the Telephone Consumer Protection Act (TCPA) that, among other items, makes it "unlawful for any person to make any call (other than a call made for emergency purposes or made with express prior consent) using any automatic telephone dialing system or any artificial or prerecorded voice message to wireless numbers" (Federal Communications Commission, 2016). Recently, however, the express prior consent portion of this rule came into question.

In 2008, the express consent was deemed granted only if the consumer provided the creditor with their wireless number and only related to the debt that was owed. The burden was on the creditor to show that they received the necessary express consent. Fast forward to 2014, the Federal Communications Commission interpreted the rules to allow creditors to utilize a wireless number through the express consent of an intermediary. There was a stipulation that actual consent still must be obtained and that the intermediary couldn't provide this consent on behalf of another party.

Mount Carmel Hospital in Columbus, Ohio, obtained signed consent forms as a part of their admission process that indicated they could use the information provided by the patient "for [as] many reasons as needed." Another consent form used was more specific in that patients allowed the release of their health information to companies that provided billing services in connection with their treatment. The hospital provided cell phone numbers to their anesthesiologists based on this consent and the anesthesiologists provided the cell phone numbers to the debt collectors. Even though the debt collectors never "directly" received the cell phone number from the patient, the Sixth Circuit held that the debt collectors did not violate the TCPA. "The Sixth Circuit held that the hospital did not violate the TCPA because the patients had given their 'prior express consent' to receive collection calls on their cell phones when they provided their cell phone information to the hospital" (Wolin, 2016).

In summary, if you don't want someone to call you on your cell phone, don't give your number out. As a provider, if you want to utilize cell phone information to contact the patient, ensure that the patient provides consent to utilize their phone and that they are made aware of the use of the information they provide. Be vigilant in monitoring your credit reports and respect your credit.

Internet of Things

> There is no Internet of Things. There is only the Internet of Data.

> **—Aral Balkan (Balkan, 2016)**

From a vision of interconnected computers known as the "Galactic Network" written down in a series of memos by J.C.R. Licklider of MIT in August of 1962, the underlying idea of the Internet was born. Heading the computer research program at the Defense Advanced Research Projects Agency (DARPA), Licklider was able to convince Ivan Sutherland, Bob Taylor, and Lawrence G. Roberts that this concept of networking was important. They had to do something that was not done before—make two computers talk to each other. In 1965, Roberts, with the help of Thomas Merrill, connected a TX-2 computer in Massachusetts to a Q-32 computer in California across a telephone line. Unfortunately, the circuit switching capabilities of the telephone systems at that time were inadequate to handle the packets by which the computers communicated.

Roberts went to DARPA in 1966 and plans were started for the Advanced Research Projects Agency Network (ARPANET). The first node to join ARPANET was the Network Measurement Center at UCLA in September 1969. The Stanford Research Institute (SRI) provided a second node. One month later, the first host-to-host message was sent. Two additional nodes, one from UC Santa Barbara and one from the University of Utah, were connected giving birth to the Internet (Internet Society, 2016).

From its earliest beginning, the Internet was intended for research and sharing of information, data, applications, ideas, etc. It was never intended or built with security in mind. Security was an afterthought and the founding developers of the Internet could not have imagined what the Internet has become today. Security for the Internet is an add-on or a plug-in. Sometimes it works and sometimes it doesn't. Just like most things that are bolted on or added later, without a good foundation, these additional items often times don't work out as well as those that are baked into the original platform itself.

Fast forward to the present day, from a NBC News report July 2, 2015, the American Registry for Internet Numbers (ARIN), the organization that issues Internet Protocol (IP) addresses in North America, has run out of numbers to assign (Johnson, 2016). For those that don't know what an IP address is, this is the number that identifies every device on the Internet. It is synonymous with a telephone number and for any device to connect or communicate with another device, it must be assigned an IP address on the Internet. This is pretty significant in that the highest possible number of devices assigned an IP address under the current standing IPv4 addressing scheme is 4.3 billion. This means that we have met this threshold in just over thirty (30) years since the Internet was developed. *So what happens now?* Not to fear, IPv6 is here. With 340 trillion trillion trillion possible addresses, the Internet will be able to grow even larger.

Some may say this a good thing since we have dawned the age of the "Internet of Things" (IoT). Per a *Wired magazine* article titled *The Internet of Things Is Far Bigger than Anyone Realizes*, Daniel Burrus writes, "The Internet of Things revolves around increased machine-to-machine communication; it's built on cloud computing and networks of data-gathering sensors; it's mobile, virtual, and instantaneous connection; and they say it's going to make everything in our lives from streetlights to seaports 'smart'" (Burrus, 2016b).

Other security and privacy experts may say (and I'm one of them) that the convenience of making our lives "smarter" isn't necessarily a good thing. When the smartphone devices used by an estimated 3.4 billion people out of the world's population of 7.3 billion know almost everything about you, where you are, where you've been, who you were with, or maybe who you plan to vote for in the upcoming election, then maybe we *might have an issue with privacy*.

Take for instance Dstillery, a company that sells data intelligence for targeted advertising. As we are in the midst of the presidential primary elections while I'm performing research for this book, I found it interesting to note that this company is using their technology to track voters' behaviors. Tom Phillips, CEO of Dstillery, states, "We watched each of the caucus locations for each party and we collected mobile device ID's…It's a combination of data from the phone and data from other digital devices" (Ryssdal, 2016). *Are they able to predict election results?* Maybe not as of yet since correlation doesn't always indicate causation, but there were some interesting items discovered in Iowa, such as individuals that loved to grill, do yard work, or watched or supported NASCAR voted for Donald Trump. There were some unexpected results such as those that watched or supported NASCAR also supported Hillary Clinton. As Elad Yoran, executive chairman of Koolspan, Inc., states, "You can extract enough information on a typical person's phone that you can construct a virtual clone of that individual" (Storhm, 2016).

This is one of the reasons why law enforcement investigators, namely, the Federal Bureau of Investigations (FBI), are in a battle with Apple Inc.: to follow a court order demanding Apple to unlock the iPhone of the shooter in the San Bernardino, CA, massacre of fourteen (14) coworkers back in December. Although I was a former law enforcement officer and understand the rationale behind the request, as a security and privacy professional, I also understand the ramification of the request. As Apple warns, "anything it does to override the encryption of its smartphones could help hackers" (Storhm, 2016). Hackers don't need any more help in this area, *really*—they do a pretty good job already.

From an article written by Dylan Love titled *Hackers Love the Internet of Things Because Security Doesn't Sell Toasters*: "Businesses spend time and money on speed and convenience because that's ultimately what consumers want. Security seems to mostly matter when it fails. This approach might be best summed up as 'no harm, no foul'" (Love, 2016). From the same article, Dan Guido, CEO of a cybersecurity research and development firm Trail of Bits, indicated that "if you want to break into an iPhone or into Internet Explorer, it takes months of effort. If you want to break into the latest Wi-Fi-enabled scale, it takes one week with no prior experience" (Love, 2016). The article goes on to say that compromising modern IoT devices is known around network security circles as "junk hacking" since it is pretty unremarkable.

Big pharmaceutical companies are seeing the opportunities within the "Medical Internet of Things." Novartis, a Swiss drug company, has teamed up with Qualcomm, a U.S. technology firm, "to develop an internet-connected inhaler that can send information about how often it is used to remote computer servers known as the cloud" (Reuters, 2016). The company sees huge potential with "Big Data" as it relates to the "huge amounts of information about a medical condition and the efficacy of a drug or device being wirelessly transmitted to a database from potentially thousands, even millions, of patients" (Reuters, 2016).

Novartis is not the only pharmaceutical company teaming up with tech firms. Roche, a domestic rival of Novartis, has also teamed up with Qualcomm, Novo Nordisk (a Danish diabetes drug manufacturer) is working with IBM, and Medtronic (the world's largest medical device manufacturer) is partnering with Glooko, a U.S. data-analytics company. Qualcomm appears to also be discussing a potential $1 billion joint venture with GlaxoSmithKline. With these types of opportunities come some risks. Rick Valencia, senior vice president of Qualcomm Life, said, "[Medical Devices] weren't designed with the idea that they would be going over the network and the information would be residing in cloud infrastructure" (Reuters, 2016). Unfortunately, this is just increasing the vast amount of confidential and personal information being stored in databases somewhere on remote servers in the "cloud."

What if doctors can obtain critical health information from a patient relayed wirelessly from a device that is smaller than a grain of rice and that can dissolve after a few days? Does this sound like a sci-fi story? Well, these transient sensors (essentially being made up of elements and minerals that we are already used to eating or drinking) could transform the way doctors "can measure pressure, temperature, pH, motion, flow, and potentially specific biomolecules" (Mole, 2016). As opposed to attaching patients to wires that must be removed, which could increase the risks of infections, these sensors could transmit information wirelessly to a device that sits on top of the skin. Rory Murphy, chief resident of neurosurgery at Washington University School of Medicine, and colleagues teamed up with John Rogers' group at the University of Illinois at Urbana–Champaign. "The researchers successfully implanted devices that measured temperature and pressure from inside the rat's brain and transmitted the information wirelessly" (Mole, 2016). Showing this concept is possible, they hope the technology will be ready for human testing in three (3) to four (4) years.

In a related article titled *Wi-Fi Standard Could Make Internet of Things Things Even Easier … for Hackers,* John Leyden writes about a new Wi-Fi standard known as 802.11ah, or commonly referred to as *HaLow,* which has been touted as the wireless technology standard for the "Internet of Things." Rather than utilizing dedicated gateways, this new standard has the ability to build wireless functionality within home routers themselves. It also significantly improves

Wi-Fi distance and lower power usage. Although these improvements appear to be great on the surface, for attackers this means that they no longer need sophisticated antennas for "drive-by" wireless attacks. It can also mean that low power usages imply low processing power that could lead to manufacturers of IoT devices cutting corners in security. As all of these devices are interconnected to networks, once a device is compromised on that network, it could lead to a compromise of other devices on that same network (Leyden, 2016). *How many home users have the technical skills to segregate or isolate IoT networks from other devices on their home network? How many home users have the network knowledge to appropriately configure their wireless network in a secure fashion?*

What if the security devices that we purchase to keep us secure are actually not as secure themselves? Let's take webcams for example. A lot of individuals purchase these security-related cameras to help us protect our homes or maybe we purchase them to keep an eye on our sleeping babies. Now comes Shodan, a search engine that allows users to search any type of Internet-connected devices. This includes being able to search for cameras that are connected to the Internet that may use the Real-Time Streaming Protocol (RTSP). Without getting too technical, this protocol generally runs on port 554 and may share video streams without requiring a password to authenticate the user. By utilizing Shodan, one may be able to view the video feed of cameras of unsuspecting individuals. According to Dan Tentler, a security researcher who has investigated webcam security over the past several years "estimates there are now millions of such insecure webcams connected and easily discoverable with Shodan. That number will only continue to grow" (Porup, 2016).

It was coincidental while performing research for this book, I was alerted by one of my associated security researchers that they just saw a disturbing image while perusing the Shodan search engine. They provided the following link: https://www.shodan.io/host/189.70.248.193. I went to the site to see what all the fuss was about and discovered, to my own dismay, an image of a screen showing an x-ray image. The screen I was viewing was apparently found in the Shodan search engine looking for devices that were operating virtual network computing (VNC—a remote desktop solution) running on port 5900 with no authentication required. This means that anyone could obtain access to this device and operate it just as though you were physically standing in front of the computer itself. It appeared that this system was an x-ray device currently being used to image a patient. The device appeared to be located in Brazil and the patient name also appeared to be present on the image.

In another example of security systems themselves being vulnerable, a report in Forbes indicated that possibly more than 300,000 customers of a "smart" alarm provider, SimpliSafe, may be vulnerable to burglaries. This company makes home security alarm products that can warn customers via cellular technology. Dr. Andrew Zonenberg, a senior security consultant at IOActive, indicates that these alarm systems may be turned off at a distance of up to two hundred (200) yards. In addition, the alarms were installed with a chip that may not be able to be patched or updated to correct the flaw discovered. Although Zonenberg indicates that an attacker would need to purchase their own SimpliSafe system along with other devices for under $50, within a few hours' work, a criminal could develop a solution to circumvent the security system. This could be done by harvesting the PINs entered to enable or disable the alarm and basically replay the PINs in the vicinity of the system. SimpliSafe responded to the reported flaw by indicating they were going to release firmware that could be updated and that a customer would receive notification that their alarm was deactivated. In addition, PINs can be changed by the customer at any time making the recorded PINs void (Fox-Brester, 2016).

If you are one of those cautious individuals when it comes to utilizing the Internet, you are not alone. In a recent survey of 41,000 U.S. households conducted by the Department of Commerce's National Telecommunications and Information Administration (NTIA) collected in July 2015 by the U.S. Census Bureau with households reporting having at least one Internet user, concerns over privacy and security have changed the behavior of almost half of the respondents. Basic Internet activities like buying online, posting to social networks, communicating controversial opinions, or performing financial transactions are no longer taking place because people are losing trust in the Internet. As Rafi Goldberg, a policy analyst with the NTIA, said, "But for the Internet to grow and thrive, users must continue to trust that their personal information will be secure and their privacy protected" (Peterson, 2016a). Figure 1.4 shows the major

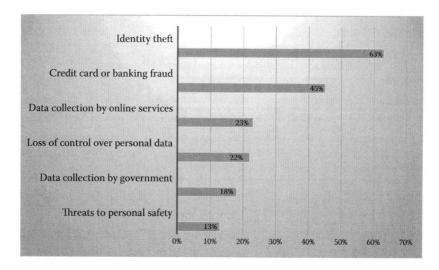

Figure 1.4   Major concerns related to online privacy and security risks. (From Goldberg, R., Lack of trust in internet privacy and security may deter economic and other online activities, Retrieved from U.S. Department of Commerce National Telecommunications & Information Administration, https://www.ntia.doc.gov/blog/2016/lack-trust-internet-privacy-and-security-may-deter-economic-and-other-online-activities, May 16, 2016.)

concerns regarding online privacy and security risks the respondents in the survey indicated.

With these concerns in mind, individuals are avoiding certain online activities. With almost twenty percent (20%) of the respondents indicating they were victims of identity theft, Figure 1.5 illustrates the avoidance rate of all respondents, those that have multiple concerns including privacy and security, and those that have experienced a security breach.

As the report indicates, "In addition to being a problem of great concern to many Americans, privacy and security issues may reduce economic activity and hamper the free exchange of ideas online" (Goldberg, 2016).

These concerns over Internet security and privacy may be justly warranted in the age of "always-on" connections. "The 'Big One' is going to be something far more personal, or even lethal," warns Lee Gruenfeld, vice president of Strategic Initiatives at Support.com, on the topic of security around the IoT (Gruenfeld, 2016). Gruenfeld references how Millennials don't necessarily value privacy as much as other generations and that there haven't been major news stories over

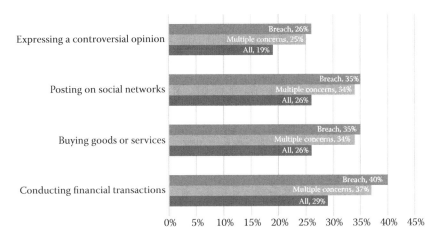

Figure 1.5 Avoidance of online activities due to privacy and security concerns. (From Goldberg, R., Lack of trust in internet privacy and security may deter economic and other online activities, Retrieved from U.S. Department of Commerce National Telecommunications & Information Administration, https://www.ntia.doc.gov/blog/2016/lack-trust-internet-privacy-and-security-may-deter-economic-and-other-online-activities, May 16, 2016.)

the compromise of devices that have directly affected them although concern is increasing. He provides an example of a criminal breaking into a house after turning off the security alarms through an interconnected thermostat: "everyone who makes connected thermostats is going to suffer" (Gruenfeld, 2016). *What about medical devices that are connected to the Internet?*

Medical Devices

This "no harm, no foul" mantra may be alright for devices such as a toaster or a refrigerator, but as mentioned in the previous example, *what if this is the same for devices that are actually attached to humans for tracking, monitoring, or other healthcare purposes?* It is not only about privacy, but the security of devices themselves. As Scott Erven, a security researcher, stated to Ars Technica UK, "As we expand the connectivity, when we get into systems that affect public safety and human life—medical devices, the automotive space, critical infrastructure— the consequences of failure are higher than something as shocking as a Shodan webcam peering into the baby's crib" (Porup, 2016).

According to a study performed by Arxan, a security vendor, more than half of the 815 consumers who polled "expect their health apps to be hacked in the next six months" (Zieger, 2016). The study indicated that seventy-six percent (76%) of consumers would change providers over a security issue with their applications and eighty percent (80%) would choose another provider if they discovered those providers' applications were more secure. Security should be a high priority for mobile health applications and devices as they become more entrenched within the healthcare industry. Consumers are paying attention.

I'm sure everyone has heard of Fitbit, and their mission is as follows: "To empower and inspire you to live a healthier, more active life. We design products and experiences that fit seamlessly into your life so you can achieve your health and fitness goals, whatever they may be" (Fitbit, 2016). According to an article written by Brian Krebs, Fitbit found itself a target of warranty fraud when it discovered a large amount of customer data posted to Pastebin in the latter months of 2015 (Krebs, 2016b). It should be noted that the wearable Fitbit devices themselves were not hacked, but rather individual account passwords appeared to be compromised through theft, guessing, or brute-force attempts. There was no indication that the account passwords were compromised from the Fitbit systems according to Stephen Cobb in his article *What Does Fitbit Hacking Mean for Wearables and IoT?* From a statement provided by Fitbit on the incident: "This is not a case of Fitbit emails or servers being hacked and it would be inaccurate to state or imply otherwise. Our investigation found that the accounts were accessed by an unauthorized party using previously stolen or compromised credentials (email addresses and passwords) from other third-party sites unrelated to Fitbit" (Cobb, 2016b). According to Cobb, "the fact that Fitbit has only recently taken the defensive measures mentioned earlier [plans to introduce two-factor authentication] suggests that the product line may not have been developed according to the principles of privacy by design (PbD)" (Cobb, 2016b).

On a recommendation of a friend, I purchased an Amazon Echo. If you aren't aware of this device or have seen it on commercials, it is an "always-on" device that is connected to the Internet. Utilizing sophisticated speech recognition software, you can ask "Alexa" to perform many different tasks. I like to have Alexa play our music collection while I'm enjoying cooking with my wife. If I need a timer set, I ask Alexa to set a timer. If I want to know what the weather is going to be, I just ask. If I want to get news updates, I just ask. It is a very impressive device, but as a security and privacy professional I always have to wonder what personal information Alexa is capturing.

With all of its amazing functions, the Amazon Echo could also be utilized in the clinical environment. From a report written by David Chou, *The Amazon Echo—Bringing Sci Fi Reality to Healthcare*, "From a clinical perspective, the Echo can assist the medical provider by reciting the medical education transcribed by the doctor to the patient, such as: the side effects of a prescription drug the patient should expect for the next month after surgery" (Chou, 2016). Chou suggests that the Echo could be utilized to replace a nurse call system or to allow for patients to order their meals. Echo did not market itself as a "medical device" but rather a consumer product utilized in the home. As you may see the benefits of the functionality and voice activation technology features integrated into the Echo, making it readily adaptable to other uses such as within a medical environment, you must also ask *what type of security or privacy features are implemented with this device?*

The Mayo Clinic, being probably one of the few hospitals in the nation with the clout to enforce security requirements for its medical devices before purchasing such devices, assembled an "all-star" group of "white hat" hackers. These are the researchers that are hired to find vulnerabilities in systems and hopefully make recommendations to fix the problems. Billy Rios was one of these researchers that worked on the Mayo Clinic's project to "hack" about forty (40) different medical devices. He accounts his story in an article from *Bloomberg Businessweek, It's Way Too Easy to Hack the Hospital*, written by Monte Reel and Jordan Robertson. After an endless number of vulnerabilities, "defenseless operating systems, generic passwords that couldn't be changed, and so on," Rios reflected, "sooner or later, hospitals would be hacked, and patients would be hurt." "Hospitals seemed at least a decade behind the standard security curve" (Robertson, 2016).

After his experience at the Mayo Clinic, Rios went home and ordered an infusion pump from an online retailer. This type of pump is utilized to provide intravenous drips of medication or other fluids into a connected patient's bloodstream. After connecting the machine to his computer network, Rios was able to manipulate the device into releasing an entire vial of medication remotely just as if someone was standing in front of the device delivering the medication in person. Rios notified the Department of Homeland Security (DHS)'s Industrial Control Systems Cyber Emergency Response Team (ICS-CERT) of his findings. The report was forwarded to the Food and Drug Administration (FDA) and then forwarded to the manufacturer of the pump. Unfortunately, Rios received no indication of any actions taken to correct the issue discovered.

This apparently wasn't the only such case of a medical device being "hacked"; the Bloomberg article describes how a researcher demonstrated an insulin pump that delivers diabetic medication could be manipulated to potentially deliver a lethal dose of drugs. Another researcher demonstrated that a pacemaker could be remotely hacked to deliver an unintended shock. This same researcher, unfortunately, passed away before he was able to unveil what he promised to be a way to "pinpoint any wirelessly connected insulin pumps within a 300-foot radius, then alter the insulin doses they administered" (Robertson, 2016).

Rios followed up with DHS about his findings, but it appeared that they weren't interested in seeing if other pumps were vulnerable. After Rios ended up in the hospital himself, he kept on DHS and FDA. He created a video and sample code explaining the vulnerability on the pump and eventually got a response back from the FDA. The FDA issued an unprecedented advisory calling out a specific product referencing a cybersecurity issue urging hospitals to stop using the pump because it "could allow an unauthorized user to control the device and change the dosage the pump delivers" (Robertson, 2016).

In a packed conference session titled "Biomedical Devices: Could Lack of Security Harm Patients?" at Healthcare Information and Management Systems Society (HIMSS) 16 Cybersecurity Symposium held in Las Vegas, Stephen Grimes, principal consultant at Strategic Healthcare Technology Associates, explained to the audience the risks healthcare is facing with networked medical devices. "There are 10 to 15 million medical devices in U.S. hospitals today. The average is 10 to 15 devices per bed, so a 500-bed hospital could have 7,500 devices—most of them networked. A 2,000-bed health system might have 1,500 infusion pumps alone" (Miliard, 2016a). Grimes indicated, "There are no real effective standards for integrating medical devices... especially when related to security" (Miliard, 2016a). Although the FDA maintains responsibility over the medical devices, there may be gaps between the biomedical engineers, the clinicians utilizing the devices, and IT individuals not knowing what devices are in use at their facilities. Grimes recommends that accurate inventory on medical devices needs to be performed, including the type of data being handled by these devices. Grimes reiterates, "You can't manage what you can't measure" (Miliard, 2016a).

Congress may be finally getting the message. The Senate Health, Education, Labor, and Pensions (HELP) Committee recently approved some legislation. An amendment to one of these pieces of legislation called for a postmarket surveillance system for medical devices that will "utilize electronic health data from applicable sources to provide timely and reliable information on medical device safety and effectiveness" (Snell, 2016d). In addition, when healthcare data are involved, they need to be protected by following the HIPAA regulations.

To be fair to the FDA, they have the challenge of drafting meaningful regulations that meet the demands of ever-changing threats. Things get even more complicated when device manufacturers and hospitals have shared responsibilities or ownership of security. Of course the hospitals say that manufacturers should be held to a higher standard when implementing security on their devices while the manufacturers indicate that hospitals need to improve their network protection since in order to compromise the device, an attacker must first breach the hospital's firewalls and other security controls. The FDA has recently issued its draft guidance outlining cybersecurity recommendations for medical device manufacturers.

FDA Draft Guidance

The U.S. FDA issued draft guidance on January 15, 2016, "outlining important steps medical device manufactures should take to continually address cybersecurity risks to keep patients safe and better protect the public health" (FDA, 2016). This guidance is voluntary and "*recommends* that [medical device] manufacturers *should* implement a structured and systematic comprehensive cybersecurity risk management program and respond in a timely fashion to identified vulnerabilities" (FDA, 2016). To paraphrase the list of critical components of the recommended cybersecurity risk management program, a medical device manufacturer should do the following:

- Apply the 2014 National Institute of Standards and Technology (NIST) *voluntary Framework for Improving Critical Infrastructure Cybersecurity*. This includes the core principles of identification, protection, detection, response, and recovery as it relates to cybersecurity.
- Identify and detect cybersecurity vulnerabilities and risks by monitoring cybersecurity information sources.
- Understand, assess, and detect the presence and impact of vulnerabilities.
- Establish and communicate vulnerability intake and handling processes.
- Develop mitigation strategies for clearly defined essential clinical performance areas that enable protection, response, and recovery of cybersecurity risks.
- Adopt a coordinated vulnerability disclosure policy and practices.
- Deploy mitigation early and prior to exploitation that address cybersecurity risks.

Public and private information sharing groups known as Information Sharing and Analysis Organizations (ISAOs) were also emphasized and recommended to organizations by the FDA. The FDA has recognized the growing concern over threats to medical devices. As cyber threats evolve, the FDA insists that manufacturers can not only incorporate controls into the design of a product, but should also consider improvements during maintenance and throughout the device's entire life cycle. As Suzanne Schwartz, MD, MBA, associate director for science and strategic partnerships and acting director of emergency preparedness/operations and medical countermeasures in the FDA's Center for Devices and Radiological Health, states, "All medical devices that use software and are connected to hospital and health care organizations' networks have vulnerabilities—some we can proactively protect against, while others require vigilant monitoring and timely remediation" (FDA, 2016).

Hippocratic Oath for Connected Medical Devices

Created in the late fifth century BC, the Hippocratic Oath was sworn to by physicians to follow a standard of ethics. I Am The Cavalry, "a grassroots organization that is focused on issues where computer security intersect public safety and human life" (I Am The Cavalry, 2016a), developed a modern version of the Hippocratic Oath for connected medical devices. "As connected technologies are increasingly the instruments of delivering this care, it stands to reason that the design, development, production, deployment, use, and maintenance of medical devices should follow the symbolic spirit of the Hippocratic Oath" (I Am The Cavalry, 2016a).

The Hippocratic Oath for connected medical devices offers five core cybersecurity capabilities:

1. *Cyber safety by design*: Inform design with security life cycle, adversarial resilience, and secure supply chain practices.
2. *Third-party collaboration*: Invite disclosure of potential safety or security issues, reported in good faith.
3. *Evidence capture*: Facilitate evidence capture, preservation, and analysis to learn from safety investigations.
4. *Resilience and containment*: Safeguard critical elements of care delivery in adverse conditions and maintain a safe state with clear indicators when failure is unavoidable.
5. *Cyber safety updates*: Support prompt, agile, and secure updates (I Am The Cavalry, 2016a).

As an international company that manufactures medical and safety devices, Dräger exemplifies the responsibilities companies have when developing technology, as their tag line states, "Technology for Life," and to Dräger "It means assuming responsibility for the lives of those who use our products and depend on them" (Dräger, 2016). Stefan Dräger, the executive board chairman, explains, "Everything we do, we do with passion—and we do it for life" (Dräger, 2016). They've built a successful company on a culture of "customer intimacy, employees, innovation and quality" (Dräger, 2016).

Royal Philips of the Netherlands (or commonly referred to as just Philips) is another company "focused on improving people's lives through meaningful innovation in the areas of Healthcare, Consumer

Lifestyle and Lighting" (Philips, 2016a). While some companies attempt to discourage testing or "hacking" of their products, Philips "encourages vulnerability testing by security researchers and by customers, with responsible reporting to Philips" (Philips, 2016b). Philips is committed to ensuring security and safety over their products and maintains a website at www.philips.com/security so that issues can be reported. In addition, Philips explains the steps they will take to follow up on reported vulnerabilities and, if requested, will also "provide full credit to researchers who make a vulnerability report or perform testing, in publicly released patch or security fix release information" (Philips, 2016b).

I had the pleasure of talking with Brian Knopf, a very experienced security researcher. Knopf is an expert on embedded device security and is passionate about making these devices more secure. His interest became more apparent after his wife was involved in an accident and had to have a medical device implanted. The realization came to him that the work he was performing on researching device vulnerabilities could have far-reaching effects, including the ability to hurt someone he loves. This got Knopf thinking about the impact of his work and how it could be balanced to protect his family.

Knopf started to think about ways that companies could become more responsible and better stewards of security over their products. Utilizing the same concept as a "five-star" test used to rate vehicles, Knopf started working with other security professionals to develop a system to rate the "IoT" security and privacy for consumers. By establishing this rating system, it will allow consumers to become more aware of these devices' security levels. Knopf indicated that device manufacturers will be invited to submit their devices for testing and researchers will test them against certain criteria. A preliminary report will be issued to the manufacturer providing the opportunity to respond and/or mitigate issues discovered, and then a final report will be published online for individuals to review that may want to purchase the device.

The standards will have a base set of requirements and then be classified based on the type of device under review. Knopf indicated that the standards must be simple, but also be specific with the ability to grow over time as new technology is developed. It follows the security by design principles along with building threat models. It also considers privacy and safety as part of the rating. For instance, under privacy, manufacturers need to be open about what data are being collected, how the data are being collected, why is there a need for the data, and what the data are being used for so that consumers can make informed decisions about the use of the device. As an example, Knopf describes water meters that could be utilized to analyze water usage. If a company wants to sell their products to assist a consumer in saving money on their water utilities, the only thing the company really needs is the zip code of the consumer to assist them in getting impressions of their product in front of the consumer. The company could provide discounts for their products based on water usage and regional area; they don't need the specific details of the consumer allowing the consumer to maintain their privacy.

Under safety, the criteria will look at items like reliability. Knopf explains that most IoT devices utilize User Datagram Protocol (UDP), which is a simple connectionless transmission protocol that doesn't guarantee delivery of the data used in low-latency and loss tolerating connections. For most devices, this isn't an issue; if the transmission doesn't occur, no problem, the data will be resent, but in cases of medical devices where reliability and error checking are required, Transmission Control Protocol must be used. The difference between the two (2) protocols could be a decision between life and death. Knopf hopes that these standards will be published within the next six (6) months and should be available by the time of this book's publication (Knopf, 2016).

Cyber Independent Testing Laboratory

After winning a contract for "Consumer Security Reports" from the U.S. Air Force, awarded on behalf of the DARPA, Peiter Zatko left Google to start Cyber Independent Testing Laboratory LLC in Waltham, MA, modeled after Underwriters Laboratories. Zatko's intention with this new entity "is to provide them [the public] with the information and tools they need, in a non-partisan fashion, and without profit incentives getting in the way of providing unbiased and quantified ratings of the software and systems they are purchasing"

(Castelli, 2016). Firmware, software, operating systems, applications, services, and the IoT devices (although hardware is not the primary focus, it could be within scope depending on the circumstance) could be included in evaluations.

Zatko goes on to say in his interview with *Inside Cybersecurity*, "We will be making the results and methodologies publicly available. This will provide consumers, companies, insurance and actuarial teams, with quantifiable measurements of 'how much risk' different products or solutions introduce to your environment" (Castelli, 2016).

Privacy by Design

As suggested as another possible solution to device concerns in an earlier section, "Privacy by Design (PbD) is an approach to protecting privacy by embedding it into the design specifications of technologies, business practices, and physical infrastructures. That means building in privacy up front—right into the design specifications and architecture of new systems and processes" (IPC, 2016). The seven (7) foundational principles of PbD are paraphrased here:

1. Privacy risks should be anticipated in a proactive way to prevent privacy issues from happening, rather than reacting to or remediating issues once they've occurred.
2. Privacy should occur automatically without any individual user intervention built as a default within the systems.
3. Privacy is embedded in systems and not, as we previously discussed, added on after the fact.
4. Privacy is not a trade-off of security, but rather the objective is a positive sum where systems are both private and secure.
5. Privacy is embedded from the start and security is implemented throughout the entire data life cycle management process.
6. Privacy should be trusted but verified in that processes and technology should operate according to stated promises/objectives validated by independent sources.
7. Privacy should focus on the users with secure settings, notifications, and ease of use (Information and Privacy Commissioner of Ontario, 2016).

Cobb provides some sage advice for consumers to consider before purchasing a wearable device, which is paraphrased here:

- Make informed purchasing decision by investigating any reported vulnerabilities, frauds, or scams.
- Ensure you use an obscure username and unique password that is hard to guess.
- Read the privacy policies provided by the device manufacturers.
- Do not use features or applications that could potentially expose your sensitive information.

In addition, Cobb advises that manufacturers of wearable devices should prepare their incident response plans to react to any data breaches appropriately (Cobb, 2016b).

Further evidence to substantiate the claim that the IoT may not be as secure as one would expect comes in the form of a recent report that stated "eighty-four percent (84%) of U.S. FDA-approved health apps tested by IT Security vendor Arxan Technologies did not adequately address at least two of the Open Web Application Security Project top 10 risks" (Siwicki, 2016). The analysis was conducted on one hundred twenty-six (126) popular health and finance apps from the United States, the United Kingdom, Germany, and Japan. According to the report, "ninety-five percent [95%] of the FDA-approved apps lack binary protection and have insufficient transport layer protection, leaving them open to hacks that could result in privacy violations, theft of personal health information, as well as device tampering and patient safety issues" (Siwicki, 2016). Patrick Kehoe, chief marketing officer at Arxan Technologies, indicated that "...mobile apps should bake application self-protection security measures into their apps before releasing them 'into the wild'" (Siwicki, 2016). You may have noticed a recurring theme that security should be "baked into" and "embedded into" devices, applications, and solutions prior to releasing them into the public. Kehoe also advised that applications should be hardened and the security over the communication between the mobile application and the back-end servers should be improved. He indicated that utilizing standard security over application programming interfaces (APIs) that do not hide cryptographic keys within the application or in memory could be utilized to compromise sensitive data on the servers.

Based on a report, *The State of Web and Mobile Application Security in Healthcare*, written by Veracode from a survey of two hundred (200) IT executives conducted by HIMSS, the top three (3) security-related concerns of a cyber breach are "loss of life due to compromised networks or medical devices, brand damage due to the theft of patient information and regulatory enforcement" (Veracode, 2016). Application security was the number one concern for healthcare providers. Lee Kim, the director of privacy and security at HIMSS, asks, "When the application was built, was it built with security in mind or was it an application that was designed quickly and security concerns were overlooked?" (Ms. Smith, 2016).

Ethical Design Manifesto

The Ethical Design Manifesto is an ethical approach to the design of technology software and products. Taking a similar track as Maslow's hierarchy of needs, the Ethical Design Manifesto speaks of the *three Rs of design*:

1. Respect human rights—The base foundation of the software/product.
2. Respect human effort—Software/products can't be so difficult to use that no one wants to use them.
3. Respect human experience—The objective is to make the software/products that are developed as beautiful as possible.

All of this comes together to give us HOPE: the hierarchy of product ethics. "Sell products, not people" (Ind.ie, 2016). The Ethical Design Manifesto is shared here, under the *Creative Commons Attribution 4.0 International License* (Creative Commons, 2016), which goes on to challenge developers to do the following:

- Design, don't decorate—Design without ethics is decoration. Decoration makes inequality palatable; design challenges it.
- Be diverse, not ethnographic—Design without diversity is imperialism. Diversity is not altruism; it is competitive advantage. A diverse team designing for themselves will meet the needs of a diverse audience. You cannot compete with a

competent design team designing for themselves if you are designing for *The Other.*

- Design the organization, the product will follow—Ethical Design is holistic or it is nothing. Ethical Design is not what ethical designers do; it is the system of values and processes at the heart of ethical organizations. It begins with the design of the organization itself.

Design your organizations so that your core values are respect for human rights, respect for human effort, and respect for human experience (Ind.ie, 2016; Figure 1.6).

Open Web Application Security

In addition to a beautiful design, software and products must be secure. As mentioned in the previous section, "the Open Web Application Security Project (OWASP) is a 501(c)(3) worldwide not-for-profit charitable organization focused on improving the security of software" (OWASP, 2016a). Their "mission is to make software security visible, so that all individuals and organizations worldwide can make informed decisions about true software security risks" (OWASP, 2016a). The OWASP Top 10 is free to use and licensed under the Creative Commons Attribution-ShareAlike 3.0 License. In basic

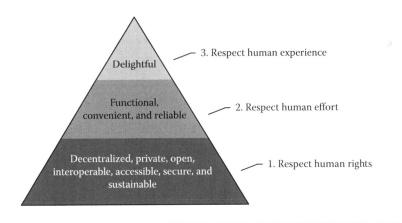

Figure 1.6 Ethical design manifesto. (From Ind.ie., Ethical design manifesto, Retrieved from https://ind.ie/ethical-design, January 29, 2016.)

terms, OWASP provides a list of the top ten (10) most critical web application security vulnerabilities as follows (Figure 1.7):

1. *Injection*—Injection flaws occur when an attacker's data can trick an interpreter into executing unintended commands or accessing data without proper authorization.
2. *Broken authentication and session management*—This occurs when application functions related to authentication and session management are not correctly implemented to allow an attacker to compromise passwords, keys, or session tokens. This can also occur when an attacker is able to exploit other implementation flaws to assume other users' identities.
3. *Cross-site scripting (XSS)*—XSS occurs whenever an application sends untrusted data to a web browser that have not been properly validated. An attacker exploiting this vulnerability could execute scripts within a victim's browser that could lead to a hijack of the user's session, deface of websites, or redirection of users to malicious sites.
4. *Insecure direct object references*—This occurs when a developer exposes an internal implementation object reference such as a file, directory, or database key. An attacker may be able to manipulate these references to access data.
5. *Security misconfiguration*—Secure settings should be defined, implemented, and maintained for applications, frameworks, servers, and platforms.
6. *Sensitive data exposure*—Sensitive data such as credit cards, tax IDs, and authentication credentials need extra protection such as encrypting it at rest or in transit along with special precautions when exchanging this information with a browser.
7. *Missing function level access control*—Applications need to perform access control checks on the server when a function is accessed. If these requests are not verified, an attacker may be able to forge requests in order to access functions without proper authorization.
8. *Cross-site request forgery (CSRF)*—CSRF occurs when an attacker is able to force a victim's browser that is currently logged on to a server to send a forged request to a vulnerable

	A1-Injection	A2-Broken authentication and session management	A3-Cross site scripting (XSS)	A4-Insecure direct object references	A5-Security misconfiguration	A6-Sensitive data exposure	A7-Missing function level access control	A8-Cross-site request forgery	A9-Using components with known vulnerabilities	A10-Unvalidated redirects and forwards
C1-Verify for security early and often	★	★	★	★	★	★	★	★	★	★
C2-Parameterize queries	★									
C3-Encode data	★		★							
C4-Validate all inputs	★		★							★
C5-Identify and authentication controls		★								
C6-Implement access controls				★			★			
C7-Protect data						★				
C8-Implement logging and intrusion detection	★	★	★	★	★	★	★	★	★	★
C9-Leverage security features and libraries	★	★	★	★	★	★	★	★	★	★
C10-Error and exception handling	★	★	★	★	★	★	★	★	★	★

Figure 1.7 Outline of the OWASP top 10 controls mapped to the OWASP top 10 vulnerabilities that they prevent or mitigate against. (From OWASP Proactive Controls—Top 10 Mapping 2016, Retrieved from https://www.owasp.org/index.php/OWASP_Proactive_Controls#tab=Top_10_Mapping_2016, October 10, 2016b.)

web application. This forged HTTP request may include the victim's session cookie or other authentication information. This allows an attacker to force the victim's browser into generating requests the vulnerable application may think is legitimate.

9. *Using components with known vulnerabilities*—Using components with known vulnerabilities that are exploited could lead to serious data loss or server takeover. In most cases, components such as libraries, frameworks, or software modules run with full privileges enabling a wide range of possible attacks along with damaging impact.

10. *Unvalidated redirects and forwards*—Without proper validation, an attacker may be able to redirect victims to phishing or malware sites. An attacker could also use forwards to access unauthorized pages. This could occur due to the frequency of web applications that redirect/forward users to other pages/websites.

In addition, OWASP also publishes its top 10 proactive controls that should be included in every software development project to help prevent against one or more of the top 10 vulnerabilities. These are as follows:

1. *Verifying for security early and often*—As an integral part of the software engineering practice, security testing should be incorporated.

2. *Parameterizing queries*—Provide SQL injection protection by leveraging the way the Data Access Abstraction Layer parameters are interpreted before executing an SQL query.

3. *Encoding data*—Encode data before using in a parser like JS, CSS, or XML.

4. *Validate all inputs*—It should be assumed that all data input from outside of the application can be manipulated and should be considered untrusted.

5. *Identifying and authenticating controls*—Implement identity management, which includes authentication (process of verifying an individual is who they claim to be), session management, identity federation, single sign on, password management tools, identity repositories, and more.

6. *Implementing access controls*—Process to grant or deny access. A "positive" access control design should be considered at the initial stages of application development (*again with designing security from the start*). Some examples of these design requirements include the following:
   a. Force all requests to go through access control checks.
   b. Deny by default.
   c. Avoid hard-coded policy-based access control checks in code.
   d. Check on the server when each function is accessed.
7. *Protecting data*—Encrypt data at rest or in transit.
8. *Implementing logging and intrusion detection*
9. *Leveraging security features and libraries*—Utilize secure coding libraries that have been updated and kept current, instead of starting from scratch.
10. *Error and exception handling*

According to an analysis performed by the research firm IDS, the IoT is expected to grow to a $1.7 trillion market by 2020 (Hulme, 2016). With this type of growth expected, it is not surprising that many companies will be trying to get their products, devices, and applications out to consumers as quickly as possible. Although there will be many consumer devices going to market, there will also be a lot of business devices. According to Gartner, there is an estimated 1.6 billion business-connected IoT devices and this number will reach 8 billion by 2020 (Hulme, 2016). The pure number of devices that will be going online over the next four years will create real security risks. Although we've heard rumors for quite some time of possible attacks on these devices, we have become witnesses to ever-increasing proof of vulnerabilities with these devices. With the amount of data that these IoT devices will generate, there is going to be an ever-increasing concern over how these data are being maintained, secured, or even analyzed despite the movement to keep your personal information private.

How many people actually read the "terms of use" policies for the devices and/or applications they use? By using the device or application (especially in cases where they provide these applications/services for free), do you surrender your rights to privacy? Could these companies utilize the information they gather on you to perform analytics on your behavior, sell this information to the highest bidder, or even direct market to you based on your activities/preferences? How are your data being collected, where are they being stored, and who has control over your information? We'll continue to explore these concerns and more throughout this book.

Legal/Constitutional Issues

What if the information collected by your fitness trackers can be used against you in a court of law? Law firms are already utilizing these data to show how their clients have been affected by an accident or injury. Comparing the activity (or inactivity) of an injured person as to the average individual of comparable age and/or job could assist in determining damages in a lawsuit. According to Bruce Hagen, an attorney with a firm that specializes in bike accidents, "This [fitness tracker] is the same as the black box data you would get on a car or a truck or an airplane" (CBS47 Fox30 Action News, 2016).

A Florida woman reported a sexual assault against her boss after she was staying at her boss's house. Detectives doubted the woman's story and noticed that she was wearing a fitness tracker. They asked the woman for permission to check her activity. Although the detectives thought they had enough probable cause to obtain a search warrant for the information, the woman gave them her logon credentials. As the detectives suspected, the tracker showed that the woman took around 1000 steps after she told law enforcement that she went to bed and before she called 911 to make the report. From the data obtained, it showed evidence that the woman was setting her boss up for a crime he didn't commit. The woman was charged with making a false report and tampering with evidence (CBS47 Fox30 Action News, 2016). Attorney Chris Simon explained, "If you are allowing it to be written down, it is accessible to somebody in the future. We are voluntarily allowing people to track our every movement, and that's scary" (CBS47 Fox30 Action News, 2016).

What if your mental health status is shared with a national database and is utilized to determine your eligibility to own a firearm? On January 4, 2016, a press release was issued by Jocelyn Samuels, director at Office for Civil Rights on the Department of Health and Human Services website, explaining the administration's commitment to move forward on modifying "the Health Insurance Portability and Accountability Act (HIPAA) Privacy Rule to expressly permit certain covered entities to disclose to the National Instant Criminal Background Check System (NICS) the identities of those individuals who, for specific mental health reasons, already are prohibited by Federal law from having a firearm" (Samuels, 2016). The post makes it clear that the rule modification only applies to a small subset of HIPAA-covered entities that are designated by their states to report such information to NICS or make the determinations that disqualify persons from having a firearm. In addition, only a limited amount of nonclinical information is reported to NICS. "The rule does not apply to most treating providers and does not allow reporting of diagnostic, clinical, or other mental health treatment information" (Samuels, 2016).

Some have concerns over the new measures introduced by executive order. The American Legion believes that this new rule may prevent veterans from seeking treatment. The American Legion's National Commander Dale Barnett said in a statement posted on their website, "Nobody wants violent criminals or those with extreme mental disorders to have firearms, but The American Legion strongly believes that treatment for Post-Traumatic Stress Disorder or depression by itself, which a number of wartime veterans experience, should not be the sole factor in denying a veteran the right to purchase a firearm" (The American Legion, 2014). The American Legion wants to ensure the Second Amendment rights are protected. Commander Barnett continues, "Barring some additional circumstances that would indicate that a veteran represents a dangerous threat, veterans should not have to forfeit their Second Amendment rights. We fear an 'over fix,' which would bar any veteran from owning a weapon" (The American Legion, 2014).

As I was performing research for this book, Antonin Gregory Scalia, associate justice of the U.S. Supreme Court, passed away. Justice Scalia was a big supporter of the Fourth Amendment right of protection against unreasonable search and seizures by the government. As an example of his support, Justice Scalia, in a 5–4 decision, wrote for the majority that using thermal sensors to detect heat patterns from inside a home required the issuance of a warrant in *Kyllo v. United States*, 533 U.S. 27 (2001). He also wrote for the majority where a warrant is required to attach a GPS surveillance device to a car in *United States v. Jones*, 132 S. Ct. 945 (2012).

Daniel J. Solove, the John Marshall Harlan research professor of law at George Washington University Law School and founder of *TeachPrivacy*, a privacy/data security training company, opines that Justice Scalia "had a narrow view of original intent [of the 4th Amendment]...*Kyllo* turned heavily on the fact that the thermal sensor was used on a home...*Jones* turned on the placement of the GPS device on a car—a trespass to a person's property" (Solove, 2016c). Solove points out that Justice Scalia missed an important point in his decision with Jones: "it's not the device that matters; it's the data!" (Solove, 2016c). See, Justice Scalia was worried about the physical trespass of the car when a device was affixed, but the government could get the data from the third-party GPS provider. *How is this possible?* By way of the "third-party doctrine."

The U.S. Supreme Court has set precedence for "the third-party doctrine" that states individuals have no expectation of privacy when their information is provided to a third party. Under the decision made in *United States v. Miller*, 425 U.S. 435 (1976), the court ruled "the Fourth Amendment does not prohibit the obtaining of information revealed to a third party and conveyed by him to Government authorities." Again, in *Smith v. Maryland*, 422 U.S. 735 (1979), when the government obtained from a phone company the list of numbers dialed by a person, the court ruled people "know that they must convey numerical information to the phone company" and cannot "harbor any general expectation that the numbers they dial will remain secret."

Solove raises concerns that a new justice may "tip the balance" in favor of (or against) enhanced Fourth Amendment protections, especially when it comes to information held by third parties in our vast data collection age. Solove contends, "The third party doctrine is, in my view, the most significant and wrongheaded impediment to effective 4th Amendment regulation of government surveillance" (Solove, 2016c). He provides further details of his view in an article he published in Volume 75:1083 of the *Southern California Law Review* (2002) titled *Digital Dossiers and the Dissipation of Fourth Amendment Privacy*. Solove concludes "One of the most significant threats to privacy of our times, government information-gathering and-use, is inadequately regulated" (Solove, 2002). He proposes, "A new architecture of power must be constructed, one that effectively regulates the government's collection and use of third party records" (Solove, 2002).

To test the far-reaching implications of government or law enforcement with obtaining information from third parties, in a recent turn of events, Apple is opposing a court order requiring them to build a "backdoor" that would allow law enforcement to circumvent security of their iPhone devices. In what Tim Cook, the chief executive officer of Apple, describes in a letter to their customers, "an unprecedented step which threatens the security of our customers" (Cook, 2016). The court order came after the FBI investigated the terror attack that occurred in San Bernardino in December 2015. The mass shooting and attempted bombing incident took fourteen (14) lives and seriously injured another twenty-two (22). The letter claims that Apple has "done everything that is both within our [Apple] power and within the law to help them [FBI]" (Cook, 2016), but the FBI is now using "the All Writs Act of 1789 to justify an expansion of its [the FBI's] authority" (Cook, 2016).

The All Writs Act, 28 U.S. Code § 1651, states the following: "The Supreme Court and all courts established by Act of Congress may issue all writs necessary or appropriate in aid of their respective jurisdictions and agreeable to the usages and principles of law" (Legal Information Institute, 2016). Although Apple believes the FBI has "good intentions" for the request, they believe that the request has far-reaching implications and should be discussed in public or the request should come through some legislative actions by Congress. Apple concludes the letter, "we fear that this demand would undermine the very freedoms and liberty our government is meant to protect" (Cook, 2016).

Unfortunately, there may be some law enforcement officials that feel very strongly about corporations like Apple to make sure they assist them in investigations that involve their products. An outspoken Central Florida sheriff, Grady Judd of Polk County, issued a warning to Apple's CEO, Tim Cook, after being involved in a murder investigation where the suspects took pictures with a cell phone of the victim's body. Although the cell phone was not an iPhone and the suspects provided the passcodes to gain access to the device, Sheriff

Judd promised, "I can tell you, the first time we do have trouble getting into a cell phone, we're going to seek a court order from Apple. And when they deny us, I'm going to go lock the CEO of Apple up... I'll lock the rascal up" (Levin, 2016).

The day before a legal hearing on the matter, the FBI appeared to be able to obtain the information on the phone by hiring a third party to, supposedly, exploit a vulnerability of the iPhone to gain access to its content. Although it is being claimed that the method works on limited iPhones, it is "highly unlikely the technique will be disclosed by the government to Apple or any other entity" (McCarthy, 2016b). The FBI still appears to be fighting with Apple over different phones and versions of the operating system. This raises other questions about the possibility that the FBI had previously known about a vulnerability in the iPhone and didn't report it to Apple as the push for sharing such type of information has come to the forefront of public and private cooperation in cybersecurity matters. As karma may have it, there apparently was nothing of use that was gained by accessing the phone in question in the first place.

Apple is not the only company that has the issue with sharing certain information with the government. While writing this book, a *Complaint for Declaratory Judgment* appears to have just been filed by Microsoft Corporation against the U.S. Department of Justice (DOJ) in the U.S. District Court Western District of Washington at Seattle. This complaint raises the issues around the constitutionality of "gag" orders. In the complaint, attorneys with the law offices of Davis Wright Tremaine LLP indicated that over eighteen (18) months between September 2014 and March 2016, Microsoft received 5624 federal demands for customer information. Of those "requests," 2576 contained secrecy orders, and of these, two-thirds (2/3) had no fixed time limits. The complaint argues, "These twin developments—the increase in government demands for online data and the simultaneous increase in secrecy—have combined to undermine the confidence in the privacy of the cloud and have impaired Microsoft's right to be transparent with its customers, a right guaranteed by the First Amendment" (Davis Wright Tremaine LLP, 2016). The complaint asks the court to rule that 18 U.S.C. § 2705(b) of the Stored Communications Act (SCA), as part of the Electronic

Communications Privacy Act (ECPA) of 1986, is unconstitutional under the First and Fourth Amendment. The ruling in this case is pending, but the decision could have a major impact on privacy.

In other recent changes that could have a great impact on our personal liberties and freedoms, the U.S. Supreme Court approved the changes U.S. federal courts made to Rule 41 of the Federal Rules of Criminal Procedures (FRPC) requested by the DOJ. Rule 41 limited the jurisdiction of search warrants issued for subjects located within the jurisdiction of the issuing judge; however, according to Senator Ron Wyden (D) of Oregon, "Under the proposed rules, the government would now be able to obtain a single warrant to access and search thousands or millions of computers at once; and the vast majority of the affected computers would belong to the victims, not the perpetrators, of a cybercrime" (Wyden, 2016). Large technology companies and groups like the American Civil Liberties Union (ACLU) see the changes going against our protections over inappropriate searches along with expanding law enforcement powers to conduct mass surveillance. The DOJ described the modifications as minor indicating that the "changes wouldn't permit searches that aren't already legal" (Khandelwal, 2016). The amendment to the rule will go into effect December 1, 2016, as proposed if Congress doesn't take any actions on it.

On the heels of this controversy over privacy, President Obama's administration is taking steps to relax long-standing procedures over its executive orders related to the Foreign Intelligence Surveillance Act (FISA). This act was narrowly focused on wiretaps on American soil involving collection of communications, both domestic and international. The rest of the surveillance conducted by the National Security Agency (NSA) was guided by procedures related to Executive Order 12333. This order can be changed by the administration and does not need to go through Congress.

Up to now, the NSA would filter information it received (without a warrant) and share "sanitized" information of Americans who were not involved in terrorism with other law enforcement agencies like the Central Intelligence Agency, the FBI, the Drug Enforcement Administration, and the Internal Revenue Services. When explaining how the information was obtained as in drug cases, these agencies would utilize the term "parallel construction" to circumvent the Fourth Amendment. Although it has been "rumored" that law enforcement agencies were receiving information from the NSA on Americans related to crimes other than terrorist activities from warrantless wiretaps, the proposed changes have made it clear that the administration is no longer worried about making this activity public. This just exemplifies how granting certain powers to the government in the name of national security can be expanded. Once "Pandora's Box" is open, it is very hard to close: "extraordinary powers we grant government in wartime rarely go away once the war is over. And, of course, the nifty thing for government agencies about a 'war on terrorism' is that it's a war that will never formally end" (Balko, 2016).

Recently, the Judiciary Committee of the House of Representatives unanimously approved bill HR 699, the *Email Privacy Act*. This law requires, for the first time, law enforcement to obtain a warrant to gain access to e-mail and text messages from a third-party service provider in reference to a criminal investigation. This bill also has support in the Senate as indicated in a joint statement by Senators Patrick Leahy (D-VT) and Mike Lee (R-Utah) that the bill ensures the "same privacy protections that apply to documents stored in our homes extend to our emails, photos and information stored in the cloud" (Chabrow, 2016a).

Not to be outdone and to go one step further in response to the FBI versus Apple conundrum, the Senate is also taking up the *Compliance with Court Orders Act of 2016*. This bill proposed by Senators Richard Burr (R-NC) and Dianne Feinstein (D-CA) states, "to uphold both the rule of law and protect the interests and security of the United States, all persons receiving an authorized judicial order for information or data must provide, in a timely manner, response, intelligible information or data, or appropriate technical assistance to obtain such information or data; and covered entities must provide responsive, intelligible information or data, or appropriate technical assistance to a government pursuant to a court order" (The Daily Dot, 2016). The bill goes on to define what crimes are included within the scope of a court order that would require compliance such as what is paraphrased here:

- Crimes involving (or the threat of) death or serious bodily harm
- Foreign intelligence, espionage, and terrorism

- Federal crime against a minor (including sexual exploitation and physical safety threats)
- Serious violent felonies
- Serious Federal drug crime (including criminal enterprise)
- The same state crimes

The bill defines a covered entity as

- A device manufacturer
- A software manufacturer
- An electronic communication service (or provider of wire or electronic communication services)
- A remote computing service (or a provider of remote computing services)
- Any person who provides a product (or method) to facilitate communication, processing, or storage of data

Although the bill discusses design limitations in that it doesn't authorize, require, or prohibit any specific design (or operating system) to be used, to meet the mandate of "decrypting" data, some argue that this bill requires covered entities to implement "backdoors" within their products or communication technology. When vulnerabilities are intentionally placed within certain technologies to be utilized for "good," it can also be utilized by criminals for "bad" purposes. The bill appears to have a low probability of becoming a law and doesn't have the support of the White House. There are still a lot of influential experts that believe in the importance of strong encryption, but these topics are being discussed by lawmakers and only time will tell as to what decisions may be made around our privacy.

Fingerprints Are Not Protected by the Fifth Amendment

Under the Fifth Amendment of the U.S. Constitution, a person is not compelled in any criminal case to be a witness against himself. In the age of technology where biometric elements such as fingerprints are utilized as "keys" to protect sensitive or possibly incriminating information, *how is it that the courts can compel us to give up our fingerprints to unlock these devices*? Easy, fingerprints are classified as "real or physical evidence" that don't require warrants, unlike communications or knowledge that falls under Fifth Amendment protections.

As Albert Gidari, director of privacy at Stanford Law School's Center for Internet and Society, explains, "Unlike disclosing passcodes, you are not compelled to speak or say what's 'in your mind' to law enforcement. 'Put your finger here' is not testimonial or self-incriminating" (Winton, 2016). Other legal experts argue that by unlocking a device that contains certain content shows that you have control over that information and being compelled to use your fingerprint to unlock it goes against Fifth Amendment protections.

There have been few court cases that have been decided based on the issue of forcing individuals to unlock their devices with a fingerprint or a passcode. In 2014, a judge in Virginia ordered David Charles Baust to unlock his phone with his fingerprint; however, he wasn't ordered to disclose a passcode. Baust was accused of attempting to strangle a woman in his room that was equipped with surveillance equipment believed to be connected to his phone. The judge reasoned that providing a fingerprint was like a "key," while a passcode revealed knowledge and would be considered testifying. Baust was acquitted on the charges.

In another case related to invoking Fifth Amendment rights, a former police sergeant was held in contempt of court after failing to decrypt hard drives that law enforcement contends stored indecent images of children. After investigators only suspected the man had the images, they seized his computer equipment along with two encrypted hard drives. Although the district courts ruled the man was not compelled to decrypt the drives, investigators obtained a warrant from a federal court invoking the *All Writs Act of 1789*. The court indicated that under this law, individuals can be forced to cooperate with a criminal investigation. *Remember, this was the same law that we just discussed involving the federal government requesting Apple to decrypt their iPhones.*

The man was taken to the district attorney's office to decrypt the drives. After entering passcodes that failed to work and refusing to testify to the explanation, he was incarcerated. Keith Donoghue, the man's attorney, states, "His confinement stems from an assertion of his Fifth Amendment privilege against self-incrimination" (BBC, 2016). The Electronic Frontier Foundation (EFF) agrees, "Compelled decryption is inherently testimonial because it compels a suspect to use the contents of their mind to translate unintelligible evidence into a form that can be used against them" (BBC, 2016). An appeal has been filed to release the man from jail until a decision is made over the enforcement of decrypting the drives. Based on the appeal, investigators may not have any proof indecent images are stored on the drives, and as the EFF states, "Complying with the order would communicate facts that are not foregone conclusions already known to the government" (BBC, 2016).

2
PRIVACY CONCERNS

Without privacy there was no point in being an individual.

—Jonathen Franzen, *The Corrections*

Information…Information…Everywhere

We live in the "Information Age" where tons of information about anything you ever wanted to know is readily available at a click of a button. This includes a lot of personal information. The Millennial Generation (or Generation Y) has basically been brought up with a smart phone or electronic device at their fingertips, and Generation Z has pretty much been born with one in their hands. As soon as they could use their fingers and see a screen, they were introduced to electronic devices connected to the Internet. They are not afraid to use these devices as many of their predecessors were, and they love to socialize through apps that are freely available. Everything you want to know (and things you may not want to know) about a person can be shared with the rest of the world. Nothing is private and there is almost nothing that is off-limits.

This is the utopia of the world we live in, but there are still some of us that like our privacy. We don't want everybody to know about our personal lives. We don't want people to know when we woke up, when we went to bed, or when we last ate (or where and with whom). This is our private life and we don't want to share it with the rest of the world.

This includes our visits to the doctor or trips to the hospital. With the ever-increasing digitization of our medical information and the advancements in the interoperability between different healthcare providers of our healthcare information, our personal medical information is getting harder to keep private.

A blog post from a company very experienced with data collection and storage, Iron Mountain, stated, "Healthcare is already a data-rich environment, but the waves of data the industry is experiencing today are nothing compared to the swells on the horizon" (Lynn, 2016a). The post goes on to predict that there is going to be an increase in the information residing in electronic health records, but also within other ancillary healthcare systems, that is, labs, pharmaceuticals, imaging, etc. Shifting toward a value-based care model throughout the health-care industry, providers will have access to all the medical information related to a patient through the sharing of this information through health information exchanges and the increased interoperability through the electronic health records themselves.

As we already alluded to in a previous section, medical devices, remote monitoring, fitness trackers, and other Internet of Thing devices will increase the amount of data already being captured on individuals on a daily, hourly, and down to the minute basis. "Is it really beyond the realms of possibility that we could visit same medical clinic and in [five] 5 years be able to provide a year[']s worth of data that reveals your exact exercise patterns, weight fluctuations, blood pressure, resting heart rate patterns, and blood oxygen levels?" (Burrus, 2016a) asks Daniel Burrus. In some cases, however, reveal-ing too much information about yourself might be a bad thing. Take for instance insurance premium fees. Burrus raises the possibility that insurance companies may "be empowered to charge higher premiums for those living what it deemed an unhealthy lifestyle" (Burrus, 2016a).

The Iron Mountain post goes on to say, "Further, healthcare is starting to see pockets of genomic data. Eventually, this informa-tion will be required in every healthcare organization" (Lynn, 2016a). Instead of just treating the patient, a healthcare provider will need to take into account environmental and societal factors. If a patient has no heat at home and has fallen ill, *would it make any sense to send that patient home or would it be better to admit them to a care facility until they get well?*

Healthcare information is not only maintained within healthcare organizations, but this information is also found in many other indus-tries and companies that maintain employee records and wellness programs. These companies may not even realize that they are storing this information or doing enough to ensure that this information is protected. A survey performed by the Vanson Bourne group on behalf of security vendor Sophos indicated that "midsized companies do a better job protecting their customer information than that of their own employees or their internal intellectual property" (Higgins, 2016a). The survey indicated that of the companies with 100–2000 employees, "nearly one-third don't regularly encrypt their employee's bank information" (Higgins, 2016a). Of these same companies, "[forty-three percent] (43%) don't always encrypt their human resource files" (Higgins, 2016a). In addition, "nearly half say they don't routinely encrypt employee health information" (Higgins, 2016a). The survey included companies from "the US, Canada, India, Australia, Japan, and Malaysia" (Higgins, 2016a).

Healthcare is progressing in front of our eyes and it is being driven by data. Through data collection, data sharing, and ultimately data analytics, we are in the early stages of developing capabilities for healthcare analytics to improve healthcare quality and hopefully reduce healthcare costs. Although the current collection and sharing of healthcare information has not significantly improved quality or reduced cost, as stated on the website of Health Catalyst, a healthcare analytics company, "the real promise of analytics lies in its ability to transform healthcare into a *truly data-driven culture*" (HealthCatalyst, 2016). From the website of another healthcare analytics company, explorys—An IBM Company, "The ability to use big data and compete in the new healthcare economy depends on having the capability to acquire, aggregate, standardize, and make the data available to the people who shape strategies and deliver care" (explorys, 2016).

Unfortunately, as security expert Bruce Schneier states, "data is a toxic asset and saving it is dangerous" (Schneier, 2016). Since the name of the game is "Big Data" and it has become relatively cheap to store the data, there is a lot more of it available. This makes it very enticing to attackers, including foreign intelligence agencies. This can also get into the realm of national security when data analysis is being performed. "That's because when combined with other data from a broad variety of sources it can be used to paint an accurate picture of individual government employees in extreme detail" (Rash, 2016a). Dipto Chakravarty, CA Technologies' senior vice president of engineering for security, states "cyber-security is the hardest challenge for national security…national security has to begin with cyber" (Rash, 2016a).

Since it can be very difficult to defend against attacks, attackers always have the advantage. "The data is vulnerable, and the company is vulnerable. It's vulnerable to hackers and governments. It's vulnerable to employee error. And when there's a toxic data spill, millions of people can be affected" (Schneier, 2016). The challenge is to deny the attackers the ability to obtain the data. As Schneier points out, "there's no better security than deleting the data" (Schneier, 2016).

So, *why is this information being saved?* Schneier points to three (3) reasons: the "hype" of Big Data, underestimating the risks, and the motivation of profit. Companies believe that information is valuable even though there is diminishing return at some point in collecting too much information. Companies may not realize the impact a breach may have on their organization. If a company is a new start-up, they may take riskier actions over the data they collect or maintain. Since they may not be profitable "out of the gate," they may not have anything to lose taking chances with the data or circumventing regulations. Schneier further contends that we need to regulate corporations more throughout the entire life cycle of data and hold executives personally responsible. By prohibiting certain business practices, companies may be less compelled to surveil their customers.

New Social Disorder

If I told you something in private, I would expect that you kept that information to yourself, or kept it in confidence. Unfortunately, communication on the Internet doesn't necessarily work like that. What we have are platforms that the information is "relayed" through multiple systems to hopefully get to the person we are trying to have a private conversation with. It is unlike us sitting in our own home and speaking to each other across a table with no one else around; on most of these social platforms, we are in a stranger's home "who pays the rent by knowing as much about us as he can" (Balkan, 2016). As we discussed in the Preface of this book, these platforms or services are offered to us with the intention of making money off of the data we share. Although this information may be meant to be private (i.e., between you and me only), this is far from the case.

Utilizing some of these services may not only affect you. Sure, I might be OK with sharing my most intimate personal information through the "spying eyes" of these "data collectors," but what if I ask someone else to share their *own* personal information with me? I give them my e-mail account through one of these services and they send me their information. Of course, the platform or service can allow viewing of the information going out and coming in; in essence, I've not given my friend a choice over their privacy. They could decide not to send me their information, but they are my friend; *they trust me*? They trust I would keep their information private, not realizing the channel I'm using to communicate isn't private as we might expect. Once you lose control of your information, you can never get it back.

Samsung, a manufacturer of Internet-connected devices, developed its *SmartTV* with a pretty interesting feature—voice activation. We no longer need to use a remote, but rather we can just tell the TV what to do. Unfortunately, this feature may record everything it hears along with personal conversations. In the original privacy statement about the voice recognition feature, Samsung warned, "Please be aware that if your spoken works include personal or other sensitive information, that information will be among the data captured and transmitted to a third party through your use of Voice Recognition" (O'Connor, 2016b). Over concerns raised by consumers, Samsung removed the statement from their Privacy Policy and indicated they may collect and capture voice commands to improve on their voice recognition features.

Just because Samsung removed this sentence from their privacy statement doesn't mean that the ability for the TV to capture your information goes away. Samsung indicated that they collect the commands *only* when a search request is made by activating the feature and speaking into the remote control's microphone. This feature can be disabled; "however, this may prevent you from using some of the Voice Recognition features" (Samsung, 2016). Furthermore, Samsung does admit in its new privacy statement that voice commands are transmitted to a third party, Nuance Communications, Inc. that converts voice to text, but only to the extent necessary to enable the voice recognition feature.

If you live in the United States, you are now, and have been living for quite a while, in a police state. You are being surveilled and your activities are being tracked, even at one of the most "happiest places on Earth"—Disneyland. Documents released by The American Civil Liberties Union (ACLU), after winning a court battle, prove the use of *dirtboxes* by the Anaheim Police Department. A dirtbox is described as a spying tool that can intercept a cell phone's information. More advanced dirtboxes can compromise a cell phone's encryption. These devices can be installed in planes that can allow them to "spy" on several hundred phones at a time. Anaheim Police apparently received a grant from the Department of Homeland Security to purchase this device and indications allude to the fact that "millions of tourists passing through Disneyland would've been within reach" (Knibbs, 2016) of this covert spying technology.

California passed a law that went into effect January 1, 2016 requiring police to obtain warrants for the use of surveillance tools like dirtboxes. It is unclear if any warrants were ever sought previously for the use of these devices prior to the passing of this law. Several law enforcement agencies were known to utilize this technology, such as the FBI, Chicago Police, and Los Angeles Police, but it appears that other departments are also using these tools. Kate Knibbs expresses concern in her article, *Disneyland's Local Police Force Caught Secretly Using Powerful Phone Spying Tools*, "The terrifying news is that we need new laws to protect our privacy from the people supposedly protecting us" (Knibbs, 2016).

Medical Records

Your medical record has been digitized. It is now referred to as your electronic health record. It is chock full of all types of personal information; however, the most important information for any physician to make accurate medical diagnosis for a particular illness is a detailed history. Per a post written by Dr. Wixon, "An expert doctor knows how to effectively use 'heuristics', tools which we develop as a result of personal experiences" (Chris Wixon, 2016). He goes on to say that, "Heuristics simplify the decision-making process and allow the physician to identify small nuances in a medical history to narrow a list of potential diagnoses into a single diagnosis" (Chris Wixon, 2016).

Unfortunately, a lot of electronic health record solutions don't do a good job in capturing this historic record. At the core of the solution, there is a database that collects massive amounts of information.

To enter the information into the database or to retrieve the information out of the database, the solution relies on database management software (DBMS). This is where, in many cases, the solution fails. Since there are a lot of uncertainties in medical data, electronic health record solutions don't always do a good job in capturing the little intricacies that physicians require. Medical histories are not just "snap shots" in time, but must be able to describe an individual over intervals. *Are symptoms getting worse? Is treatment improving?* Dr. Wixon noted that "the new system [electronic health record] failed to accurately capture the subtle nuances associated with the patient's story" (Chris Wixon, 2016). He further described that "it flattened a three dimensional history into a two dimensional template and ignored the cause and effect which remains so vital" (Chris Wixon, 2016).

Dr. Wixon opines that there are three (3) distinct tenants or challenges that need to be worked out within electronic health records: data querability, degrees of freedom, and time. Being able to search certain fields of a database (querability) along with having the ability to "efficiently get information out of the physician's head and into the database" (Chris Wixon, 2016) (degrees of freedom) are the challenges these software developers face. Throwing in a third variable, time, to the mix makes the challenges even more complex (Figure 2.1).

Dr. Wixon proposes that a possible solution to the problem can be found in the concept of a knowledge base. "Think of it as an intricate

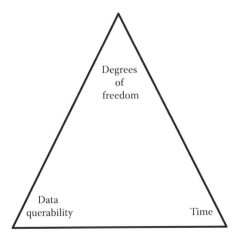

Figure 2.1 Electronic health record tenants.

map of symptoms, locations, severity, laterality, etc. The physician navigates a predetermined map in order to arrive at a particular diagnosis or plan of treatment. It is the very fabric on the EHR [electronic health record]" (Chris Wixon, 2016).

Beyond the functionality and capabilities that an electronic health record solution can offer, there are other major concerns—security and privacy. According to a Pew Research Center survey of four hundred sixty-one (461) U.S. adults and nine (9) online focus groups of eighty (80) people, "Just over half of Americans feel it would be acceptable for doctors to use health information websites to manage patient records" (Davis, 2016c). Twenty percent (20%) of the respondents indicated that managing patient records through the use of health information websites would depend on the scenario and another twenty-six percent (26%) said this would be unacceptable to them (Figure 2.2).

The Pew study showed varied circumstances by which Americans would allow information sharing or monitoring in return for something of value. "An overwhelming number of respondents said their comfort in sharing information depended on the scenario—trust, circumstances, how the data is stored and how it is used" (Davis, 2016c). In basic terms, they want to ensure the site is secure and the data is kept private.

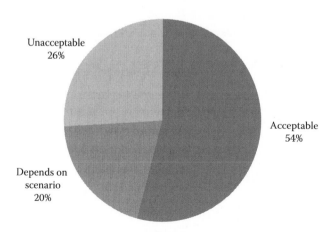

Figure 2.2 Americans' opinions on the use of health information websites to manage patient records.

The sharing of information is also dependent on relationships. We may find that individuals don't necessarily have a problem sharing their deepest, darkest secrets with family and friends on social media outlets where they may feel this information is kept in confidence, but some may fear how this information could be utilized in such cases as obtaining a job, insurance coverage, or even credit. The Pew study also showed that respondents over fifty (50) years of age or those (in all age groups) with some college education were more acceptable to sharing personal health data. As one respondent adamantly professed, "My health records are my business and no one else's. No website is totally secure" (Davis, 2016c).

Elizabeth Snell, in her article *How Health Data Sharing Relates to Healthcare Privacy*, writes: "One of the key aspects to health data sharing is ensuring that it is done in a secure way that will not compromise patient information" (Snell, 2016c). She indicates that using encryption may help, but under the Health Insurance Portability and Accountability Act of 1996 (HIPAA) this implementation specification is considered *addressable* as opposed to being required. As a side note, under these regulations, an addressable specification does not mean "optional." Those organizations that fall under the scope of HIPAA must determine if it is reasonable and appropriate. If it doesn't apply, the organization must still adopt alternative measures to achieve the purpose of the standard.

Another way to secure patient information is to limit the information available or utilizing a method called de-identification. Through de-identification processes, certain elements of information that could identify a specific individual are removed. Under the HIPAA Privacy Rule, de-identified health information is no longer considered protected health information.

Before we go further, let me just take a second to discuss what the HIPAA regulations define as Protected Health Information (PHI). A broad definition of PHI is any information, in any form or medium (i.e., paper or digital), that relates to the past, present, or future physical (or mental) health, condition, provision of healthcare, or future payment for the provision of healthcare of (or to) an individual. I know it is a mouthful and you may want to go back and reread that last sentence.

To get more detailed, there are nineteen (19) common direct identifiers of individually identifiable health information that could identify (or reasonably be used to identify) an individual. As you could expect, your name, Social Security number, and medical record number are on the list, but there are several other direct identifiers of the individual or of relatives, employers, or household members of the individual that are defined under Title 45 Code of Federal Regulations (CFR) § 164.514(e)(2) as follows:

1. Names
2. All geographic subdivisions smaller than a State, including street address, city, county, precinct, zip code, and their equivalent geocodes, except for the initial three (3) digits of a zip code, if, according to the current publicly available data from the Bureau of the Census
   a. The geographic unit formed by combining all zip codes with the same three (3) initial digits contains more than 20,000 people
   b. The initial three (3) digits of a zip code for all such geographic units containing 20,000 or fewer people are changed to "000"
3. All elements of dates (except year) directly related to an individual, including birth date, admission date, discharge date, date of death, and all ages over eighty-nine (89), and all elements of dates (including year) indicative of such age, except that such ages and elements may be aggregated into a single category of age ninety (90) or older
4. Telephone numbers
5. Fax numbers
6. Electronic mail addresses (i.e. e-mail)
7. Social Security numbers
8. Medical record numbers
9. Health plan beneficiary numbers
10. Account numbers
11. Certificate/license numbers
12. Vehicle identifiers and serial numbers, including license plate numbers
13. Device identifiers and serial numbers
14. Web Universal Resource Locators (URLs)
15. Internet Protocol (IP) address numbers

16. Biometric identifiers, including finger and voice prints
17. Full face photographic images and any comparable images
18. Any other unique identifying number, characteristic, or code
19. Genetic Information (added to the definition of protected health information by the finalization of the Omnibus Rule)

De–Identification

The HIPAA Privacy Rule provides two methods to de-identify information: utilizing expert determination or through safe harbor. Figure 2.3 walks through the steps required for de-identification.

The expanded use of electronic health records really took hold when The American Recovery and Reinvestment Act of 2009 (ARRA) was enacted. This Act established incentive payments to eligible professionals (EPs), eligible hospitals, critical access hospitals (CAHs), and medicare advantage organizations to promote the adoption and meaningful use of interoperable health information technology (HIT) along with qualified electronic health records (EHRs). These incentive payments were part of a broader effort under the Health Information Technology for Economic and Clinical Health (HITECH) Act to accelerate this adoption (Electronic Health Records (EHR) Incentive Programs, 2016).

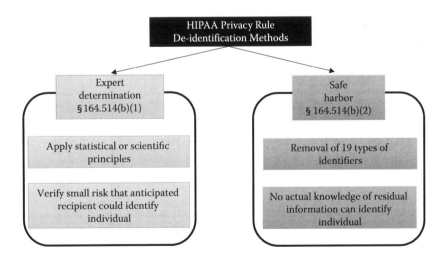

Figure 2.3 Two methods to achieve de-identification in accordance with the HIPAA Privacy Rule.

Meaningful Use

Meaningful use is defined as using certified EHR technology to

- Improve quality, safety, efficiency, and reduce health disparities
- Engage patients and family
- Improve care coordination, and population and public health
- Maintain *privacy* and *security* of patient information

Ultimately, it is hoped that the meaningful use compliance will result in:

- Better clinical outcomes
- Improved population health outcomes
- Increased transparency and efficiency
- Empowered individuals
- More robust research data on health systems (HealthIT.gov, 2016)

The meaningful use incentive program is overseen by the Centers for Medicare & Medicaid Services (CMS) and evolved in three (3) stages over five (5) years:

- Stage 1 (2011–2012): Data capture and sharing
- Stage 2 (2014): Advance clinical processes
- Stage 3 (2016): Improved outcomes

As of December 31, 2015, CMS has dulled out more than $21 billion in Medicare EHR Incentive Program payments and more than $10.3 billion in Medicaid EHR Incentive Program payments actively registering more than 559,000 eligible professionals, eligible hospitals, and critical access hospitals (CMS, 2016). On January 12, 2016, Acting Centers for Medicare and Medicaid Services Administrator Andy Slavitt announced at *the J.P. Morgan Healthcare Conference* in San Francisco, "Now that we effectively have technology into virtually every place care is provided, we are now in the process of ending Meaningful use and moving to a new regime culminating with the MACRA [Medicare Access & CHIP Reauthorization Act of 2015] implementation. The Meaningful Use program as it has existed, will not be effectively over and replaced with something better" (Slavitt, 2014). The details on this new transformation are a little sketchy at this point and are supposed to be put out over the next few months;

however, with the emphasis being placed on a new Merit-Based Incentive Payment System and alternative payment models, Slavitt indicated that a new streamlined regulatory approach is needed.

Slavitt explained a few guiding themes of the new implementation. First, focus will be put toward outcomes that are achieved with patients as opposed to rewarding providers for the use of technology. Second, technology must be user-centric and support physicians by giving them the capabilities of customizing their solutions for their own goals and build technology around the individual practice needs as opposed to the government needs. Third, Slavitt provides a recommendation that will level entry into the market space for healthcare technology companies by requiring open Application Program Interfaces (APIs) to allow solutions to get data in and out of an EHR securely. Finally, emphasis will be placed on interoperability. The practice by some technology companies to block data will no longer be tolerated.

In a blog post on the Center for Medicare and Medicaid Service's website, Slavitt and Karen DeSalvo, Acting Assistant Secretary for Health at the U.S. Department of Health and Human Services (HHS), reminded everyone that the current law requires the existing set of standards be utilized to measure meaningful use, and while MACRA could adjust payment incentives, it doesn't eliminate the existing incentives. In addition, MACRA only addresses Medicare physician and clinician payments and doesn't affect Medicaid and Medicare hospitals. Slavitt and DeSalvo further indicated that these changes won't occur immediately and requirements under meaningful use Stage 3 are still in effect, but Congress has provided some new authority over granting hardship exceptions.

Slavitt and DeSalvo end the blog by reiterating, "The challenge with any change is moving from principles to reality. The process will be ongoing, not an instant fix and we must all commit to learning and improving and collaborating on the best solutions" (Desalvo, 2016). They are looking forward to collaborating with stakeholders and advancing the changes.

21st Century Cures Bill

The news doesn't end here. There is a bill called the "21st Century Cures Bill" that has been passed by the U.S. House of Representatives and is now being considered in the Senate. This bill is intended to provide drug researchers more accessibility to certain health information, but it raises some concerns over patients' privacy. As long as appropriate security/privacy safeguards are met and PHI is not copied (or retained) by the researcher, the legislation will allow researchers to obtain health information. Currently, protected health information is only permitted to be used or disclosed (without a patient authorization) for treatment, payment, or healthcare operations. If information is required for research purposes, the information must be de-identified or the patient must authorize the disclosure.

A statement on the website of the Energy & Commerce Committee states "the 21st Century Cures Act, will bring our health care innovation infrastructure into the 21st Century, delivering hope for patients and loved ones and providing necessary resources to researchers to continue their efforts to uncover the next generation of cures and treatments" (Energy & Commerce Committee, 2016). Unfortunately, the Minnesota-based Citizens Council for Health Freedom (CCHF) believes otherwise. In a letter written to a select number of Congressman in opposition to the bill states: "While a focus on rare diseases is mentioned, the bill does not limit it to such, creating the possibility of broad research on anyone with any 'disease'. The requirement that the Secretary [of Health and Human Services] provide advice on 'addressing associated patient privacy concerns' is insufficient, as neither the bill nor HIPAA require informed written patient consent" (Snell, 2016a).

In another letter by the American Hospital Association (AHA), Executive Vice President Rick Pollack, overall, commends the House Energy & Commerce Committee's efforts, but raises some concerns over the broad definition of "information blocking." He indicated that this "would result in penalties for providers' reasonable business practices and beneficial modifications to information technology (IT) systems that improve patient care" (Snell, 2016a). Pollack recommends different definitions of information blocking:

1. Limit or restrict electronic sharing, through certified EHRs, of patient information necessary for the care of the patient that is permissible to be shared under relevant federal and state privacy laws, insofar as the technology and supporting infrastructure have the capability to carry out such electronic sharing

2. Limit or restrict patients' access to their electronic records, as specified in existing federal and state privacy laws, insofar as the provider has current capability to efficiently and effectively share the data electronically (Pollack, 2016b)

Khaled El Emam, CEO of Privacy Analytics and a data de-identification expert, contends in an interview with Information Security Media Group, "A possible side-effect of the HIPAA changes proposed in the 21st Century Cures bill is a watering down of that de-identification requirement, putting PHI at a higher potential privacy risk when used for research" (McGee, 2016f). El Emam says, "A lot of these efforts are pushing for greater access to data, and using data to accelerate research … by getting access to multiple sources," but he also goes on to say, "…some of the changes won't necessarily help increase access to information, and instead have unintended consequences" (McGee, 2016f). El Emam provides an example that if de-identification requirements for research purposes went away, "this will allow a lot more PHI [protected health information] to be shared with researchers at different organizations, external organizations, companies—without any de-identification." Without some of these controls, El Emam fears that "it becomes very dangerous, very risky" (McGee, 2016f). De-identification still plays a very important role in keeping a large amount of information secure and private as may be needed for secondary purposes like research.

Cybersecurity Information Sharing Act 2015 (CISA)

December 18, 2015, the Consolidated Appropriations Act, 2016 was signed into Law (Public Law No: 114-113). This 2,009-page bill was primarily an omnibus spending bill; however, it did include an important piece of legislation known as the Cybersecurity Information Sharing Act 2015 (CISA). *Section 405: Improving Cybersecurity in the Healthcare Industry* laid out a plan to lower cybersecurity risks and to improve protection from the compromise of sensitive information. In my honest opinion, this new act is not Earth-shattering and doesn't really do enough to combat the threats we are facing in terms of cybersecurity in the healthcare industry. If Congress really held cybersecurity as important, they would have passed this bill on its own merits and discussed "real" solutions to the problem as opposed to attaching it as a "line-item" to the Consolidated Appropriations Act, 2016.

A healthcare industry cybersecurity task force will be established by the Secretary of the Department of HHS in consultation with the Director of the National Institute of Science and Technology (NIST) and the Secretary of Homeland Security within ninety (90) days of the bill's passage. Task Force members were recommended by subject matter experts from HHS, the Department of Homeland Security (DHS), and NIST utilizing the following criteria:

- Serving in an influential position at an organization with broad healthcare and public health sector representation
- Experience with health information security including technical, administrative, management, and/or legal aspects
- Knowledge of major health information security, best practices, trends
- Ability to actively participate in meetings and contribute to products of the Task Force (PHE, 2016)

The Task Force is made up of chief information security officers or equivalent with some having expertise in clinical medicine, software development, and other related experience. The members represent a variety of organizations to include hospitals, insurers, patient advocates, security researchers, pharmaceutical companies, medical device manufacturers, technology vendors, laboratories, and federal agencies (PHE, 2016). The Healthcare Industry Cybersecurity Task Force is assigned the following duties:

- Analyze how various industries outside of healthcare have implemented strategies to address cybersecurity threats. This is truly nothing amazing and you can find a lot of information already available on the safeguards that other industries utilize to keep their information secure. The financial services industry has guidelines issued from the Federal Financial Institutions Examination Council (FFIEC) and fall under security regulations of the Gramm–Leach–Bliley Act (GLBA), also known as the Financial Services Modernization Act of 1999. Governments, themselves, already have such strategies as the Federal Risk and Authorization Management Program

(FedRAMP), which is meant to standardize an approach for assessing the security of cloud services, and the Federal Information Security Management Act (FISMA), which defines a framework to protect information from natural or man-made threats.

- Analyze the challenges and barriers private entities (excluding state, tribal, or local government entities) in healthcare face when securing themselves against cyberattacks. I'm not sure why there is a stated exclusion here and the focus is only on *private entities*, but I can name two specific challenges/barriers that the task force can start with: the financial resources allocated to security and the lack of security experts available within the healthcare industry.

- Review challenges that covered entities and business associates face in securing networked medical devices and other software or systems that connect to an electronic health record. One such challenge is the security over medical devices. We'll discuss this in more detail in a later section of this book, but currently the Food and Drug Administration (FDA) has regulatory oversight of these devices and has decided not to issue mandatory guidelines over security; they are voluntary. Healthcare organizations that utilize these devices find themselves to have minimal ability to establish appropriate controls over these devices.

- Provide the Secretary with information to disseminate to healthcare-industry stakeholders of all sizes for the purpose of improving preparedness for, and response to, cybersecurity threats affecting the healthcare industry. Although this sounds great on paper, *how is this information going to be obtained and by what process is this information going to be delivered to healthcare organizations?*

- Establish a plan for implementing title I of this division, so that the federal government and healthcare-industry stakeholders may share actionable cyber threat indicators and defensive measures in real time. In basic terms, the government is encouraging organizations to share information with immunity against prosecution in an effort to combat hackers. By sharing this information, organizations will get advance notice of possible vulnerabilities and upcoming cyberattacks. Opponents fear that this is a way that government can surveil private individuals under the guise of cybersecurity. There is also some concern over reaching a data sharing agreement with the European Union.

- Report to the appropriate congressional committees on the findings and recommendations of the task force regarding the actions taken on these tasks.

The task force will be operational for one (1) year and expires March 2017, but there is no indication as to the final outcome of this work. Without ongoing resources dedicated to combat cyber threats, these tasks may be nothing more than a "snapshot" in time.

The law establishes for the aligning of healthcare industry security approaches by developing a common set of *voluntary*, consensus-based, and industry-led guidelines, best practices, methodologies, procedures, and processes. Intended to serve as a cost-effective resource to reduce cybersecurity risks, this common-set approach will be developed for a wide range of healthcare organizations. Unfortunately, no two organizations within the healthcare industry do things the exact same way. There is too much flexibility within the industry creating a challenge to interpreting the intentions of certain security requirements.

This common set of security approaches is offered up for *voluntary* adoption and intended to address security threats by improving safeguards. There are already several guidelines, best practices, methodologies, procedures, and processes that are available to the healthcare industry for *voluntary* adoption. Examples of these are the HITRUST Common Security Framework (CSF), the National Institute of Standards and Technology (NIST) standards, the International Organization for Standardization (ISO) standards, and others that can be adapted from other industries such as the financial industries or government agencies that can serve healthcare organizations' needs.

Healthcare organizations have been slow to adopt standardized security frameworks and this voluntary approach only lends itself to organizations ignoring additional guidance due to requirement fatigue. *Why would healthcare organizations want to volunteer to make things more complex in an already complicated and stressed indus-try?* It is important to note that the law specifically states that the Secretary of HHS has NO AUTHORITY to provide for audits to ensure that healthcare organizations are in compliance. The Secretary can't even mandate, direct, or condition the award of any federal grant, contract, or purchase, pertaining to compliance with a common set of security approaches. Unfortunately, compliance can sometimes only be mandated, and without enforcement, there is no compliance. I've gone into more detail on this topic in an article I wrote titled *Cybersecurity & Healthcare: Does Cybersecurity Act Help or Hurt?*, published by InformationWeek's DarkReading at this link: http://www.darkreading.com/endpoint/cybersecurity-and-healthcare-does-cybersecurity-act-help-or-hurt/a/d-id/1324292.

Seventeen (17) advocacy groups including the American Civil Liberties Union (ACLU), the Center for Democracy and Technology, FreedomWorks, and others drafted a letter to members of the U.S. House of Representatives calling for the repeal of the Cybersecurity Act of 2015. The letter included five (5) provisions they believed to be unacceptable "to the technology community, privacy and open-government advocates, as well as ordinary Americans" (Groups, 2016), paraphrased to include the following:

1. Expanded surveillance on Americans through new avenues of collection of information and communications content
2. The immunity from liability of companies that share too much private information with the government
3. No limitation on the type of information shared to include online personal communications
4. The authorization for law enforcement to investigate and/or prosecute crimes of information received unrelated to cybersecurity
5. Measures that undermine government accountability and transparency such as exemptions to the Freedom of Information Act that may preempt state/local laws on disclosures

The letter explains, "Measures to strengthen cybersecurity should not come at the expense of exposing law-abiding Americans' private information to government surveillance" (Groups, 2016).

Health Information Technologies Standards Committee

As is the basis of this book, the healthcare industry hasn't taken security seriously and the lack of formal compliance enforcement has led to major concerns over the privacy and security of healthcare information. Without any motivation, incentives, or enforcement over compliance efforts, the state of cybersecurity in the healthcare industry is going to be hard pressed to improve.

There may be some relief when it comes to the security and privacy of data being maintained in an electronic health record solution. As mentioned earlier, the meaningful use program was pivotal in enforcing some level of security on electronic health record solutions through its certification process. This certification program was managed by the Office of the National Coordinator for Health Information Technology (ONC-HIT) and although meaningful use is transitioning to a new program, the certification program will continue. It appears, in fact, that the certification program will be expanded to include "health information technology" certification above and beyond just electronic health record solutions as is being finalized in the rules. As indicated by Dixie Baker, a senior partner at the consulting firm Martin, Blanck and Associates and a longtime member of the HIT Standards Committee that advised the ONC, "And most important for privacy and security, they [ONC] are changing the way that products are certified against the security standards and criteria" (McGee, 2016c). This all sounds very promising and reassuring, but "some CISOs [chief information security officers] insist that EHR [electronic health record] vendors still have a long, long way to go when it comes to protecting patient data" (McGee, 2016c).

Improving Health Information Technology Act

When it comes to sharing of health information, a Senate Bill to watch, which was just approved by the Senate Health, Education, Labor, and Pensions (HELP) Committee, is the Improving Health Information Technology Act (S.B. 2511). This bill calls for more interoperability of healthcare records and to establish a trusted exchange network for health information. It also calls for better awareness over misunderstandings of health information exchanges.

There are some critics of this bill namely the National Partnership for Women & Families (NPWF) that "call for changes to the draft's definition of information blocking and interoperability to explicitly include consumers as users and address operational and technical barriers that impact their ability to send, receive, find and use their health data" (National Partnership for Women & Families, 2016). NPWF further cautioned the committee over privacy recommending that OCR and FTC perform a six (6) month study to determine appropriate methods of protecting privacy when consumers use certain applications that may not have a privacy framework.

The College of Healthcare Information Management Executives (CHIME) also warned the committee over the definition of information blocking that may be too broad that could be left up to legal interpretation. CHIME writes in a letter to the Chairman and Ranking Member of the HELP Committee, "Currently providers find themselves questioning the bounds of state and federal privacy laws as it relates to the flow of patient data. Thus we encourage ONC and HHS to provide clear guidance to allow providers to delineate circumstances of expected exchange and those exceeding the limits of such regulation" (CHIME, 2016).

Governmental Issues

The regulators and governmental agencies that not only develop security standards but also enforce these standards are the ones that need to follow them the most. According to SecurityScorecard, a security risk benchmarking company, as compared to seventeen (17) major private industries (including healthcare, retail, and transportation), federal, state, and local government agencies ranked the lowest when it comes to online security practices. Malware infections, network security, and software patching were found to be the biggest areas of concern. "Shockingly, 90 percent of state organizations scored an 'F' in Software Patching Cadence, and 80 percent received the same score in Network Security" (Chang, 2016).

Out of the six hundred (600) governmental organizations reviewed, the National Aeronautics and Space Administration (NASA) was the worst followed by the U.S. Department of State and the state systems of Connecticut, Pennsylvania, and Washington. Senior Data

Scientist at SecurityScorecard, Dr. Luis Vargas explains, "The data we uncovered clearly indicates that while some are improving their security postures, too many are leaving themselves dangerously exposed to risks and vulnerabilities, especially at the larger federal level" (Chang, 2016). I guess the old adage of "do as I say; not as I do" sort of applies to the security state of affairs of the government.

Healthcare.gov

How many of you reading this book visited healthcare.gov? How many of you actually provided or entered personal information into this site in hopes of determining qualifications and/or purchasing healthcare insurance? If you answered "yes" to these questions, you might want to skip over what we are about to discuss next.

The Affordable Care Act, or more affectionately referred to as *ObamaCare*, launched the healthcare.gov website in 2013 to provide for and allow for the purchase of healthcare insurance through the provisions of the act. Based on documents acquired by Judicial Watch, a governmental "watchdog" group, the website went into operation without the appropriate "authorization to operate" (ATO) from the agency's security officials.

The documents were obtained from the Department of HHS as a response to a court order after HHS failed to respond to a Freedom of Information Act (FOIA) request. Based on the information and e-mails provided in the request, just ten (10) days before the launch of the site, "Centers for Medicare and Medicaid Services (CMS) information security officer Tom Schankweiler discussed with deputy chief information officer Henry Chao 17 initial 'moderate' security issues findings and two 'high' security issues" (Judicial Watch, 2016). Although some of these findings were resolved, a separate analysis discovered seventeen (17) "high" issues. This prompted Chao to question, "What are we actually signing off on…?" (Judicial Watch, 2016). CMS's security officer Teresa Fryer refused to approve the Authorization to Operate (ATO) after concerns of the number of security issues discovered with the site.

An e-mail from the acting chief technology officer of CMS to a colleague, George Linares, six weeks after the launch indicated that healthcare.gov "is operating without an ATO [Authorization to

Operate]...Operating without an ATO is a serious issue and it represents a high risk to the agency" (Judicial Watch, 2016). Apparently, "Judicial Watch also uncovered the previously secret involvement of the Department of Homeland Security in the Obamacare site and how the Obama White House further weakened privacy protections of Healthcare information on the Healthcare.gov website" (Judicial Watch, 2016).

In a statement by Judicial Watch President Tom Fitton, "The Obama administration is prosecuting private companies for the same security lapses it knowingly allowed with its own Healthcare.gov. Will Justice Department prosecutors now investigate the Obamacare website security scandal? In the meantime, Americans should be warned about the high risk of using Healthcare.gov" (Judicial Watch, 2016).

So, *where does the information go that is entered on healthcare.gov? What steps have been taken since its launch to make it more secure and protect the information obtained?* To answer the first question, we must look at the $110 million Multidimensional Insurance Data Analytics System, or MIDAS. Although MIDAS doesn't store medical records, it does contain personally identifiable information such as names, Social Security numbers, date of births, and the "financial account information of customers on Healthcare.gov and state insurance marketplaces" (Hall, 2016b). An Office of Inspector General's (OIG) report dated September 2015, titled "The centers for Medicare & Medicaid services' implementation of security controls over the multidimensional insurance data analytics systems needs improvement," indicated the following deficiencies:

- Unnecessary generic accounts in the test environment were not disabled.
- User sessions were not encrypted.
- Automated vulnerability assessments that simulate known attacks, which would have revealed vulnerabilities (e.g., password weaknesses and misconfigurations) specific to the application or database that support MIDAS were not conducted.
- A shared read-only account for access to the database that contained the personally identifiable information was used.

Further, the OIG identified twenty-two (22) high, sixty-two (62) medium, and fifty-one (51) low vulnerabilities discovered (Office of Inspector General: Report A-06-14-00067, 2015).

To be fair, attached to the end of the OIG report is a response to the findings dated May 8, 2015, from Andrew M. Slavitt, acting administrator of CMS, to Daniel R. Levinson, inspector general: "The privacy and security of consumers' personally identifiable information (PII) are a top priority for CMS. No person or group has maliciously access personally identifiable information from HealthCare.gov or its related systems" (Office of Inspector General: Report A-06-14-00067, 2015). Slavitt goes on to say that "CMS worked with the OIG during the security testing and within a week of the findings being identified, CMS had addressed all the high vulnerabilities identified. CMS had addressed a majority of the remaining findings within 30 days of identification. All of OIG's findings in this report were addressed by February 2015. In addition, all of the recommendations in this report were fully implemented prior to the draft report being issued" (Office of Inspector General: Report A-06-14-00067, 2015).

As with any site that you want to share information with, you need to be aware of the risks. You need to be able to trust the sites and ensure that the organizations maintaining your information have your best interest in mind. *Maybe the agencies involved in the security of healthcare.gov have taken care of all their issues? Maybe they are abiding by good security practices to ensure the continued safeguard of your information?* You'll need to determine this yourself and weigh out your own risks, but one thing is for certain, with the amount of information potentially stored in MIDAS and the publicity that a government site like healthcare.gov gets, rest assured that this system is a prime target for hackers.

OPM Data Breach

As a possible example of how inept the government may be in protecting personal information it collects, the Office of Personnel Management (OPM), the federal agency that "works in several broad categories to recruit, retain and honor a world-class workforce for the American people" (OPM, 2016a), started making notifications of a cybersecurity incident on September 30, 2015. Back in June 2015, OPM discovered not one, but two related incidents involving the theft of "background investigation records of current, former, and prospective Federal employees and contractors" (OPM, 2016b). The incident affected 21.5 million individuals that went through a Federal background investigation since 2000. Sensitive information including Social Security numbers were stolen from the background investigation database to include 19.7 million individuals that applied for a background investigation and 1.8 million nonapplicants (such as spouses or cohabitants of the individuals). Approximately 5.6 million records included fingerprints, some included findings from interviews, and usernames/passwords individuals used to fill out the applications were stolen.

Beyond making notifications, OPM indicated that individuals affected will be automatically eligible for some services and will need to enroll themselves in others. They would provide assistance to those involved and continue to strengthen their defenses. They also suggested some steps for individuals to follow in protecting their identity. I wanted to list a couple of items that I thought were a little amusing in that the OPM should have minded their own advice: "Get up to speed on computer security" and "Learn how to keep your information safe from exploitation" (OPM, 2016b).

As a result of an internal review following this disclosure, the Defense Department will take on the responsibility of storing information and a new entity, the National Background Investigations Bureau, will be formed to conduct government-wide background investigations. One critic of the change, Representative Jason Chaffetz (R-Utah), House Oversight and Government Reform Committee Chairman, indicated that the change may only be solving a perception problem rather than real reform. In a report by The Washington Post, Chaffetz stated, "simply creating a new government entity doesn't solve the problem…The administration needs to undertake meaningful reforms to protect citizens' most sensitive personal information" (Yoder, 2016).

Welcoming the change, Representative Adam Schiff (D-Calif.), the ranking Democrat on the House Intelligence Committee, said: "OPM was never designed, nor intended to be, an intelligence or national security agency. By entrusting the cybersecurity of this new bureau to the Pentagon, we will be better able to ensure that the personal information of those who work to secure all of us is protected" (Yoder, 2016).

The Washington Post goes on to report that OPM characterized their systems "as being out of date and incapable of providing the latest security protection" (Yoder, 2016). At a proposed budget request of $95 million, the Defense Department will apparently build on improvements that OPM had been trying to make to its security as a result of the breach.

Einstein Program

OPM is not the only governmental agency having issues with cybersecurity. The Government Accountability Office (GAO) has pointed out many shortcomings in the U.S. Department of Homeland Security's (DHS) National Cybersecurity Protection System (NCPS). The NCPS has cost taxpayers more than $5 billion over the past years and as stated on DHS's website, "is an integrated system-of-systems that delivers a range of capabilities, including intrusion detection, analytics, intrusion prevention, and information sharing" (Department of Homeland Security, 2016). Commonly referred to as the EINSTEIN program, it is intended "to secure and defend the federal civilian government's information technology infrastructure against advanced cyber threats" (Department of Homeland Security, 2016). The GAO report indicates that the network traffic monitored by the EINSTEIN program is only compared to known signatures as opposed to detecting anomalies in behavior. The report also indicated that the signatures utilized in alerting may not even address many of the common vulnerabilities. "Intrusion prevention capabilities, meanwhile, currently do not cover malicious web traffic—although this is planned for 2016" (Muncaster, 2016).

Although information sharing was an important capability in the EINSTEIN program, this appears to be nonexistent and DHS is unable to prove the return on investment of the program since performance measures don't "gauge the quality, accuracy, or effectiveness of the system's intrusion detection and prevention capabilities" (Muncaster, 2016). Furthermore, not all traffic appears to be running through the NCPS sensors due to lack of guidance, which in turn limits the effectiveness of the EINSTEIN program.

IRS

Not to get too far off topic, but since I'm writing this book around tax season, I thought the following information to be relevant in the course of our discussions. *Interesting tidbit*: Under the frequently asked questions (FAQs) of the Social Security Administration, Social Security Cards issued in 1946 contained a legend at the bottom of the card that read "FOR SOCIAL SECURITY PURPOSES—NOT FOR IDENTIFICATION." This was discontinued in the beginning of 1972 and the legend has not appeared on a Social Security Card since. I bring this up because one of the most common ways that the IRS sees income tax fraud is through the use of a Social Security number along with a counterfeit W2 form. In basic terms, the criminal files a tax refund before the victim files. *How does this occur?*

Figure 2.4 explains how tax fraud occurs.

To walk through this figure, your company must send your official W2, either in paper or electronic form, no later than February 29 and March 31, respectively, to the Social Security Administration (SSA). Here is the issue, your W2 isn't sent to the Internal Revenue Service directly. It takes the Social Security Administration until July before it sends these W2 forms over to the IRS. In the meantime, individuals are filing their returns with their own copies of W2 forms. In a case of a criminal targeting a victim for tax identity theft, they steal the Social Security number, make up a fake W2 form that will produce a return, and send this to the IRS before the "true" individual. The IRS processes the refund back to the criminal, in this example. The IRS doesn't get to reconcile the "real" W2s with the individually filed W2s for several months after they receive them from the SSA in July. At this point, the refund has already been issued.

In a report from *USA Today*, "According to the General Accountability Office (GAO), the IRS paid out 5.8 billion dollars in bogus refunds to identity thieves for the tax year 2013" (Weisman, 2016). This, of course, may be higher since it is only the fraud that was detected. Unfortunately, it takes victims on an average of 278 days to resolve an identity theft claim. This is much higher than the 180 days that the IRS has indicated to be the average resolution time.

The fraud problem is compounded not only against the IRS themselves, but also against unsuspecting tax payers. After years of advising tax payers that the IRS won't call them by phone, legislation was passed that mandated the IRS hire private collection agencies to collect taxes on their behalf. You may have already received a call from a scammer advising you that you are delinquent on your taxes and if you don't pay immediately, you will be arrested. (I know I have

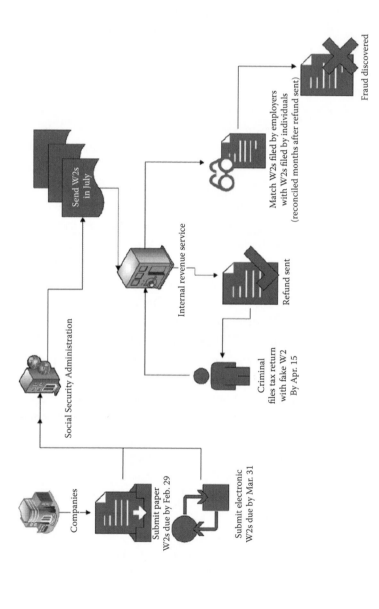

Figure 2.4 Tax fraud process. (From Weisman, S., What the IRS isn't telling you about identity theft, Retrieved from *USA Today*, http://www.usatoday.com/story/money/columnist/2016/01/30/what-irs-isnt-telling-you-identity-theft/79306984/, February 06, 2016.)

received these calls along with other friends and family members.) The Treasury Inspector General for Tax Administration (TIGTA) has warned of these phone call scams and since October 2013 has received approximately 896,000 complaints. TIGTA has also indicated that they know "of at least 5,000 victims who have paid more than 28.5 million dollars to the scammers" (Weisman, 2016).

To solve this issue, Congress could have easily required employers to send W2s to the IRS directly. There they could match the "real" W2s with the ones submitted by an individual. Any discrepancies could be addressed before a refund was issued. Instead, in the recent Omnibus Spending Bill signed into law on December 19, 2015, Congress just moved the date up that W2s must be filed with the Social Security Administration (SSA) for tax year ending 2016 to January 31, 2017. The SSA must still forward these returns to the IRS and the IRS still attempts to refund ninety percent (90%) of the returns within twenty-one (21) days of filing. *So what can you do to protect yourself from tax identity theft?* Not much, short of filing your tax returns early (or before a criminal files one on your behalf).

Telemedicine

Another rapidly growing phenomenon in the healthcare industry is telemedicine. From the American Telemedicine Association, "telemedicine is [formally defined as] the use of medical information exchanged from one site to another via electronic communications to improve a patient's clinical health status. Telemedicine includes a growing variety of applications and services using two-way video, email, smart phones, wireless tools and other forms of telecommunications technology" (American Telemedicine Association, 2016). The association further indicates that there are four (4) fundamental benefits of telemedicine driving its rapid growth: improved access, cost efficiencies, improved quality, and patient demand.

States are also recognizing the importance that telemedicine could have on their citizens. In Kentucky, legislatures are considering "a proposal related to Medicaid telemedicine that would cover remote patient monitoring (RPM)" (Open Minds, 2016a). The proposal would provide Medicaid coverage of RPM services at home and outside of medical facilities. Missouri is also taking up two proposals that would allow "RPM to be covered [by Medicaid] for individuals with specific conditions and at least two risk factors" (Open Minds, 2016b). RPM "is projected to reach 1.8 million patients worldwide by 2017" (Open Minds, 2016b).

In fact, telemedicine practices utilized at the International Space Station are setting an example to provide care to people in isolated parts on Earth. As you can imagine, handling medical emergencies in space comes with its own set of challenges "such as engineering and space constraints, limited bandwidth for data transmission, a lack of advanced diagnostic equipment and the absence of a physician. How space station crewmembers overcome these challenges may present a model to Earth-bound programs" (McCarthy, 2016a). Connectivity issues are a major obstacle since data transmission is not always continuous or very slow; however, "medical data and ultrasound images are routinely transmitted to ground-based flight surgeons for diagnostic and training purposes" (McCarthy, 2016a). Despite these communication concerns, crew members have been able to perform complex examinations through assistance of "just-in-time" education modules. Dr. Alfred Papali, MD, with the Division of Pulmonary and Critical Care Medicine at the University of Maryland, School of Medicine, indicated that "these modules could be adapted to terrestrial environments with limited connectivity. In addition, NASA has tested virtual remote guidance (i.e. recorded instructional videos for use by crew members using wearable technology) as a means of overcoming connectivity barriers; this technique will soon be used in Haiti to study remote guidance of endotracheal intubation" (McCarthy, 2016a).

In a technical brief on telemedicine written by The Agency for Healthcare Research and Quality (AHRQ), they identified 1,305 citations about telehealth and 44 systematic reviews. "The majority of studies found that telemedicine produced positive results for the conditions studied…The most positive results were noted for patients with multiple medical problems (mixed chronic conditions), diabetes, and mental health" (Jeremy C. Storhm, 2016). The study does provide some recommendations for further research in areas such as "sub-specialty consultation, acute care (online urgent care visits), maternal health, and pediatrics" (Jeremy C. Storhm, 2016). The study also recommended more research for new care and payment models. Telemedicine, or telehealth as referred to in the study, is touted as "the key needed to unlock the Triple aim (improved outcomes, decreased costs, and patient experience)" (Jeremy C. Storhm, 2016).

Telemedicine can provide great benefits; however, it can also bring its own set of risks. Since data transmission is an issue over slow or low bandwidth connections and in some cases, encryption creates an overhead for the data, a concern might be raised over the security transmission of the medical information being shared through tele-medicine. Just as a case in point, Chris Roberts, a researcher at secu-rity intelligence firm One World Labs, touted the claim of hacking NASA and messing around with the temperature on the space sta-tion. NASA apparently disputes the claims, but Roberts reportedly stated, "If they're going to leave it open that's not encrypted that's their own damn silly fault" (Austin, 2016).

NASA

Roberts isn't the only individual that claims that they've hacked NASA. According to *Infowars*, a group that goes by the name of *AnonSec* claims to have over 276 GB worth of data collected over sev-eral months of alleged compromise of NASA's internal network. The data includes videos, flight logs, and employee contact information. According to the report, hackers also attempted to crash a drone into the Pacific Ocean; however, NASA has denied the claim that the drone was compromised. Although the reported attempt and data breached may have been a bonus, the real objective of this hack was to obtain information on climate engineering. "NASA even has sev-eral missions dedicated to studying Aerosols [sic] and their affects on the environment and weather, so we targeted their systems" (Thalen, 2016).

Weather modification apparently has been utilized before as was the case in "Operation Popeye" during the Vietnam War where the United States used the weather against the Viet Cong to disrupt sup-ply channels by seeding clouds with silver iodide to create heavy rains. There are also reports that the Chinese government, to mitigate a drought, covered Beijing in snow by seeding the clouds. Some in the international science community support proposals to study climate manipulation in an attempt to counteract the greenhouse effect caused by man-made emissions. Studies have already appeared to be initiated to determine the feasibility and effects of certain geoengineering techniques. There could be some very good reasons to control the weather, but this knowledge in the wrong hands could be dangerous as well.

Medical Information Is Highly Coveted

In a 2013 report titled "Hackers Sell Health Insurance Credentials, Bank Accounts, SSNs and Counterfeit Documents, for over $1,000 Per Dossier" written by Dell SecureWorks, an information security services company, Don Jackson, senior security researcher, discovered in the criminal cyber underground, "the current asking price for a complete identity theft kit, containing the health insurance credentials, is in the range of $1,200 to $1,300 each" (Clarke, 2016). The report also addresses other prices for stolen credential as paraphrased in this list (see Table 2.1 for additional information).

A more recent article written in Reuters, *Your Medical Record Is Worth More to Hackers than Your Credit Card*, echoes the value of medical information by stating, "Your medical information is worth 10 times more than your credit card number on the black market" (Finkle, 2016). As Dave Kennedy, CEO of TrustedSEC, LLC and an expert on healthcare security, explains, cyber criminals want to target the $3 trillion U.S. healthcare industry "because of the ability to sell large batches of personal data for profit...Hospitals have low security, so it's relatively easy for these hackers to get a large amount of personal data for medical fraud" (Finkle, 2016).

This medical fraud rationale for the value of personal information is backed up from research published February 2015 in the *Fifth Annual Study on Medical Identity Theft* by the Ponemon Institute, an independent research and education firm. From a survey of 1,005 adult respondents that were victims of identity theft for fiscal year 2014, the highest three (3) areas explaining the reason for stealing their information were the following: fifty-nine percent (59%) indicated that their medical information was stolen to obtain healthcare services or treatments, fifty-six percent (56%) indicated criminals stole their information to obtain prescription pharmaceuticals or medical equipment, and fifty-two percent (52%) identified

Table 2.1   List of Prices and Related Information of Stolen Credentials on the Black Market

ITEM	INFORMATION	PRICE RANGE	SPECIAL REQUESTS
"Kitz"	Verified: • Health insurance • Social Security number • Financial information (account numbers or credit card information including PINs) • Driver's license information • Contact information (name, date of birth, address, phone, e-mail) Physical Documents (Counterfeit): • Insurance card • Credit cards • Driver's license	$1200–$1300 for package	Rush orders: Add $100–$500
"Fullz"	Verified: • Health insurance • Social Security number • Financial information (account numbers or credit card information including PINs) • Driver's license information • Contact information (name, date of birth, address, phone, e-mail) No Counterfeit Documents included.	$500 each	Based on information included
Health Insurance Only	Health Insurance Credentials: • Names • Date of birth • Insurance numbers/ information (contract, group, type of plan, copay, etc.) • Contact information on insurer	$20 each	Add $20 for associated coverage—dental, vision, other
Credit Cards	U.S. with CVV Code Non-U.S. with CVV Code Prestige Cards (Platinum, Diamond, Black with verified available balance)	$1–$2 each $2–$10 each $20–$400 each	With full track 2 and PIN: $5–$50; Some prices based on 4%–12% of balance

(Continued)

Table 2.1 (*Continued*) List of Prices and Related Information of Stolen Credentials on the Black Market

ITEM	INFORMATION	PRICE RANGE	SPECIAL REQUESTS
Online Bank Account	Less than $10,000 available PayPal, verified balance	$250–$1000 each $20–$200 each	Some prices based on 4%–12% of balance; Additional for associated e-mails; Additional for ACH bill pay or wire transfer abilities
Compromised Computer	Proxy only (prices can depend on bandwidth and location)	$1–$100 each	Additional for admin/root access
Game Accounts	Examples: XBOX, PSN, etc.	$5–$1000 each	Rare items sold separately
Skype Account	Premium	$1–$10 each	

the criminals obtained government benefits such as Medicare or Medicaid. The remaining reasons were as follows:

- Medical records access/modified—Twenty-three percent (23%).
- Opened fraudulent credit accounts—Fourteen percent (14%).
- Credit report accessed/modified—Five percent (5%).
- Five percent (5%) didn't know why their medical identity was stolen (Ponemon Institute, 2015a).

Another report released, *Verizon 2015 Protected Health Information Data Breach Report*, indicated that "stolen medical information is a much more widespread issue than previously thought, affecting [eighteen] 18 out of [twenty] 20 industries examined" (Brumfield, 2016). This first-time detailed analysis from Verizon's Data Breach Investigations Report (DBIR) team examined 1931 confirmed incidences involving 392 million protected health information records across 25 countries and indicated that ninety percent (90%) of these industries experienced a breach involving protected health information. In most cases, organizations outside of healthcare didn't even realize they held this type of personal information. Such information was found in employees' records that could include related health information on workers' compensation or possibly wellness programs.

In a *Private Industry Notification* alert dated April 8, 2014 (PIN#: 140408-009) from the Federal Bureau of Investigations (FBI), "Health Care Systems and Medical Devices [are] at Risk for Increased Cyber Intrusions for Financial Gain" (Federal Bureau of Investigations, 2016). The alert goes on to say, "Cyber actors will likely increase cyber intrusions against health care systems—to include medical devices—due to mandatory transition from paper to electronic health records (EHR), lax cybersecurity standards, and a higher financial payout for medical records in the black market" (Federal Bureau of Investigations, 2016).

The FBI alert additionally referenced a SANS Institute Report dated February 2014, titled "Health care cyberthreat report: Widespread compromises detected, compliance nightmare on horizon," which, based on the analysis of the report, indicated "health care security strategies and practices are poorly protected and ill-equipped to handle new cyber threats exposing patient medical records, billing and payment organizations, and intellectual property" (Federal Bureau of Investigations, 2016). The alert ends by referencing an EMC2/RSA White Paper published in 2013 titled "Cybercrime and the healthcare industry," where they cite an analysis performed by the World Privacy Forum by stating "Cyber criminals are selling the [health] information on the black market at a rate of $50 for each partial EHR [electronic health record], compared to $1 for a stolen social security number or credit card number" (Federal Bureau of Investigations, 2016). The FBI further warns, "EHR theft is also more difficult to detect, taking almost twice as long as normal identity theft" (Federal Bureau of Investigations, 2016).

Ease of Obtaining Information

Throughout my years working in the information security industry and assisting healthcare clients in their security efforts, I've had the privilege to work with some outstanding organizations. Unfortunately, I've found that almost all of these clients were unprepared and lacking in their information security efforts. To delve a little deeper, there is a big difference between being compliant and being secure. The organization can be in compliance with several regulations, but still be very vulnerable to exploitations of their systems. In retrospect, organizations could be pretty secure, but may lack the requisite documentation or perform activities needed for compliance. Although security and compliance are complimentary elements, I tend to put more emphasis on "real security" over "check box" compliance efforts.

According to a survey conducted at the 2015 Annual Black Hat Conference, Thycotic, an IT security solutions company, indicated that forty-five percent (45%) of hackers believe that privileged account credentials are their most coveted items during an attack, and nine (9) out of ten (10) hackers believe it is easy to obtain these privileged account credentials. The survey goes on to indicate that ninety-four percent (94%) of the hackers surveyed find these types of credentials in files that are maintained in an unsecured fashion (Thycotic, 2016). The survey also indicated that hackers believe the healthcare industry is a prime target leading with twenty-nine percent (29%), followed closely by financial services at twenty-five percent (25%), and government at twenty-four percent (24%) (Thycotic, 2016).

Security versus Privacy

Not to side track the conversation, but it is important that we pause to understand that security and privacy are vastly different. You can be very private, but not secure or vice versa. An analogy that I saw once in a video clip explaining the difference between privacy and security involved a desk with a computer monitor facing out toward a courtyard. The office had a sliding glass door that provided a way in or out toward the courtyard. The desk and monitor were facing in such a way that the monitor could be seen through the glass door. Now, let's say that we have blinds installed that could cover the door so that the monitor can't be seen from the outside.

In this scenario, we closed the blinds and we locked the sliding door. We might say that we are both private and secure. No one can see the monitor on the desk from the outside and to get into the office, you must have a key to open the door. As a counter example, if we left the blinds open and unlocked the door, we might conclude that someone could see the monitor screen from outside and there would be nothing prohibiting someone from walking into the office since the door isn't locked. In this case, we don't have any privacy or security.

In our next scenario, we lock the door, but we leave the blinds open. Here we might say that we are secure, but not private. Although someone couldn't open the door without a key, they could see through the glass to view what may be on our monitor. Now, let's unlock the door and close the blinds. Someone from outside can't see our monitor, but they could always open the unsecured door and come into the office. We might say that we are private, but not secure.

When it comes to privacy and security, I've found almost all of my clients to be lacking the fundamental concepts or implementing the necessary controls to adequately maintain their patients' health records. Although I might contend that I'm a pretty good "ethical" hacker (or a professional security expert that assists organizations in finding vulnerabilities along with providing recommendations to mitigate security/privacy-related deficiencies), I'm far from the best. I know that if I was able to easily compromise the systems that I was hired to test, it would be simple for an attacker to do the same if they made my clients a target.

Consumer Scores

Not only is health information valuable to criminals, but as we already discussed, "Big Data" is power. Enabling corporations to build profiles on consumers from the large amount of data available on them is key. This profiling was explained in detail in a report dated April 2, 2014, from the World Privacy Forum titled "The scoring of America: How secret consumer scores threaten your privacy and your future." The authors of the report, Pam Dixon, founder and executive director of the World Privacy Forum, along with Robert Gellman, a privacy and information policy consultant, describe consumer scores as being scores built from predictive modeling that takes a large amount of data and passes it "through analytical methods to predict the future, based on past information" (Gellman, 2016). Dixon and Gellman explain that "the World Privacy Forum defines a consumer score as follows: a consumer score that describes a single individual or sometimes a group of individuals (like a household), and predicts a consumer's behavior, habit, or predilection. Consumer scores use information about consumer characteristics, past behaviors, and other attributes in statistical models that produce a numeric score, a range of scores, or a yes/no" (Gellman, 2016). These scores can segment a group of individuals and companies (or governments) can use these scores to make decisions. Such decisions can be important and consumer scores could be used for almost anything, like identifying fraud or predicting healthcare costs. Dixon and Gellman warn, however, that unlike a common score for credit, "consumer scores remain largely secret and unregulated" (Gellman, 2016).

Almost every American of adult age has one or more scores attached to them. "Fed by the masses of consumer data now available," Dixon and Gellman said, "consumer scoring is quickly becoming a form of shorthand to make sense of a sea of information" (Gellman, 2016). As it relates to health information, health risk scores do not appear to fall under current regulations. Dixon and Gellman contend, "Even if the input to a score is accurate, consumers do not know or have any way to know what information derived from their lifestyle, health status, and/or demographic patterns is used to infer patterns of behavior and make decisions that affect their lives" (Gellman, 2016). Some of the other issues brought up in the report are secrecy over the score, accuracy of the score, identity theft, fairness/discrimination, sensitive health information, and consent for the use of the data being utilized in the scoring.

We'll go into more detail about the Health Insurance Portability and Accountability Act of 1996 (HIPAA) in a later section, but as it relates to information being maintained by data brokers outside of healthcare organizations, this information is not covered by the Privacy Rule protection that falls under HIPAA. For instance, if you provide your health information by completing a survey or other online registration activity, this information is not protected under HIPAA. It could be utilized on a consumer score with undesired consequences. Unfortunately, analysts may utilize demographic information as opposed to patient records to create a score where the score itself has no bearing or relevance to the records. The Affordable Care Act (ACA) health risk score, for example, is used to determine how much it will cost to provide healthcare to an individual, but may not utilize any specific healthcare records of the individual to determine their score. The ACA health risk score is supposed to be phased out over the next four (4) years and if an insurer maintains control over the risk score, it could be argued that the score is considered protected health information under direct identifier number eighteen (18)—any other unique identifying number, characteristic, or code; thus, an individual would be able to request to see their score. Since this score is so new, it is not yet determined how this score might be utilized in the future or if the federal government will phase out the use of this score as expected.

3

Healthcare Armageddon

Technology is neither good nor bad, nor is it neutral.

—*Dr. Melvin Kranzberg, Six Laws of Technology* **(Kranzberg, 2016)**

2015 Year of the Hack: Medical Breaches

"There were 736 million records exposed in 2015 due to a record setting 3,930 data breaches," according to the *CSO Online's 2016 Data Breach Blotter* (CSO Staff, 2016). This is a total number of breaches across all industries, so *how did the healthcare industry fair?* In a related study, "there were 258 large breaches of protected health information (PHI) last year [2015], and 113,208,516 patient health records were breached in total in 2015" (Goldman, 2016). These numbers may be a little skewed since the single largest healthcare-related incident to date occurred to Anthem in 2015 with 78 million records breached, but *are we facing a healthcare security crisis?* It seems like every day we are hearing a new report of a breach of our healthcare information. Since starting the research and writing of this book in the middle of January 2016, I've already read about several reported healthcare-related breaches. Table 3.1 describes these recently reported breaches.

Another recent reported breach occurred to NCH Healthcare Systems that operates two (2) hospitals in Naples, FL. Apparently, data was taken from two (2) computer servers located in a data center in Kansas City, MO. Medical records were involved including an employee and staff credentialing database (Olenick, 2016). 21st Century Oncology Holdings, a cancer treatment provider, notified 2.2 million patients and employees that their personal information such as names, Social Security numbers, diagnosis, and insurance records were compromised by a cyberattack. This provider was asked to delay notification until an investigation was completed and is offering three

Table 3.1 Listing of Recent Breaches That Were Reported over the First Few Weeks of 2016

ORGANIZATION	DESCRIPTION	NUMBER OF RECORDS INVOLVED	CAUSE
Centene	Payer	950,000	Loss of six (6) unencrypted hard drives
Michael Benjamin, MD	Hematology and oncology physician	1,300	Paper charts stolen from office
Alaska Orthopedic Specialists	Provider	Undetermined	E-mail of patients sent to personal account
Brigham and Women's Hospital	Hospital	1,009	Unauthorized access of credentials—phishing
St. Luke's Cornwall Hospital	Hospital	Undetermined	Stolen thumb drive
Maine General Health	Health system	Updated 2,000; total 120,000	Data discovered on external website
New West Health Services	Health plan	25,000	Off-site computer stolen
Blue Shield of California	Insurer	21,000	Data breach
Hillsides	Child welfare	502 clients; 468 employees	E-mail sent to personal account
Indiana University Health Arnett Hospital	Hospital	29,000	Missing thumb drive

Source: Jayanthi, A., 10 latest data breaches, Retrieved from Becker's Health IT & CIO Review, http://www.beckershospitalreview.com/healthcare-information-technology/9-latest-data-breaches-1-25-16.html, February 1, 2016.

(3) years of credit monitoring to those that were affected (Osborne, 2016). Premier Healthcare, LLC, a multi-specialty healthcare group in Bloomington, Indiana, reported a theft of a laptop containing approximately 205,748 records, of which, 1,769 records contained Social Security numbers or other financial information. Even though the laptop was password protected, it was not encrypted (Slavin, 2016).

Although not a cyberattack, providers need to secure all records containing personal information, including those on paper. Radiology Regional notified more than 480,000 patients when their medical and financial records started littering Fowler Street as a result of being blown out of a solid waste truck that was hauling these records off to the dump. Three (3) searches were conducted to ensure records were retrieved, but it begs the question: *Why weren't these records being disposed of properly (i.e., shredded)* (Payne, 2016)?

As it is shaping out, 2016 is going to be another "banner year" for breaches. According to a recent Ponemon Survey, we are trending at about one (1) healthcare-related cyberattack per month (Snell, 2016e). If all of these examples aren't enough to demonstrate that we have some issues with security, within the healthcare industry, let me point your attention to the Office for Civil Rights breach portal at: https://ocrportal.hhs.gov/ocr/breach/breach_report.jsf. This portal is affectionately referred to as the "wall of shame." It reports on incidents involving five hundred (500) or more individual records affected by a breach. Some troubling statistics can be uncovered from the reports of breaches collected on this site. "According to *Bitglass' 2016 Healthcare Breach Report*, [ninety-eight percent] 98% of record leaks were due to large-scale breaches targeting the healthcare industry" (Seals, 2016).

These large-scale breaches affected more than ten (10) million records each resulting in more than one hundred thirteen (113) million records breached or, in other words, one (1) in three (3) Americans that fell victim to a healthcare-related data breach (Korolov, 2016b). In 2015, there was an increase of data breaches of eighty percent (80%) and as Nat Kausik, CEO of Bitglass, explains, "As the [internet of things] revolution compounds the problem with real-time patient data, healthcare organizations must embrace innovative data security technologies to meet security and compliance requirements" (Seals, 2016).

Raj Samani, CTO for Intel Security EMEA, states the same concern: "In 2016 we're only going to see the further exploitation of people's data and the expansion of what we call the 'data economy', especially as the Internet of Things becomes part of our day-to-day lives with smart home fast becoming a reality" (SC Magazine UK, 2016). Samani contrasts society in that we are outraged by the amount of data breaches that occur, but we trade our personal information for free applications or services.

David Mount, director, security solutions consulting EMEA, Micro Focus, contends that we leave security to the decisions made by the end users. Unfortunately, people are considered the weakest link in the security chain and as Mount explains, "As an industry [security], when we consider users to be the last line of defence, the technology has failed" (SC Magazine UK, 2016).

Based on the analysis performed by *Information Is Beautiful* on the *World's Biggest Data Breaches* (website: http://www.informationis beautiful.net/visualizations/worlds-biggest-data-breaches-hacks), 2015 was a record-breaking year. Cases in point:

- Anthem, Inc., a large insurance company, reported the theft of eighty (80) million Social Security numbers and other sensitive information. It appears as though credentials were compromised allowing queries to be run against databases that stored the data (Krebs, 2016a).
- Premera Blue Cross, another large insurance company, reported a breach of eleven (11) million records containing medical and financial information (Vinton, 2016).
- CareFirst, a Blue Cross Blue Shield health plan, reported a breach of a little over one (1) million records containing customer contact information and date of births (Abelson, 2016).
- Medical Informatics Engineering (MIE), a software development company, reported a breach of four (4) million patient records of more than two hundred thirty (230) hospitals and other providers. Almost a quarter of the state of Indiana's population was affected by the breach (Paul, 2016).

Chief Legal and Compliance Officer of Greenway Health, LLC, Sam Snider, believes breaches like these reiterate the importance to increase security efforts such as assessing and monitoring the network. Upon closer examination, however, Snider contends "that fundamental security awareness still matters…basic security awareness training remains the most important tool in an organizations [sic] cybersecurity program" (Snider, 2016). Attackers have gotten more sophisticated in targeting end users through phishing and spoofing domains to trick users into believing their malicious attachments or links are from legitimate company personnel.

Another Search Engine to the Rescue

Although the Office for Civil Rights publicizes breaches that affect more than five hundred (500) records, there are still a lot more complaints or violations that take place within healthcare providers and other related healthcare service organizations reported to the

Department of Health and Human Services. ProPublica developed the HIPAA Helper, (website: https://projects.propulbica.org/hipaa), to assist individuals in finding out which organizations might be violating your privacy. Taken from information obtained through the Freedom of Information Act, this search engine provides data from the U.S. Department of Health and Human Services Office for Civil Rights, the California Department of Public Health, and the U.S. Department of Veterans Affairs. It also provides such information as the organizations receiving the most privacy complaints, notable incidents, and top ten (10) lists.

Proponents of this site may claim it will bring awareness to individuals about concerns over their privacy and motivate organizations to do better at protecting information, while opponents may argue that it may hurt the reputation of the organizations. "There's been concern that the government does not do enough to deter HIPAA violations. The increased transparency ProPublica has helped provide might do wonders to counter that" (Baum, 2016).

Hackers Are the Problem

Referring back to the Bitglass' 2016 Healthcare Breach Report, findings showed that "98 percent of record leaks were due to large-scale breaches targeting the healthcare industry" (Pennic, 2016). Luke Brown, VP & GM, EMA, India and LATAM at Digital Guardian notes, "The past twelve months [2015] have seen some of the biggest data breaches on record, across a wide range of global industries and sectors" (Brown, 2016). Looking at some of the trends, it is apparent that the healthcare industry is one of the top targets for hackers and cyber criminals.

According to a report published by Raytheon/Websense, a security company, that based their analysis on live feeds from global healthcare organizations, Carl Leonard, principal security analyst, revealed that the healthcare industry "sees 340 percent more security incident and attacks than usual" (Korolov, 2016a). The report goes on to indicate that healthcare is more likely to fall victim to the items demonstrated in Figure 3.1.

According to the *Sixth Annual Benchmark Study on Privacy and Security of Healthcare Data* conducted by the Ponemon Institute issued May 2016 (Figure 3.2), "89 percent of responding organizations

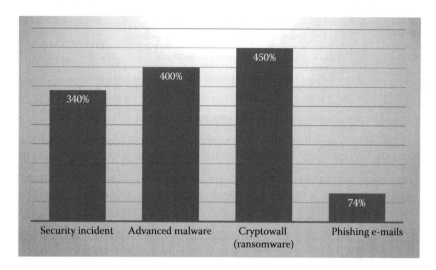

Figure 3.1   The likeliness that healthcare organizations will fall victim to certain attacks. (From Korolov, M., Healthcare firms three times more likely to see data breaches, Retrieved from CSO Online, http://www.csoonline.com/article/2985401/cyber-attacks-espionage/healthcare-firms-three-times-more-likely-to-see-data-breaches.html, February 2, 2016.)

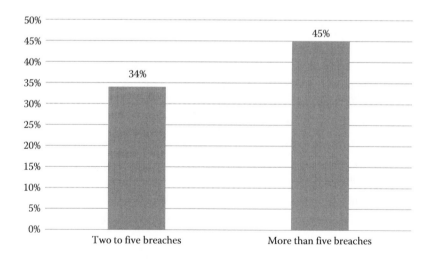

Figure 3.2   Percent of healthcare organization respondents experiencing multiple data breaches. (From Raths, D., Sixth annual ponemon survey: Criminal attacks cause 50% of breaches. Retrieved from Healthcare Informatics, http://www.healthcare-informatics.com/article/sixth-annual-ponemon-survey-criminal-attacks-cause-50-breaches?utm_source=feedburner&utm_medium=feed&utm_campaign=Feed%3A+healthcare-informatics+%28Healthcare+Informatics%29, May 27, 2016.)

experienced data breaches, and the number of breaches tied to criminal attacks continues has reached 50 percent" (Raths, 2016).

What may be more distressing is that out of fear over risks of patient safety regarding misconfigurations or false positives of security solutions, up to seventy-five percent (75%) of network traffic for hospitals is not monitored. This increases the threat to these organizations since suspicious activities may go unnoticed for a long period of time. If by chance activity is discovered, the attackers are usually long gone and answering the questions *who, what, when, how, where,* and *why* becomes an even greater challenge to incident responders.

Although "zero-day" attacks, or a vulnerability in a system or application that is discovered that the vendor is unaware of, are sometimes used by hackers to compromise systems, generally, hackers attempt to breach systems from less obvious methods. As soon as a vendor releases a patch for the vulnerable system, the zero-day becomes null and void. For this reason, hackers will wait to find compromise vectors that make it very difficult for security teams to detect. "For example, researchers have seen an uptick in file[-]less malware attacks, in which adversaries use an OS's embedded tools to penetrate an organization's network and evade detection by traditional programs like antivirus software" (O'Connor, 2016a). Rob Joyce, Chief of the National Security Agency's Tailored Access Operations (TAO), indicated, "For big corporate networks, persistence and focus will get you in without a zero day; there are so many more vectors that are easier, less risky and more productive" (O'Connor, 2016a).

The hacking economy is primed for attackers. A report from the Ponemon Institute and sponsored by Palo Alto Networks titled *Flipping the Economics of Attacks* surveyed more than 10,000 hackers from the United States, Germany, and the United Kingdom. The report shows that specialized hacking tool kits costing on average of $1367 have increased in use by sixty-three percent (63%) of the respondents along with sixty-four percent (64%) indicating the tools are very effective (Taylor, 2016). *Is hacking lucrative?* On average, respondents indicated that they earn $28,744 per year or $40.75 per hour, which is just about a quarter of the average salary for security professionals (Taylor, 2016).

Not only do organizations need to be concerned with the external hacker threat, but they also need to worry about the trusted, insider threat. This insider threat is the biggest risk to fraud, corruption, or data loss faced by organizations, according to Ernst & Young's *2016 Global Forensic Data Analytics Survey, Shifting into high gear; mitigating risks and demonstrating returns* (Palmer, 2016). To combat this threat, companies are turning to advanced forensic data analytics (FDA) tools along with proactive monitoring. These tools assist in mining or monitoring data to identify fraud or suspicious activities that are or have occurred.

During a presentation at the *Usenix Enigma Security Conference* in San Francisco, Rob Joyce told a crowd of cybersecurity professionals what they can do to keep unauthorized people out of their systems. A lot of his recommendations would seem pretty straight forward to most individuals in the cybersecurity industry and it sort of begs the question as to why it may be so easy for the National Security Agency (NSA) and others to compromise these systems? This is sort of "Security 101" tips, but these are the items Joyce reminded security professionals of the following (paraphrased):

- Systems classified as important should only be accessed by individuals that need to access these systems.
- Networks and data should be isolated, providing segmentation.
- Keep systems and applications updated.
- Configure "white lists" where only applications on the list should be allowed to run on a system. All other applications not on the list will be prohibited from running.
- Disable or change all default/hardcoded accounts/passwords. In most cases, systems and applications that are initially installed are installed with "default" credentials. These should not be available in production systems.
- Upgrade protocols that do not utilize encryption to secure credentials or sensitive information that are transmitted across the wire or that transmit across public networks.
- Configure systems that monitor for suspicious activities and ensure that someone is reviewing these logs on a continuous basis.
- Don't ignore the items you believe are insignificant; these items may just be the foothold an attacker needs to compromise a system. Even the temporary openings that are provided for vendor remote fixes could be an entry point.

- Personal devices that a company can't control, which are allowed to connect to a corporate network, are targeted by attackers. The integrated systems for AC/heat, or alarm systems, could be leveraged as a vector of attack if it doesn't come to mind for security consideration (Zetter, 2016b).

Patients Trust Healthcare

Even with the number of record breaches taking place in the healthcare industry, individuals still apparently trust their doctors. A survey performed by the National Cyber Security Alliance (NCSA) indicated that seventy-four percent (74%) surveyed "trust healthcare providers the most with personal information" (Davis, 2016b). Michael Kaiser, NCSA Executive Director, said, "I think the expectation is that when they [patients] provide personal information [to their providers], it's protected" (Davis, 2016b). In most cases, you provide more personal information to your healthcare provider than you do to your banker and this information is expected to be kept private and secure.

This is sometimes easier said than done as we've been discussing. One of the concerns that we see in the healthcare industry is that most organizations don't have a clue as to where their information is located. They don't know where this information is being stored, maintained, or who has control over this information. They can't tell you who has access to the information and don't even touch on the concept of how this information is protected. These issues are compounded when the information is exchanged with other healthcare providers through health information exchanges or other sharing solutions. Once this information leaves the compounds of the healthcare provider's four walls, no one knows where the information ends up. As we've alluded to throughout our conversation thus far, this information will most likely end up somewhere in the "cloud."

In a survey of 2000 respondents conducted by OnePoll, approximately eighty-seven percent (87%) indicated they would not or very likely not do business with a company that has suffered a breach of credit or debit card details. Tim Critchley, CEO of Semafone, a UK-based fraud prevention company, stated, "...the reputational damage suffered by companies who fail to protect personal data can translate directly into a loss of business" (Drinkwater, 2016). Data breaches can also result in a loss of reputation. The Ponemon Institute's report, *The Aftermath of a Mega Data Breach: Consumer Sentiment*, indicated that environment disasters, poor customer service, and data breaches are on par for impacting reputation (Drinkwater, 2016). *Fallout: The Reputational Impact of IT Risk*, a Forbes Insights Report, showed a breach has damaged the reputation of forty-six percent (46%) of companies and another nineteen percent (19%) have suffered brand damage from a third-party breach (Drinkwater, 2016). Jane Frankland, managing director of consultancy KnewSmart and formerly of Sensepost and NCC, reiterates, "A favorable corporate reputation is a valuable, yet intangible asset. It plays a vital role in attracting the best talent, suppliers and investment" (Drinkwater, 2016).

Healthcare, at its core, is about human beings and not computers or technology. Although technology in medicine is important, physicians primarily went into medicine to help humans and not play with computers. At times, information technology professionals forget this, leaving a huge gap between technology and clinical areas that needs to be closed to make any progress possible. As Dr. Suneel Dhand explains, "Health care is an intensely personal and human arena. It is about relationships and very raw emotions of illness and sickness" (Dhand, 2016). This mind-set also impacts the security controls around the systems.

I can't tell you how many times I have performed an assessment on a healthcare organization only to hear that we can't enforce strong passwords because the physicians complain (or can't remember the password they use). The securities of these systems suffer and are trumped by flexibility/operational necessity. (Of course, my response to this is a little less politically correct—I usually ask the physician that complains the most to write down his/her favorite diagnosis. This medical term is always at least eight (8) characters long and of course, the doctor spells it correctly. I then, jokingly, mention to the doctor that this is now their new password—of course, they need to capitalize it and put a number at the end along with a symbol, like an exclamation point. I convince them that they are able to remember this advanced medical term, that I am confident that they can remember this password in the future.)

If this doesn't get the point across, I play a little hard ball. I find out who is ultimately in charge and tell them that they've just been breached. They need to write out a nice big check, say in the area of $500,000 (it was a small breach). As the room grows silent and I see the decision makers figuring out what line items will need to be cut in the budget to come up with this amount, I relieve the tension by telling them that it was a "false alarm"; however, if they keep things "status quo" and don't improve their security posture, the next time someone says that they were breached—it will be for real.

The Standard Response

Unfortunately when a breach occurs, companies react with the same old "song and dance." In basic terms, the company, albeit required by regulations, acknowledges that they have had a breach. It is more often than not someone else discovered the breach and advised the company that they had a problem. Of course, these are the activities the company is aware of, but *what about suspicious activity that they aren't aware of?* The company will go on to say that it was a "sophisticated" or "advance" attack. They will never say that they didn't have policies/procedures in place, they didn't follow appropriate physical safeguards, or they didn't have any technical controls in place to not only stop the attack from occurring or detect the attack immediately once it commenced.

The company is required to provide details of the breach, of course if the details of the attack are available. In most cases, the company will hire a computer forensic company to identify the cause of the attack, if possible. This can generally only occur if appropriate logs or monitoring systems are in place; however, from my experience, this is rarely ever implemented within healthcare organizations.

Sometimes the company will respond that all systems are secure based on the opinion of the forensic company performing the investigation or any remediation efforts that internal staff have performed. One of the surefire way of making sure that systems are secure would be to reimage all systems back to a known secure state. This takes a lot of time and resources to undergo. In most cases, systems will be tested and provided an "all clear" based on the results of the tests. These tests may not always catch that a system has been compromised or is still compromised.

As an example, Affinity Gaming, a Las Vegas casino, hired a security company, Trustwave, to investigate and contain a breach of credit card data on their network. Based on the forensic report produced by Trustwave, the source of the data breach was identified and the malware responsible was contained. A year later, Affinity Gaming had a second breach. This time, Affinity Gaming hired a competing security firm, Mandiant, which indicated that the malware was not fully removed. The lawsuit filed by Affinity Gaming claims that Trustwave's work was "woefully inadequate" (Goodin, 2016). It goes on to say that Trustwave lied about properly diagnosing the breach, stating the breach was contained (when apparently it wasn't), providing recommendations to remediate the breach (that appeared to be worthless), and failed to identify the source of the breach. In *The Financial Times*, Trustwave officials denied the claim stating, "We dispute and disagree with the allegations in the lawsuit and we will defend ourselves vigorously in court" (Goodin, 2016).

Companies that have had a breach will attempt to set the minds at ease of individuals affected by indicating that there is no evidence that the data was or will be used inappropriately. Since the information is out there under someone else's control, it is not fair for these companies to make this assumption. They can't tell what, how, or when this information will be used. A cybercriminal may sit on this information for years, may gather or data mine other information, and as we've discussed, may put all of this information into "kitz" to sell it at a higher price in the black market. There is no telling how this information can or will be used against the victims and let's face it, *who has requested to change their Social Security number when they have been involved in a breach?*

It is a requirement that companies must notify all individuals affected by a breach. This notification must be done, in the case of a healthcare data breach, through first class mail. Hopefully the notification comes to the individual affected because if not, they may not even know that they were impacted by a breach. As a part of "good will" and not that it is required, a company may provide credit monitoring services "free of charge" for a certain amount of time. Unfortunately, credit monitoring may not be enough to protect an individual from medical identity theft. In addition, a cybercriminal may wait out the limited time that credit monitoring is offered. Credit monitoring may only last a couple of years, but in most cases, your personal information stays with you for a life-time.

Companies will usually end their responses that they take the security and privacy of your information very seriously and that they are going to do everything they can, in the future, to prevent a breach from occurring again. *Wouldn't it had been nice that they did all of this before the breach occurred in the first place? Why wasn't the protection of your information a priority before the incident as opposed to being one after an incident?* As John Lynn, the founder of the *HealthcareScene.com* blog, said as it relates to companies' responses to a breach, "Unfortunately, far too many [companies] are living in an 'ignorance is bliss' state right now. What they don't tell you is that ignorance is not bliss if you get caught in your ignorance" (Lynn, 2016b).

EU Doesn't Trust U.S. Privacy: Agreement Made

Over the past fifteen (15) years, the European Union (EU), through a Safe Harbor Agreement, permitted data on citizens and businesses of the EU member countries to be stored with companies in the United States provided they complied with the EU's data privacy laws. In October 2015, however, the European Court of Justice (ECJ) invalidated this agreement. In basic terms, the privacy laws of the United States were inadequate to protect the privacy of the EU member's data. It isn't the issue that companies aren't complying with the privacy laws of the EU, but rather, U.S. surveillance laws are the concern. Danny O'Brien, international director of the Electronic Frontier Foundation, stated, "What's important about this is that without US legal reform, the Safe Harbor—and all the other proposals to move personal data from the US to the EU—fail" (Peters, 2016b).

With the passing of the Cybersecurity Act of 2015 (CISA), the sharing of information between the EU and the United States became more difficult. CISA provided the ability to share information with the government without requiring this information to be sanitized of personally identifiable information. In addition, it provided protection against organizations that voluntarily share this information.

The EU General Data Protection Regulation (GDPR) is replacing the EU Data Protection Directives and the fines for violating privacy are steep. Fines being proposed could be up to four percent (4%) of a company's annual global revenue or $21.76 million, whichever is greater. Neil Stelzer, general counsel for data classification firm Identity Finder, stated, "privacy is a right that is protected more strongly there [in the EU]" (Peters, 2016b). In fact, the GDPR expanded the definition of personal data to include "other factors that could be used to identify an individual, such as their genetic, mental, economic, cultural, or social identity" (IT Governance, 2016).

The EU and the United States have come to an agreement for data transfer known as the EU-U.S. Privacy Shield. Some skeptics believe that this new agreement will not be upheld by the EDJ as valid. Others like Vera Jourová, European Union Commissioner for Justice, Consumers, and Gender Equality, indicated that it "lives up to the requirements of the ECJ" (Peters, 2016a). Jourová further explained that the U.S. Office of the Director of National Intelligence will provide written assurance to the fact that safeguards will be established on access to EU citizens' information. The Privacy Shield will be different from Safe Harbor in that it will require stronger obligations from companies and is considered a "living mechanism" whereby the European Commission and the U.S. Department of Commerce will review it on an on-going basis.

The following is a summary of some of the important elements of the Privacy Shield:

- Enhanced obligations on processing data along with guaranteeing individual rights. Companies will need to publish their practices that will make them enforcement under the Federal Trade Commission. Companies handling European human resource's data must comply with European Data Protection Authorities.
- Access by public authorities (i.e., law enforcement) is subject to limitations, safeguards, and oversight. The United States is giving the EU written assurance that it won't perform mass surveillance on the data transferred.
- Europeans will be provided a complaint process and if companies are discovered not meeting requirements, they could be subject to sanctions. A new Ombudsperson will be created (European Commission, 2016).

Furthermore, if the Judicial Redress bill is passed, it would enable European citizens the right to sue the United States for misuse of their information by law enforcement agencies. This appears to contradict the protection provided by CISA. Yorgen Edholm, CEO of Accellion, a cloud services firm, contends, "Ultimately, the practice of trans-Atlantic data transfer will remain controversial as long as there remains a fundamental difference of opinion between the U.S. and the EU on what is more important: national security or data privacy" (Peters, 2016a).

4
Victims

I am convinced that there are only two types of companies: those that have been hacked and those that will be.

**—Robert S. Mueller III, Former Director of the FBI
(Robert and Mueller, 2016)**

Costs

I've shared this quote from Robert S. Mueller III, former director of the Federal Bureau of Investigation, in my previous book and several times during speaking engagements. I usually take this quote one step further and talk about one additional type of companies: those that don't know they've been hacked. In the most recent annual study of data breaches, *Ponemon Institute's 2015 Cost of Data Breach Study: Global Analysis,* based on a sample size of three hundred fifty (350) organizations, the average time to identify a breach is two hundred six (206) days (Ponemon Institute, 2015a). This means that it took companies just under seven (7) months to figure out that they've been breached. In addition, it took these same companies, on average, sixty-nine (69) days to contain the breach (Ponemon Institute, 2015a).

The Center for Strategic and International Studies, a Washington research firm, developed a report funded by the security firm, McAfee (part of Intel Security), estimating the annual cost of worldwide cybercrime to be more than $445 billion. This is almost one percent (1%) of the global income (Peterson, 2016b). As you might imagine, the more technologically advanced countries such as "The United States, Germany, and China together accounted for about $200 billion of the total in 2013" (Peterson, 2016b). Figure 4.1 shows the comparison of the breakdown of the losses.

When a company falls victim to a breach, the costs are high. Based on the same Ponemon report, research indicated that companies

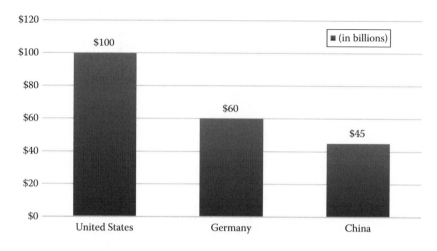

Figure 4.1 Comparison of losses to cybercrime by the top three (3) countries. (From Peterson, E.N., Report: Cybercrime and espionage costs $445 billion annually, Retrieved from *The Washington Post*, https://www.washingtonpost.com/world/national-security/report-cybercrime-and-espionage-costs-445-billion-annually/2014/06/08/8995291c-ecce-11e3-9f5c-9075d5508f0a_story.html, February 07, 2016.)

in the United States, on average, face $6.53 million in total costs related to a breach. Healthcare faces the largest average cost per record breached at $363 per individual record (Ponemon Institute, 2015a). *Can you even imagine the cost of a breach for a company like Anthem that had over 80 million records compromised?* If this calculation holds true, they could be facing costs in the area of $29 Billion (that's right, with a "B").

The Ponemon study goes on to point out that there were three (3) major areas that contributed to higher costs of a breach in 2015. First, as we've already seen, attacks on organizations to obtain the data they possess have increased. It is costing companies more to defend themselves or mitigate potential issues they find. Since healthcare is such a rich target for hackers due to the amount of data they maintain, the value of the data due to the personal nature of the information, and the complexity of the systems healthcare organizations operate, the costs to healthcare organizations have risen to protect themselves from cyberattacks.

Second, not only are their tangible costs associated with breaches, but organizations, especially in healthcare, can see high levels of attrition. Since healthcare services are primarily supported on the back of trust, if patients lose trust in their healthcare providers, they'll seek other providers. Healthcare is built on personal relationships that directly relate to the root core of privacy. One of the key assets of any good doctor is his or her reputation. Without a good reputation, the doctor won't stay in business long. Patients will leave and new patients won't seek out their help. If providers can't keep their patient information private, they won't be in business very long. As the Ponemon Report states, "The growing awareness of identity theft and consumers' concerns about the security of their personal data following a breach has contributed to the increase in lost business" (Ponemon Institute, 2015a). This is no truer than in the healthcare industry.

Finally, obtaining expert services to respond to a breach as in the case of performing forensic analysis and investigations has contributed to the additional costs of a breach. Company's management wants to know what happened to cause an incident. This is important in healthcare since regulations are in place to define an incident. For instance, breach notifications must be made after, what I refer to as a "compromise risk analysis." Since there are four (4) areas that must be considered in the case of an incident rising to the level of a breach, a full analysis of an incident must be performed. The four (4) factors to consider are

1. The nature and extent of the information involved, including the types of identifiers and the likelihood of reidentification
2. The unauthorized person who used the information or to whom the disclosure was made
3. Whether the information was actually acquired or viewed
4. The extent to which the risk to the information has been mitigated

Except as may be demonstrated through a compromise risk analysis that classifies an incident in the area of a low probability that protected health information has been compromised, breach notification is required in "all" situations. As a sidebar, compromise was defined as posing a significant risk of financial, reputational, or other harm to an individual; however, with the finalization of the Omnibus Rule of 2012, breach notification requirements utilize the analysis performed to all healthcare providers to determine their responsibilities in notifying individuals affected by a breach.

It is interesting to note that per Ponemon study, thirty-four percent (34%) of data breach costs are direct costs such as hiring experts to facilitate investigations while the other sixty-six percent (66%) are indirect costs such as accounted for in time or resources spent to handle a breach (Ponemon Institute, 2015a). Unfortunately, the cost of a breach can extend over several months beyond just the initial costs of responding to and making notifications of a breach.

A survey of sixty (60) organizations by the SANS Institute researching the costs over time for a company following a breach indicated that sixty percent (60%) still felt some related impact of the breach even after remediation steps took place. Figure 4.2 shows some of the "aftershocks" felt by companies affected by a breach.

Costs related to cybercrime not only impact the global economy and organizations, but also directly hurt individuals that fall victim to breaches involving their personal data. This personal data could be utilized in a number of ways. Of course this information can be utilized to open up fraudulent credit accounts, but as it relates to healthcare, this information is used for medical identity theft and other fraud. This information can be provided to individuals that don't have health insurance or may need to obtain medical services. It can also be used

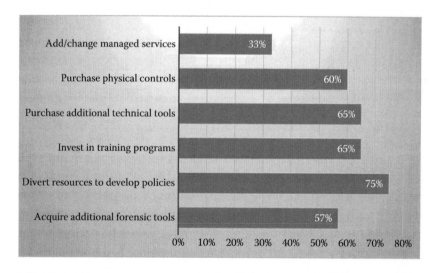

Figure 4.2 Percentage of respondents having to perform/spend/purchase items after a breach. (From Chickowski, E., Post-breach costs and impact can last years, Retrieved from Darkreading, http://www.darkreading.com/risk/post-breach-costs-and-impact-can-last-years/d/d-id/1324055, February 07, 2016.)

to obtain prescription drugs or controlled substances that could be sold back out on the streets.

According to the *Fifth Annual Study on Medical Identity Theft* published in February 2015 by the Ponemon Institute, as it relates specifically to individuals that have suffered at the hands of criminals targeted through the healthcare system, sixty-five percent (65%) of them paid on an average of $13,500 to recover from medical identity theft (Ponemon Institute, 2015b). Furthermore, it takes a lot of time to recover. On average, more than two hundred (200) hours and only ten percent (10%) reported that they were completely satisfied with the outcome (Ponemon Institute, 2015b). To make things worse, individuals may not even realize that they were victims, thirty percent (30%) didn't know when the incident occurred to them and over half of the fifty-four percent (54%) of individuals that found errors on their explanation of benefits didn't know how to go about reporting the issue (Ponemon Institute, 2015b).

Due to the amount of private information that is maintained in a person's medical record, the impact to the person can be severe. The majority of individuals that fell victim to medical identity theft also fell victim to other financial issues like fraudulent accounts being opened under their name that eventually led to decreased credit scores. In some cases, there were delays in receiving necessary healthcare services or misdiagnosis and treatments. One of the major concerns here is the lack of awareness that individuals have over their medical information. Half of the population don't realize that errors from medical identity theft can stay in their permanent record and they don't know how to protect themselves (Patterson, 2016). Further education is needed for consumers of healthcare services and the healthcare industry as a whole. This is also the mission of the Medical Identity Fraud Alliance (MIFA): "to strengthen the healthcare ecosystem by working to reduce the frequency and impact of medical identity fraud" (MIFA, 2016).

Identity Theft/Fraud

According to the U.S. Department of Justice's website regarding the topic of identity theft and identity fraud, these "are terms used to refer to all types of crime in which someone wrongfully obtains and uses another person's personal data in some way that involves fraud or deception, typically for economic gain" (Department of Justice, 2016). In 1998, Congress passed the *Identity Theft and Assumption Deterrence Act*, creating definition and subsequent punishment for "knowingly transfer[ring] or us[ing], without lawful authority, a means of identification of another person with the intent to commit, or to aid or abet, any unlawful activity that constitutes a violation of Federal law, or that constitutes a felony under any applicable State or local law." Under 18 U.S.C. § 1028(a)(7), the punishment for identity theft carries a maximum term of 15 years' imprisonment, a fine, and criminal forfeiture of any personal property used or intended to be used to commit the offense. In some cases, according to the Department of Justice, these crimes may also violate other statutes such as identification fraud, credit card fraud, computer fraud, mail fraud, wire fraud, or financial institution fraud.

According to reports from the Department of Justice, "17.6 million U.S. residents were identity theft victims in 2014, at a cost of $15.4 billion" (Wilber, 2016). Replacing credit cards is easy; fixing credit scores is another issue. According to U.S. Secret Service Agent Matthew O'Neill, "What Americans may not understand is that it's really, really easy to buy this [identity] information. And once it's stolen, it's nearly impossible to be sure that you can reclaim your stolen identity" (Wilber, 2016).

Why is identity theft so easy to commit? I think we've answered this question for the most part already. People are generally "too trusting." We've already discussed how "free" applications are utilized to collect all types of information about us and how willing individuals are to give away this information. In public, individuals talk about themselves to connect with others. *How many times have you sat behind people in a restaurant or at a coffee shop discussing their personal matters with each other?*

As a consultant, I travel a lot. You could basically call me a "road warrior." I love airports—*no, not really*, but in the line of work I'm in, I find the place to be very interesting. It seems that as soon as you go through the Transportation Security Administration (TSA) checkpoint, you have entered a "secure zone" where everyone can let their guard down. It is a safe area where you can conduct your business affairs and share your most intimate stories, *right?* There is always that one individual in a fairly quiet waiting area that is louder than everyone else, especially if they are on a cell phone. Maybe it is a sales person talking to his boss about the new company he or she just landed. Or maybe it is a college student talking about the huge party they just attended and how drunk they got. Or maybe it is a business person calling the hotel to reserve a last-minute room.

On one of my excursions, I actually met this businessman who was sitting right next to me. Unbeknownst to him, I'm a professional ethical "hacker" and was just gearing down from performing an intense penetration test on a client. The gentleman was trying to make a reservation for the night at a hotel. Having tons of experience making these types of calls, I knew exactly what was going to come next on the other end of his cell phone—"Sir, I'll need your credit card information to reserve the room."

Being the professional that I am and always trying to keep my skills honed, I opened up a notepad application on the tablet device I had running at the time. As the unsuspecting "poor" man was reading off all the numbers and information to the customer service representative, I was typing the number right along on my tablet. The phone call ended and I was left in amazement. I had a guy who was sitting right next to me and oblivious at what he just did. He didn't even make an attempt to move to a less populated area of the terminal.

Needless to say, I erased all of the information I collected immediately. (I only collected the data to see if it *could be* done; I had no intentions of performing any illegal acts against this person.) As the gentleman was just about ready to get up to board the plane, I gently told him what he had just done. I gave him my business card and advised him that I was one of the "good guys"; however, I couldn't attest to anyone else that may have been in the vicinity that overheard his conversation. He seemed like he got the point and realized, albeit too late, that it probably wasn't a good idea giving his information over the phone in earshot of everyone. He thanked me and rushed off to his plane. I probably would guess that he was going to be on the phone with his credit card company immediately to have a new card reissued or *would he? How much inconvenience is there in changing cards especially in cases where you have cards on file with other companies for automatic payments?* This man was fortunate enough to have met me, but what if I was someone else whose mission in life is to take advantage of people.

Hieu Min Ngo, pronounced "no," is a Vietnamese hacker considered "one of the most prolific identity thieves in U.S. history" (Wilber, 2016). He made $2 million over two (2) years providing criminals access to a database containing records of two hundred (200) million Americans. Ngo plead guilty to wire/identity fraud (and other charges) and was sentenced to thirteen (13) years in federal prison in 2015. He shared some insights of his crimes during an interview with Bloomberg Politics along with writing his own e-books of his escapades to warn others.

Ngo explains that he had always had interest in computers and electronics that started at an early age. By the time he was sixteen (16), he was installing key-logging software at Internet cafe computers just to find out interesting stuff for fun. Ngo learned in high school that he could make money with his "hacking" skills by compromising credit cards from retailers' websites. While attending a New Zealand university, he continued hacking and eventually got caught for dealing in goods purchased by stolen credit cards. Ngo returned home to Vietnam and was turned on to the money that could be made by stealing U.S. Social Security numbers.

Ngo was able to compromise a company in New Jersey that maintained a consumer information database. He began selling this data to criminals and made it more efficient by setting up his own website to run the queries. The New Jersey company discovered and fixed their vulnerabilities leaving Ngo to find another victim. He discovered Court Ventures, a data broker in California. After compromising a private investigator's computer to create fraudulent papers, he was able to gain access to the data broker's database. To make matters worse, Court Ventures had an agreement in place to share data with U.S. Info Search that owned another billion records. Experian eventually acquired Court Ventures, and after learning about Ngo's scam, they stopped reselling U.S. Info Search data. Gerry Tschopp, Experian's senior vice president of public affairs, reiterated on this case, "To be clear, no Experian database was accessed" (Wilber, 2016).

Brian Krebs, a security consultant and blogger, exposed Ngo's fraudulent website that got the attention of U.S. Secret Service Agent O'Neill. Through O'Neill's investigation, Ngo was identified and a sting operation commenced. Experian was notified that their data was being used and terminated Ngo's access. O'Neill knew that Ngo would be looking for another source of data and leveraged a hacking suspect in another case to promise such a source. Unfortunately for Ngo, the deal had to be conducted in person. Ngo was concerned with extradition; however, he agreed to meet in Guam forgetting that Guam is part of the United States. Ngo was placed under arrest when he landed.

Tax Fraud

It is tax season again as of the time I started writing this book and the U.S. Federal Trade Commission (FTC) had just released some of its numbers related to identity theft over the last year (2015). In fact, the FTC indicated that it received a forty-seven percent (47%) increase over 2014 of identity theft complaints for more than 490,000 received. Edith Ramirez, the FTC chairwoman, stated that tax refund fraud is "the largest and fastest growing ID theft category" that is tracked (Krebs, 2016c). The FTC indicated that they received 221,854 tax- or wage-related identity theft complaints out of the total received that is almost double of complaints for this category in 2014. (There were 109,250 identity theft complaints related to taxes or wages in 2014.)

The Internal Revenue Service (IRS) also shows a dramatic increase in 2015 over 2014 for tax-related ID theft. In 2014, the IRS reported 242,575 ID thefts related to taxes. This number nearly doubled to 601,799 reported in 2015. With the increase of identity theft–related complaints, the FTC has responded to the public by improving IdentityTheft.gov. This site provides individuals who have fallen victim to identity theft resources for reporting the issue along with providing a step-by-step customized recovery plan. A later section of this book called "Recovery" goes into further details on what you might do and actions to take if you fall victim to identity theft.

The IRS has sent identity theft victims Identity Protection PINs (IP PINs) that would be required to be entered on the following year's tax returns. Unfortunately, these victims must obtain their IP PINs from the IRS website entering multiple choice answers to questions that could be obtained from other publicly available sources or through random guessing. Brian Krebs, a security reporter, author, and blog post writer on KrebsOnSecurity.com, attests to the ease of which to obtain personal data. In his December 2014 article, *Toward a Breach Canary for Data Brokers*, he describes how he was able to obtain personal information like Social Security numbers and phone numbers of all current members of the U.S. Senate Commerce Committee. Krebs states, "this information is no longer secret (nor are the answers to [knowledge-based authentication] KBA-based questions), and we are all made vulnerable to identity theft as long as institutions continue to rely on static information as authenticators" (Krebs, 2016c).

Healthcare Resources

Medical identity theft affects the entire healthcare ecosystem, from the patient to the provider, from the insurance company to taxpayers that subsidize healthcare costs. Healthcare resources are already pushed to the limits and are now overburdened with the extra concerns of providing services to fraudsters. Ultimately, all healthcare consumers are hit by paying higher prices for their healthcare needs.

Americans spend $2.7 trillion on healthcare (or seventeen percent [17%] of the gross domestic product). Medicare alone costs $600 billion and Medicaid costs $415 billion a year. It is no wonder that healthcare becomes a major target for criminals. Based on estimates conducted in 2012 by Donald Berwick, former head of the Centers for Medicare and Medicaid Services (CMS), and Andrew Hackbarth, from the RAND Corporation, $272 billion was spent on fraud across the entire health system (The Economist, 2016). Although this takes into all types of fraud and crimes, as described by Ann Patterson, senior vice president and program director of the MIFA, medical identity theft is growing and has cost victims "out of pocket" $12 billion (Patterson, 2016).

Ransomware, or a type of cyberattack that makes computer resources unavailable until money is paid, has seen significant increase in use within the healthcare industry. As an example of how dangerous this type of attack can be or the impact it can have on a healthcare organization, Hollywood Presbyterian Medical Center (HPMC), a Southern Californian hospital, recently had their computer resources down for more than a week due to a ransomware incident. Staff were without email and lost access to some data on patients while HPMC worked with law enforcement to identify the attackers. Emergency room systems and other critical clinical devices such as scanners, labs, pharmacy, and other systems were affected. HPMC declared an internal emergency and had to transport some patients to other hospitals. The criminals demanded 9,000 Bitcoins, or roughly over $3.6 million dollars (Ragan, 2016). HPMC finally broke down and paid $17,000 to the attacker (Osborne, 2016).

Untold Victims

"As reported by the 2013 Europol Serious & Organized Threat assessment, the 'Total Global Impact of CyberCrime [has risen to] US $3 Trillion, making it more profitable than the global trade in marijuana, cocaine and heroin combined'" (Khimji, 2016). Interesting that the illegal drug trade would be compared with cybercrime since medical identity theft is one way for criminals to get prescription drugs and other narcotics onto the streets. Furthermore, "almost a third of cyber crime victims last year [2015] were less than 18 years old and the number of online crime victims in that age group has increased by 163%" (ITV, 2016). These are relevant statistics as we move onto another topic that may not be as obvious to many as it relates to our discussions around victims of cybercrime and, more specifically, medical identity theft.

As we've eluded to, medical identity theft has been credited as a way to obtain prescription and other narcotic drugs, but did you know "the nonmedical use and abuse of prescription drugs is a serious public health problem in this country [U.S.]," states Dr. Nora Volkow, director of the National Institute on Drug Abuse (NIDA) (Volkow, 2016). NIDA's Monitoring the Future (MTF) survey shows that young people are strongly represented in the estimated fifty-two (52) million people that at least once in their lives have, for nonmedical reasons, used prescription drugs. The survey shows that Vicodin and OxyContin are the most abused by adolescents, and for the survey in 2010, one (1) in twelve (12) high school seniors reported using Vicodin and one (1) in twenty (20) used OxyContin for nonmedical reasons. "The reasons for the high prevalence of prescription drug abuse," Dr. Volkow explains, "vary by age, gender, and other factors, but likely include greater availability" (Volkow, 2016). According to the U.S. Department of Health and Human Services, "Every day, 44 people in the United States die from prescription opioid overdose and many more become addicted" (U.S. Department of Health & Human Services, 2016).

To explain the devastating effects of the prescription drugs epidemic, I wanted to share a story that is close to my heart. These real-life events happened to one of my relatives, by way of marriage, just under a decade ago. Out of respect, I will not use names, but the details provided were from individuals directly involved. I recount this story to show respect to the numerous untold victims that may no longer have a voice to be heard. I want to bring awareness to those that still can make a difference as to the tidal wave of pain that crashes through society at all levels.

A beautiful, enthusiastic, energetic, and caring sixteen (16)-year-old girl's life was cut short after law enforcement investigators determined she snorted three (3) OxyContin prescription painkiller pills. This dosage is equivalent to taking forty-eight (48) Percocet. Claims alleged that this high school sophomore bought the pills from a fellow classmate and inhaled the drug sometime between class changes. She was assisted back to her classroom by another student, but wasn't feeling well. She apparently laid her head down on her desk during class and was unresponsive. She hadn't been noticed for twenty (20) to thirty (30) minutes during the class movie (or presentation—details a little unclear) that was taking place. By the time the teacher and other students realized that there was a problem, she was already turning blue.

The girl was rushed to the hospital, but was listed in critical condition. She had suffered severe lung damage that led to cardiac arrest. She had been without oxygen to her brain for an unknown amount of time and was placed on life support. Five (5) days later, the family had to make the most painful decision of their lives. The family insists that the girl had no intentions of hurting herself and it is unclear why she needed the medication.

The student accused of selling the drugs was arrested and charged with delivering drugs resulting in death, a third-degree murder charge. The accused student was going to be tried as an adult; however, the district attorney later decided to try the student in juvenile court. Upon executing a search warrant at the suspect's house, prescription pills were found that belonged to the student's father who was on disability. Investigators, however, indicated that the potency of the pills didn't match what the girl consumed. The accused denied the allegations of selling the prescription drugs to the girl. Although a couple of witnesses came forward, there were still some inconsistencies in the case.

No one may ever know what really happened, but this tragic event changed the lives of many. A girl died, a boy was tried, and the lives of multiple members of the family were devastated by this lost. It is a very sad story that has been replayed over and over again in the minds of those that were involved. In retrospect, this incident, along with others like it, shouldn't have happened or could have been prevented. If individuals would wake up to these problems and provide real solutions (as opposed to excuses or transfer blame), we might be able to make a difference.

5

HEALTHCARE SECURITY

If we don't act now to safeguard our privacy, we could all become victims of identity theft.

—Clarence William "Bill" Nelson II, U.S. Senator, Chairman of the Senate Aging Committee

Ignorance Is Bliss: State of Healthcare Security

Based on my professional experience in the healthcare industry, I believe healthcare, as a whole, is about ten (10) to fifteen (15) years behind other organizations in other industries when it comes to information security and protecting individual's privacy. Healthcare organizations have a lot of catching up to do and in most cases, new technology always outpaces regulations when it comes to enforcing certain compliance requirements. As the U.S. Food and Drug Administration (FDA) director of Emergency Preparedness, Operations, and Medical Countermeasures, Suzanne Schwartz, MD, puts it, "hospitals and health care systems are under constant attempts at attack and intrusion of their networks" (Miliard, 2016b). The self-proclaimed hackers at Black Hat also agree with my analysis indicating that the healthcare industry is "at the top of the list when it comes to targeted industries" and the healthcare industry "seems the most vulnerable" (thycotic, 2015).

According to a report published by Verizon, globally, "more than 392 million [protected health information] (PHI) records have been disclosed during 1,931 data breach incidents" (Barwick, 2016). The data dates back to 1994, but concentrated around incidents between 2004 and 2014 from twenty-five (25) countries with a majority of the data from the United States. The report indicates that eighty-six percent (86%) of all breaches involved three (3) categories: theft, human error, and insider abuse.

It has been my experience that healthcare organizations tend to favor ignorance and take a more reactive approach to information security. If the healthcare executives don't know about it, then it doesn't exist—"ignorance is bliss." With a constant bombardment of competing priorities, healthcare IT (and more specifically cybersecurity) takes a back seat. Unfortunately, as Cohen Wood, former Defense Intelligence Agency (DIA) senior intelligence officer and Cyber Deputy Division chief, explains, "data security and privacy concerns are no longer 'just an IT issue'" (Snell, 2016g), it is an organizational concern that needs to be dealt with at the board room level. Wood urges that since lives are at stake in the healthcare industry, "cybersecurity threats are now everybody's problem" (Snell, 2016g).

One of the main concerns around data security is knowing what data you have and where the data is located. If an organization doesn't have a good handle on where their data is at, they can't protect that data. A quarterly report titled "Q4 2015 Shadow Data Report" performed by Elastica Cloud Threat Labs indicates "organizations are not aware that 26 percent of documents stored in cloud apps are broadly shared" (Blue Coat, 2016). The analysis was performed on sixty-three (63) million enterprise documents located in cloud applications. The report indicated that the top ten (10) applications used within enterprises included: Office 365, Twitter, YouTube, LinkedIn, Google Apps, Salesforce, AWS, Dropbox, Skype, and Box. The analysis defined "broadly shared" as meaning staff members are able to access the documents, the documents may be shared with external contacts (like contractors or vendors), or publicly accessible through search engines such as Google. The research also found that one (1) out of ten (10) of the documents shared contained sensitive data such as source code, personally identifiable information, protected health information, or payment card industry data (Blue Coat, 2016).

These two (2) concerns, data security and awareness, along with evolving technology, were among the highest rated concerns in a readers poll on *HealthITSecurity.com*. Even after the major healthcare breaches took place, only thirty-seven percent (37%) changed their approach to privacy/security. Forty percent (40%) responded with no changes and twenty-two percent (22%) weren't sure about their changes (Snell, 2016f).

Healthcare is going to see some changes coming in the next few years. Since 2015 set some records on breaches that occurred, according to attorney Michael J. Kline from Fox Rothschild, LLP, the healthcare industry is going to see more Health Insurance Portability and Accountability Act (HIPAA) enforcement. Not only will the Office for Civil Rights (OCR) step up enforcement activities, but other federal agencies "such as the Department of Homeland Security, the Securities and Exchange Commission and the Federal Communications Commission" will get involved in healthcare compliance efforts (Medical Practice Compliance Alert, 2016).

Fox Rothschild LLP attorney Elizabeth Litten believes that individuals will be held more accountable for compliance failures as opposed to previous concentration on entities. Based on changes announced by the Department of Justice (DOJ) in the *Yates Memo* and OCR mentioning that more attention will be placed on liability of the individual. "They're trying to put the fear in smaller entities. A small breach is as important as a big one," says Litten (Medical Practice Compliance Alert, 2016).

The healthcare industry is going to see a change in the threat landscape. Based on a trend analysis conducted over 2015, Troy Gill, manager of security research for AppRiver, predicts some of the following top information security threats for 2016 as they may relate to the healthcare industry:

- *Advanced malware*—These applications will go undetected and will work in conjunction with enhanced social engineering attacks. Mark Painter, security evangelist for security products at Hewlett Packard Enterprise, predicts, "Adversaries are evolving their tactics and embracing new technologies, and unless we shift our approach, we can't expect to see improvements" (Painter, 2016).
- *Breaches*—With the amount of sensitive information available, there will be an increase in targeted attacks. Painter points out an experiment where security researchers left USB drives in random places in four (4) major cities. Twenty percent (20%) of the drives were plugged into computers demonstrating lack of awareness by the end users over basic security controls.

- *Internet of things*—The attack surface will increase as a number of new devices will connect to the Internet. In healthcare, where life is in the balance, improperly securing these devices that may attach to an individual could be life threatening.
- *Bring your own device (BYOD)*—Organizations may see efficiencies and savings in permitting employees to bring their own devices to work; however, this raises risks of vulnerabilities being introduced into the network since these devices may not be under the direct control of the organization. Painter adds, "With 2 billion consumers expected to have smartphones in 2016…it's only a matter of time before mobile vulnerabilities impact an organization's underlying servers" (Painter, 2016).
- *New vulnerabilities*—As computer processing capabilities increase and legacy standards are not improved, additional exploits will be developed to circumvent security measures.
- *Cloud storage*—As more and more information is stored in the cloud, risk increases over the control or sharing of this information. As discussed, healthcare data is valuable and as Painter indicates, "most healthcare budgets are stretched too thin to adequately invest in the right levels of security" (Painter, 2016).

[Paraphrased and summarized from Gill (2016).]

In *The State of Cybersecurity in Healthcare Organizations in 2016* survey conducted by the Ponemon Institute, five hundred thirty-five (535) IT/security practitioners interviewed from small to medium-sized healthcare organizations across the United States indicated their top security threats as shown in Figure 5.1.

Cyberattack trending in the healthcare industry shows a logical progression that hackers will take from compromising small providers, to medium-/large-sized healthcare systems, to hospitals, and now, into electronic health record solution providers. As Mark Menke of Digital Guardian predicts, hackers will continue to increase their attacks against electronic health record vendors, "Web-based EHR [electronic health records] systems easily allow them [hackers] to access data from hundreds or thousands of health networks in one fell swoop" (Menke, 2016). These systems may be vulnerable to many

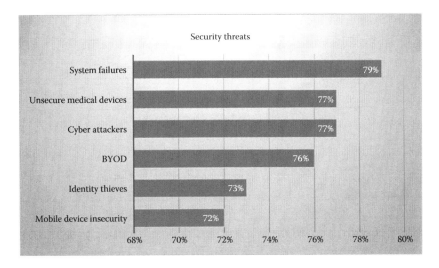

Figure 5.1 Respondents indicated their top security threats. (From Snell, E., Ponemon: Healthcare cyber attack averages one per month, Retrieved from Health IT Security, http://healthitsecurity.com/news/ponemon-healthcare-cyber-attack-averages-one-per-month, March 13, 2016.)

common attack vectors like SQL injections or cross-site scripting that could easily be exploited by hackers.

Unfortunately, according to a study issued by PwC, a consulting firm, companies may not be prepared for a cyberattack. This global survey across one hundred fifteen (115) countries, ten (10) industries, and 6300 respondents indicated that "nearly half of U.S. companies don't have an active plan to respond to cyber incidents, while [seventeen percent] 17% don't have any plan at all" (Sidel, 2016). More scary is the fact that "one in three survey respondents said they don't think they need one" (Sidel, 2016).

Constructive Ambiguity and the HIPAA Regulations

As mentioned, I received inspiration to write this book after reading *Lights Out* by Ted Koppel. In his book, Koppel used a term "constructive ambiguity" that I found appropriate to touch on here. The term appears to be credited to Henry Kissinger, one of the foremost negotiators and although I don't like to use it, *Wikipedia* appeared to have one of the most concise definitions of the term *constructive ambiguity*: "It refers to the deliberate use of ambiguous language on a sensitive issue in order to advance some political purpose" (Wikipedia, 2016b). This is relevant to explain the regulations governing the privacy and security over healthcare-related information brought to us when Congress enacted the HIPAA law of 1996 and thirteen (13) years later the Health Information Technology for Economic and Clinical Health Act (the HITECH Act), which was part of the American Recovery and Reinvestment Act of 2009 (ARRA).

I wrote an entire book on these regulations a few years back, *The Definitive Guide to Complying with the HIPAA/HITECH Privacy and Security Rules*, so I won't go into a significant amount of detail here on them; suffice it to say, the rules developed by the Department of Health and Human Services (HHS) to carry out the legislation are very *flexible* and lead to a lot of interpretation. In fact, subject matter experts often disagree on the intention of the rules or how these rules may apply to certain situations. Attorneys that get paid top dollar to provide legal opinions on the rules sometimes don't get them right and although HHS attempts to provide guidance; however, in certain areas, this guidance is minimal or nonexistent at best. Maybe without even realizing it, or maybe intentionally (I tend to favor the latter), these rules were constructed in an ambiguous way. Since healthcare is a "touchy subject" and the medical community tends to have strong lobbyist groups, it is no wonder that legislation around healthcare providers, insurers, and pharmaceutical companies may not be as stringent as in other industries.

According to *MapLight*, a nonpartisan research organization, the healthcare industry spends billions annually on lobbyists. Figure 5.2 shows the top twenty (20) healthcare companies' expenditures on lobbyists.

Another reason that healthcare regulations are not as straight forward as you might think may be found in the revelations by General Michael Hayden, former director of the National Security Agency (NSA) and Central Intelligence Agency (CIA), now principal with The Chertoff Group. In his keynote address and interview at the *S4x16 ICS/SCADA Conference*, General Hayden stated, "People ask how come government isn't doing something about it [cybersecurity]…Government will be permanently late to the need in providing cybersecurity" (Higgins, 2016b). General Hayden encourages the private industry to take the lead in protecting data since technology

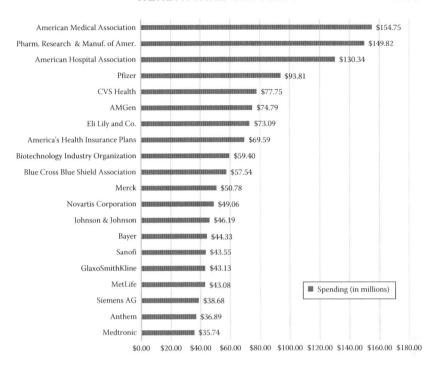

Figure 5.2 Top twenty (20) healthcare company lobbyist expenditures as of August 2015. (From Rappleye, E., Top 20 healthcare lobbyists by spending, Retrieved from Becker's Hospital CFO, http://www. beckershospitalreview.com/finance/top-20-healthcare-lobbyists-by-spending.html, February 13, 2016.)

moves faster than government. General Hayden explains, "It's the technology driving policy and political change, not the other way around" (Higgins, 2016b).

Some experts believe that one of the major reasons the HIPAA regulations aren't working to keep our healthcare information secure and private is these rules are narrowly focused. They don't cover all the cyber threats that healthcare organizations are currently facing. Being primarily a rule-based or compliance-based mandate, the HIPAA regulations don't lend themselves to a broader, organizational-wide governance framework. "The problem with this approach is that it gives false confidence to healthcare executives that HIPAA Security Rule compliance equates to effective cybersecurity risk management" states Jonathan Litchman, CEO of the Providence Group (Litchman, 2016). Litchman suggests, "In order for healthcare providers to effectively manage the full range of cybersecurity risks they must treat cyber risks as an enterprise-wide risk" (Litchman, 2016).

Ensuring that board members understand cybersecurity may become a requirement. A new bill introduced in the Senate titled the Cybersecurity Disclosure Act of 2015 (S.B. 2410) proposes to require the board members of public companies to disclose their expertise in cybersecurity. If passed, the Securities and Exchange Commission will enact rules requiring the disclosure of the expertise or experience in cybersecurity that members of the governing board (i.e., board of directors or general partner) on their annual reports. If members don't have expertise or experience in cybersecurity, they must describe what other cybersecurity steps were taken into account when identifying and evaluating nominees for membership on the governing board. Furthermore, the Securities and Exchange Commission in coordination with the National Institute of Standards and Technology will define the expertise required in cybersecurity "such as professional qualifications to administer information security program functions or experience detecting, preventing, mitigating, or addressing cybersecurity threats" (Collins, 2016).

State Requirements

Some states have recognized that the federal government is behind on passing legislation to assist with cybersecurity along with privacy and have taken steps to enhance their protection over sensitive data within their states. Here are examples of what some states are doing on this front.

California

California appears to be leading the way in privacy legislations. On October 8, 2015, California's governor, Jerry Brown, signed into law the *Electronic Communications Privacy Act* (CalECPA). The ECPA "prohibit a government entity from compelling the production of or access to electronic communication information or electronic device information, as defined, without a search warrant, wiretap, order for electronic reader records, or subpoena issued pursuant under specified conditions, except for emergency situations, as defined" (California Senate, 2016). The authors of the legislation, State Senators Mark Leno (D-San Francisco) and Joel Anderson (R-Alpine), intended to give the same protection to digital data as that provided for nondigital communications. Senator Leno stated, "For too long, California's digital privacy laws have been stuck in the Dark Ages, leaving our personal emails, text messages, photos and smartphones increasing vulnerable to warrantless searches" (Zetter, 2016a). Nicole Ozer, Technology and Civil Liberties Policy Director at the American Civil Liberties Union of California, agreed, "This is a landmark win for digital privacy and all Californians…We hope this is a model for the rest of the nation in protecting our digital privacy rights" (Zetter, 2016a). The law only applies to state law enforcement agencies, but supporters hope that other states or even the federal government will follow suit.

Californians place a lot of importance over privacy and have expanded the Fourth Amendment to the U.S. Constitution within their own State Constitution in Article I, Section 1 – Sec.31, "All people are by nature free and independent and have inalienable rights. Among these are enjoying and defending life and liberty, acquiring, possessing, and protecting property, and pursuing and obtaining safety, happiness, and privacy" (California Constitution—Cons, 2016).

There are several related privacy laws for the State of California, but for our discussion, I want to keep on point with our topic of health information. Under California's Health and Safety Codes (Regulations 1280.15), a clinic, health facility, home health agency, or hospice shall prevent unlawful or unauthorized access to, and use or disclosure of, patients' medical information. If one of these organizations did encounter any unlawful or unauthorized access to, or use or disclosure of, a patient's medical information, they need to report it to the Office of Statewide Health Planning and Development within fifteen (15) business days of being detected. The Department of Justice's Privacy Enforcement and Protection Unit enforces California state and federal privacy laws. The administrative penalties are steep for organizations that fail to comply with regulations and they could face up to twenty-five thousand dollars ($25,000) per patient whose medical information was unlawfully accessed, used, or disclosed and up to seventeen thousand five hundred dollars ($17,500) per subsequent occurrences.

One of the unique regulations in California's codes is that any business organized for the purpose of maintaining medical information along with any business that offers software or hardware to consumers, which includes mobile applications or other related devices designed to maintain medical information, are considered providers of healthcare subject to certain regulations. The business, software or hardware, must maintain medical information for the purpose of allowing individuals to manage their information or for the purpose of diagnosis and treatment of the individual. The business must maintain standards of confidentiality required of a provider of healthcare and may be subject to penalties for improper use and disclosure of medical information.* The regulations define medical information as any individually identifiable information, in electronic or physical form, in possession of or derived from a provider of healthcare, healthcare service plan, pharmaceutical company, or contractor regarding a patient's medical history, mental or physical condition, or treatment. California expands a little on the definition of individually identifiable in that medical information includes or contains any elements of personal identifying information sufficient to allow identification of the individual. Examples provided include patient's name, address, electronic mail address, telephone number, or social security number, *or* other information that, alone or in combination with other publicly available information, reveals the individual's identity.†

Another unique area to note under California's regulations is that individuals have an individual right of action against a person or entity that negligently released confidential information. There is a nominal penalty of one thousand dollars ($1000) and this is very important, the individual does not need to prove damages. Now, if the patient whose medical information was used or disclosed has sustained any economic loss or personal injury, they could recover compensatory damages along with punitive damages not to exceed three thousand dollars ($3000), attorneys' fees not to exceed one thousand dollars ($1000), and the costs of litigation. This violation is also punishable as a misdemeanor. Table 5.1 lists out other penalties that could be accessed.

It is also important to note that California's regulation provides for an affirmative defense. Although a person or entity may be responsible for any actual damages and reasonable attorney's fees, they won't

---

* From California Civil Code 56.06.
† From California Civil Code 56.05.

Table 5.1   California's Violations for Use or Disclosure of Medical Information

VIOLATION OF MEDICAL INFORMATION	ADMINISTRATIVE FINE/CIVIL PENALTY
Person/entity—negligently discloses	Not to exceed $2,500 per violation
Person/entity—knowingly/willfully obtains, discloses, or uses	Not to exceed $25,000 per violation
Person/entity—knowingly/willfully obtains/uses for financial gain	Not to exceed $250,000 per violation and subject to disgorgement of proceeds obtained
Person/entity not permitted to receive and knowingly/willfully obtains, discloses, or uses without written authorization	Not to exceed $250,000 per violation
Licensed healthcare professional—knowingly/willfully obtains, discloses, or uses	First violation—Not to exceed $2,500 per violation Second violation—Not to exceed $10,000 per violation Third violation—Not to exceed $25,000 per violation
Licensed healthcare professional—knowingly/willfully obtains, discloses, or uses for financial gain	First violation—Not to exceed $5,000 per violation Second violation—Not to exceed $25,000 per violation Third violation—Not to exceed $250,000 per violation and subject to disgorgement of proceeds obtained

Source: California Legislature, Civil code part 2.6 confidentiality of medical information [56-56.37], Retrieved from California Legislative Information, http://leginfo.legislature. ca.gov/faces/codes_displayText.xhtml?lawCode=CIV&division=1.&title=&part=2.6.&c hapter=7.&article, February 21, 2016.

be hit with any nominal damages for a violation as long as all of the following are established (paraphrased here):

- The defendant, as defined under Section 160.103 of Title 45 of the Code of Federal Regulations, is a covered entity or business associate.
- The defendant complied with notification requirements regarding release of records and the release was solely to another covered entity or business associate.
- The release of records did not involve medical identity theft.
- The defendant took appropriate actions to safeguard information consistent with the HIPAA regulations to include, but not limited to
  - Developing/implementing security policies/procedures
  - Designating a security official responsible for policies/ procedures and awareness
  - Encrypting records

- The defendant took appropriate corrective actions after release of records, and the covered entity/business associate that received records destroyed or returned the records; the receiving covered entity/business associate did not retain, use, or further release the records.
- After release, defendant took appropriate action to prevent future similar release of records.
- The defendant has not previously established affirmative defense or the court determines, considering all facts, the affirmative defense is consistent to promote reasonable conduct.

Civil penalties can be assessed in any civil action in any court of competent jurisdiction brought in the name of the people of the State of California by any of the following:

- The attorney general
- A district attorney or by agreement with a county counsel involved in actions of county ordinances
- A city attorney or a city attorney of a city/county having a population in excess of 750,000 with consent of the district attorney
- A city prosecutor, being a full-time city prosecutor or with consent of the district attorney, by a city attorney in a city/county
- Upon recommendation by the state public health officer, or his/her designee, to bring a civil action

Florida

The *Florida Information Protection Act (FIPA)* was unanimously passed and signed into law June 20, 2014. It took effect July 1 that same year and covers a wide range of organizations. In basic terms, any company (including a governmental entity) that "acquired, maintains, stores, or uses personal information" is governed by FIPA.

Under FIPA, personal information is defined as an individual's first name (or first initial) along with their last name in combination with any or more of the following:

- A Social Security number
- A driver license or identification card number, passport number, military identification number, or other similar number issued on a government document used to verify identity

- A financial account number/credit/debit card number, in combination with any required security code (password) that is necessary to gain access to the account
- Any information about the individual's medical history, mental or physical condition, or medical treatment or diagnosis by a healthcare professional
- An individual's health insurance policy number or subscriber identification number and any unique identifier used by a health insurer to identify the individual

In addition, FIPA defines personal information to be a user name or e-mail address, in combination with a password or security question/answer that would permit access to an online account.

Data that is encrypted, secured, or modified by some method or technology to remove personally identifiable information or otherwise render the data unusable is *not* considered personal information. Unfortunately, the law doesn't provide any guidance on what encryption to use, and since almost all information security experts would agree, not all encryption is the same. In fact, the Department of Health and Human Services has issued *Guidance Regarding Methods for De-Identification of Protected Health Information in Accordance with the Health Insurance Portability and Accountability Act (HIPAA) Privacy Rule*, November 26, 2012, that refers to FIPS 140-2 standards for acceptable encryption; however, FIPA doesn't refer to any such guidance.

FIPA is primarily a reactive legislation more relevant to addressing breach notification requirements as opposed to being proactive in addressing the security of confidential personal information. As opposed to requiring actions to be taken to prevent a breach, FIPA requires notifications to be made after a company has already fallen victim to a breach. For instance, FIPA could have required covered entities to perform risk assessments; implement specific administrative, physical, or technical controls; perform independent testing, auditing, or evaluations; mandate the development of information security and privacy-related policies and procedures; require an officer of the company to take responsibility over security; require the development of incident response plans; require that companies certify to an acceptable level of security; perform logging and activity monitoring; or other actions that assist in strengthening the security posture of companies.

FIPA does require each covered entity, governmental entity, or third-party agent to take *reasonable measures* to protect and secure data in *electronic form* containing personal information; however, these reasonable measures are not addressed. What may be reasonable to someone untrained in information security is not the same as what should be considered as reasonable by experts in the field. *What is the standard of reasonableness here?* In addition, FIPA defines customer records as any material, regardless of the physical form, on which personal information is recorded or preserved. I emphasized electronic form earlier since customer records can also be included within paper or as "spoken words," but this isn't covered under FIPA.

As mentioned, FIPA primarily covers breach notification and requires a covered entity to notify the Department of Legal Affairs of any breach of security affecting five hundred (500) or more individuals in the State of Florida. The notices must be made as expeditiously as practicable, but not later than thirty (30) days after the *determination* of the breach or reason to believe a breach has occurred. FIPA defines a breach as unauthorized access of data in *electronic form* containing personal information. *What happens if a company has a breach of paper records?* FIPA also defines a breach as an employer or agent of a covered entity that uses personal information for other than business purposes or for further unauthorized uses.

FIPA's determination factor may be less strict than HIPAA's discovery factor. As you may remember, HIPAA/HITECH regulations require notification in less than sixty (60) days upon discovery of a breach while under FIPA, its thirty (30) days upon determination. The concern I have with this is that there can be some time lapses between when the incident occurred, when it was discovered, and then when the incident was actually determined to be a breach under the definition of law.

Let's demonstrate this point through a breach example assuming a healthcare covered entity had their patient database containing personal information accessed by an unauthorized person (i.e., a typical hacking scenario). In most cases, if the covered entity had no activity monitoring in place, they probably wouldn't even know that the incident occurred and the attacker could be in the systems for an extended period of time. For our example, however, we are going to say the covered entity did discover the unauthorized access. Under the federal HIPAA regulations, the "clock" may start running at the point of discovery for notification purposes. The covered entity brought in a forensic expert to investigate. It took the expert forty-five (45) days to determine that someone got into the database three (3) months back and over time, copied all the patient records out of the database. If we assumed the clock started counting down, under HIPAA the covered entity would have fifteen (15) days to make notification to affected individuals.

Based on the results of the expert, the incident was reported to law enforcement. If the law enforcement agency takes the expert's opinion "at face value," the determination of a breach was made and the clock starts under FIPA. Unfortunately, in our example, law enforcement wants to conduct their own investigation. This determination might be delayed due to a possible criminal investigation. Based on the information presented thus far, we could assume that personal information is no longer under the control of the covered entity and could be susceptible to misuse and other criminal activities such as identity theft. In our scenario, the covered entity fell under the HIPAA regulations and notifications were made; however, FIPA expanded the definitions of a covered entity to include other types of companies. If this incident were to have occurred to such a company, at this point, the individuals affected by the breach may not have even been notified that their personal information has been compromised.

Under FIPA, a covered entity (or business associate) that falls under the purview of the HIPAA/HITECH regulations and made the requisite notifications under the Breach Notification Rules of HIPAA/HITECH are deemed to be in compliance with the individual notification requirements for FIPA.

FIPA does require, however, certain written notification to the Department of Legal Affairs that must include a synopsis of the event, number of individuals affected, services being offered to affected individuals (without charge), a copy of the notice provided to the individuals, and contact information for an employee or agent of the covered entity for additional information on the breach. The Department of Legal Affairs could request additional information and the covered entity must provide the following upon request: a police report, incident report, or computer forensic report; a copy of the policies in place regarding breaches; and/or steps that have been taken to rectify the breach. If the covered entity is a governmental agency such as the judicial branch, the Executive Office of the Governor, the Department of Financial Services, or the Department of Agriculture and Consumer Services, these agencies can post notification on their websites as opposed to making written notification to the Department of Legal Affairs.

The notification for a non-HIPAA covered entity must be sent by mail or e-mailed to individuals that include, at a minimum, the following items:

- Dates of the breach (or estimated date or date range)
- Description of the personal information that was accessed or reasonably believed to have been accessed
- Contact information of the covered entity to inquire about the breach

Notification in cases involving a large amount of records can get very expensive. For this reason, FIPA provides for a substitute notification where costs may exceed $250,000 or where 500,000 or more records were involved. In addition, if the covered entity doesn't have e-mail or addresses for individuals, they could post a notice on their website and provide notice in print/broadcast media where individuals may reside.

Along with notification to individuals and to the Department of Legal Affairs, any breach that affects more than one thousand (1000) individuals at a single time, notification must be made to consumer reporting agencies without unreasonable delay. This notice must include timing, distribution, and content of the notification.

The Florida State Legislatures recognized the growing risk of third-party service providers as more and more companies rely on them for services along with maintaining customer records of covered entities. FIPA includes provisions that third-party providers whom fall victim to a breach must notify the covered entities affected no later than ten (10) days. Once a third-party provider notifies a covered entity, the covered entity needs to provide appropriate notices to individuals, Department of Legal Affairs, and to credit reporting agencies. The third-party service provider could make notifications on the covered entity's behalf; however, the responsibility for notification still remains with the covered entity. Service providers have a tight window to make notifications and unlike the direct liability these service providers have under the HIPAA Omnibus Rules, the onus is on the covered entity to ensure notifications are made appropriately. Although I've always recommended to my clients that business associate agreements should contain specific time frames of notifications, if you work with covered entities (and third-party providers) that operate in Florida, you may want to consider updating your notification requirements accordingly.

If, after an appropriate investigation and consultation with relevant federal, state, or local law enforcement agencies, it is reasonably determined that a breach has not and will not likely result in identity theft or any other financial harm, no notification is required. This determination must be in writing and maintained for at least five (5) years. It also must be provided to the Department of Legal Affairs within thirty (30) days.

Being a former law enforcement officer, this caveat makes me a little nervous. I know that cybercrime investigations aren't a normal part of an officer's training and although I actually pursued training in this area, I found that generally, law enforcement agencies are way behind in this area of investigations especially at the local level. Now that I work in the information security industry, it is apparent that these agencies may not be equipped to handle such investigations as seen through the rise in identity theft crimes and the low number of arrests of cybercriminals. These types of investigations could be highly technical and complex. Unless the investigators are skilled in these specific investigations, I'm not sure how they can make an *accurate* determination of a breach. I'm not even sure if law enforcement agencies have the resources to handle the influx that may come about from investigating these types of breach incidences. *Will additional resources be provided to these agencies? Will additional training be provided to these investigators? What type of equipment and software will be needed to perform these types of investigations?* Unfortunately, FIPA doesn't address these questions.

FIPA requires that covered entities and third-party providers take *reasonable measures* to dispose of customer records. Unfortunately, FIPA is a little vague when it comes to shredding, erasing, or otherwise modifying the personal information in the records to make it unreadable or undecipherable through *any means*. As security experts, we know that unless you utilize a cross-cut shredder, perform certain wiping activities utilizing specifically approved software, or physical destruction of paper/media, the information could possibly be retrieved. FIPA lacks the appropriate guidance for proper disposal of personal information. FIPA could have easily referred to the *NIST SP 800-88: Guidelines for Media Sanitization* to offer up guidance by which these disposal methods could be better followed and enforced.

Finally, no law is complete without enforcement. A violation of FIPA is treated as an unfair or deceptive trade practice. Civil monetary penalties can be imposed not to exceed $500,000. These penalties can be assessed as provided in Table 5.2.

An interesting note is that FIPA assesses penalties on a per breach basis as opposed to HIPAA that is on a per violation basis. Just like HIPAA, there is no private cause of action. In my opinion, there should be a private cause of action. At the end of the day, we are talking about the rights of an individual to keep their personal information private and the failure of a covered entity to properly protect this information violates this right of privacy. Covered entities have an obligation and responsibility to protect the information they maintain. It is ultimately going to be the individual that falls victim to a crime and be burden with the cost of recovering from any damage that is caused by their personal information being available to criminals. Unless the legislatures were counting on individuals affected by a breach taking up personal legal actions against covered entities, I'm not sure why these *victims* would not be entitled to a private cause of action. We are already finding that the judicial system is not very supportive of individuals taking actions against companies to protect their information unless they can show specific damages caused by a breach. I argue that the damage has already occurred when an individual's personal information *has been* breached. Their fundamental right of privacy has been violated and breached. Once an individual's personal information is out in the open, it can't be taken back.

Table 5.2   FIPA Civil Monetary Penalties

FOLLOWING A VIOLATION	PENALTY
Up to 30 days	$1,000 per day
Subsequent 30-day period up to 180 days	$50,000 for each 30-day period
More than 180 days	Not to exceed $500,000

Massachusetts

Under the Commonwealth of Massachusetts, "A person shall have a right against unreasonable, substantial or serious interference with his privacy. The superior court shall have jurisdiction in equity to enforce such rights and in connection therewith to award damages" [*General Laws. Part III, Title I, Chapter 214, Section 1B*] (Massachusetts Legislature, 2016). As it relates to our topic of conversation, the Commonwealth of Massachusetts defines *personal information* as a resident's first name and last name (or first initial and last name) in combination with any one (1) or more of the following:

- Social Security number
- Driver's license number or state-issued identification card number
- Financial account number (or credit/debit card number) with (or without) any required security/access code/personal identification number/password, that would permit access to the financial account
  Exception: Personal information doesn't include any information that is lawfully obtained from public sources, or from federal/state/ local government records lawfully made available to the public.

Under 201 CMR 17.00, entities, even those that do not operate in the Commonwealth of Massachusetts, that own or license personal information about a resident of the Commonwealth, must comply with *Standards for the Protection of Personal Information of Residents of the Commonwealth*. Own or license also means receiving, storing, maintaining, processing, or otherwise has access to personal information. The standards include the following (paraphrased here):

- Develop, implement, and maintain a comprehensive, written information security program that contains administrative, technical, and physical safeguards. These safeguards must be appropriate to
  - The size, scope, and type of business
  - The amount of resources available
  - Amount of data stored
  - The need for security and confidentiality
  - Consistent with other similar safeguards set forth in any state or federal regulations the entity falls under

- The information security program shall include, but not limited to
  - Designation of employee to maintain the program
  - Identifying and assessing risks along with improving safeguards to limit risk to include such things as training, employee compliance, and detecting/preventing security system failures
- Developing security policies related to storage, access, and transportation of records
- Imposing disciplinary measures
- Preventing access of terminated employees
- Oversee services providers based on selection and retention of providers that maintain appropriate security measures along with requiring third-party service providers by contract to implement appropriate security measures
- Restrict physical access to records
- Regularly monitor the program to ensure it is operating in a reasonable manner along with upgrading safeguards as necessary to limit risks
- Review scope of security measures at least annually or whenever there is a material change to business practices that could impact security
- Document actions taken in response to an incident involving a breach along with mandatory postincident review of events to make changes to practices involving the protection of personal information

The standard is specific about computer system security requirements including any wireless systems as well. At a minimum, and to the extent feasible, computer system security should include the following:

- Secure user authentication protocols such as
  - User ID controls
  - Secure method of assigning passwords (or use of biometrics or tokens)
  - Control over data security passwords
  - Restrict access to active users only
  - Lockouts after multiple unsuccessful attempts to gain access

- Secure access control measures
  - Restrict access based on job duties
  - Assign unique identifications to each person
- Utilize encryption in transmission of data across public networks and transmitted wirelessly
- Monitoring of systems for unauthorized use or access
- Encryption of personal information stored on laptops or other portable devices
- For systems connected to the Internet containing personal information, must have up-to-date firewall protection and security patches along with malware protection (with up-to-date definitions) that is set to receive, on a regular basis, security updates
- Employee education and training for proper use and importance of personal information security (201 CMR 17.00: Standards for the Protection of Personal Information of Residents of the Commonwealth, 2016)

A *breach* in Massachusetts is considered the unauthorized acquisition or use of unencrypted data. It is interesting to note that encryption is defined within the regulations as the use of *128 bit* or higher algorithmic process transforming data and therefore providing a low probability of assigning meaning without a key. (The regulations do call out the ability of the department of consumer affairs and business regulations to revise the definition of encryption based on technology advancements.) In turn, a breach is also defined as obtaining encrypted electronic data with a key or the capabilities of compromising the security, confidentiality, and integrity of personal information. Furthermore, the compromise must create a substantial risk of identity theft or fraud against a resident of the commonwealth.

The department of consumer affairs and business regulations is tasked with adopting regulations that are primarily consistent with federal regulations with the objectives to

- Ensure the security and confidentiality of information in a manner consistent with industry standards
- Protect against anticipated threats/hazards to the security/integrity of the information
- Protect against unauthorized access/use of information resulting in harm or inconvenience to residents

As it relates to patient's rights, every patient or resident of a facility shall have the right to confidentiality of all records and communications as provided by law. In basic terms, an entity that knows or has reason to know that they've been breached must notify a resident of the commonwealth as soon as practicable and without unreasonable delay. The notice to residents shall include, but not limited to

- Right to obtain a police report
- Information on how to request a consumer security freeze
- Any fees required to be paid
  It is of peculiar note that the notice should not include the nature of the breach or the number of residents affected.

As in other breach notifications, the entity is required to notify the attorney general and the director of consumer affairs and business regulations. This notification shall contain the nature of the breach, the number of residents affected, and any steps being taken regarding the incident. The attorney general can bring action for any failure to comply with this breach notification regulation. Civil penalties could include five thousand dollars ($5000) per violation.

Nevada

Unfortunately, the term *privacy* doesn't appear in the State Constitution of Nevada; however, many may infer that privacy is part of Article 1, Section 1, describing "Inalienable rights: All men are by Nature free and equal and have certain inalienable rights among which are those of enjoying and defending life and liberty; Acquiring, Possessing and Protecting property and pursuing and obtaining safety and happiness" (Nevada State Constitutional Convention, 2016). In May 2015, Nevada Governor Brian Sandoval signed an amendment into law that provides for the expansion of the definition of personal information. In Nevada, personal information is defined as a person's first name or first initial and last name in combination with one of the following:

- Social Security number
- Driver's license number, driver authorization card number or identification card number
- Account number, credit/debit card number, in combination with any required code that would permit access to the account

- A medical/health insurance identification number
- A username, unique identifier, or e-mail address in combination with a password, code, or security question that permits access to an online account

An exemption to this definition exists that includes the last four (4) digits of a Social Security number, a driver's license number, a driver authorization card number, an identification card number, or information from federal, state, or local government records that are lawfully made public (Nevada State Legislatures, 2016a).

As in the case of medical records being maintained by hospitals in the State of Nevada, these hospitals must have procedures to ensure the confidentiality of medical records. Information from these medical records may only be shared with authorized persons and the hospital should make sure that unauthorized persons can't gain access or alter the medical records under Nevada Administrative Code 449.379.*

Nevada broadly defines *data collectors* as government agencies, institutions of higher education, corporations, financial institutions, retail operators or any other type of business entity/association that handles, collects, disseminates, or deals with nonpublic personal information. These data collectors must maintain reasonable security measures to protect records that contain personal information of a resident of Nevada from unauthorized access, acquisition, destruction, use, modification, or disclosure. There is an interesting caveat in the Nevada regulations on privacy that includes reference to the standards provided by a private corporation. More specifically, if a data collector doing business in Nevada accepts payment cards, they must comply with the current version of the Payment Card Industry (PCI) Data Security Standards.

If the data collector doing business in Nevada doesn't utilize payment cards, then for any transfers through an electronic method of personal information or movement of any data storage device containing personal information outside of the secure systems or beyond the logical/physical controls of the data collector must utilize encryption technology. The regulations provide for a "safe harbor" against damages if encryption is utilized in case of a breach. Furthermore, the

---

* From NRS § 449.0302.

regulations also call out the Federal Information Processing Standards (FIPS) issued by the National Institute of Standards and Technology (NIST) as a standard to follow in the use of encryption technology.

Nevada has its own breach notification regulations. A breach is considered unauthorized acquisition of data that materially compromises the security, confidentiality, or integrity of the personal information. A data collector that owns the data must, upon discovery and in the most expedient time possible, notify any resident of the State of Nevada where unencrypted personal information has been or reasonably believed to have been acquired by an unauthorized person. For any data collector that doesn't own the data, they must notify the owner or licensee of the information.

Notification must be in writing, in electronic form following certain requirements, or through substitution notification if costs exceed $250,000 or affect 500,000 or more records. In addition, if one thousand (1000) persons were involved at any one time, the data collector must notify consumer reporting agencies.

Nevada's regulations are a little unique in that there is civil action and restitution written into the law that provides additional protections for the data collector against persons that unlawfully obtained or benefited from obtaining personal information as a result of a breach. The data collector can bring civil action against the person and be awarded damages or restitution for the cost of notification, attorney's fees, and other punitive damages. Finally, the attorney general or district attorney may obtain a temporary or permanent injunction against a person that violates the breach notification requirements* (Nevada State Legislatures, 2016b).

Oregon

Due to the number of breaches that have taken place, many states have updated their privacy and data breach notification laws. Oregon is one among several states that have recently amended their laws on this matter. Personal information, defined under Oregon regulations, includes a consumer's (or resident of the state's) first name or first initial and last name in combination with any one or more of the following:

---

* From NRS § 603A—Security of Personal Information.

- Social Security number
- Driver license number or state identification number
- Passport number or other identification number issued by the United States
- Financial account number or credit/debit card number in combination with a code that permits access to the account
- Biometrics information such as a fingerprint or retina image that is used to authenticate identity in the course of a financial or other transaction
- Health insurance policy or subscriber identification number in combination with unique identifier that insurer uses for identification
- Any medical history, mental/physical condition, medical diagnosis/treatment information about a consumer
- Any combination of the data elements without a consumer's first name or first initial and last name that would enable a person to commit identity theft

Exception: personal information doesn't include any information that is encrypted as long as the encryption key has not been compromised.

Just like other states, pretty much any type of entity that maintains or possesses covered data that was subject to a breach must make notifications to individuals affected by the breach. Breach is defined as an unauthorized acquisition of data that materially compromises the security, confidentiality, or integrity of personal information. Inadvertent acquisition by employees or agents of an entity that owns the data that is not used in violating a law or causing harm is not considered a breach. An entity must make notice to individuals in the most expeditious manner possible upon discovery of a breach and if the number of records exceeds two hundred fifty (250), the entity needs to make notice to the attorney general. Oregon makes it pretty simple to make notification by setting up an electronic form to complete on the Oregon Department of Justice Consumer Protection website located here: https://justice.oregon.gov/consumer/DataBreach/Home/Submit. An entity must also notify consumer reporting agencies of any breaches that affect more than one thousand (1000) consumers.

Oregon has also set up a site that consumers can go to search on companies that have made a breach report. As of this writing, there were five (5) companies listed: Gyft, Inc.; Landry's, Inc. (including Golden Nugget Atlantic City, LLC, Golden Nugget Lake Charles, LLC, GNL Corp., GNLV C); HSBC Bank USA (including National Association); Accuform Manufacturing Inc.; and T-Mobile/Experian.*

If, upon appropriate investigation by law enforcement, the entity determines that there is no reasonable likelihood of harm to a consumer then the entity does not need to make a notification; however, this determination must be in writing and maintained for at least five (5) years. Covered entities under HIPAA are also exempt from other provisions of this law as long as they send a copy of the notice they sent to the consumer of a breach to the attorney general.

The amended law also updated the regulations to ensure that entities develop, implement, and maintain reasonable safeguards to protect the security, confidentiality, and integrity of personal information they own, maintain, or possess to include disposal of the information. The entity is deemed to be in compliance if they comply with more stringent regulations such as the Gramm–Leach–Bliley Act (GLBA) of 1999 and the HIPAA law of 1996. If the entity doesn't fall under stricter federal regulations, they must implement an information security program that includes

- Administrative safeguards to include
  - Designate an employee to coordinate the program
  - Identify risks
  - Assess effectiveness of controls
  - Train employees in security practices
  - Select service providers that will maintain safeguards under contact
  - Update the program as necessary
- Technical safeguards to include
  - Assess risks in network and software
  - Assess risks in information processing, transmission, and storage

---

* From https://justice.oregon.gov/consumer/DataBreach/.

- Detect, prevent, and respond to attacks
- Regularly test and monitor controls
- Physical safeguards to include
  - Assess risks to storage and disposal
  - Detect, prevent, and respond to intrusions
  - Protect against unauthorized access or use
  - Proper disposal

Failure to comply or violations of the Oregon Senate Bill 601 is considered a violation of Unlawful Trade Practices that is enforced by the attorney general (Oregon Legislature, 2016).

Texas

One of the states with the most stringent protection over medical information is Texas. Under Texas regulations, a covered entity is any person that engages in the practice of assembling, collecting, analyzing, using, evaluating, storing, or transmitting protected health information along with coming into possession, obtaining, or storing protected health information. This includes a person who for commercial, financial, or professional gain whether on a cooperative, nonprofit, or pro bono basis, whether whole or in part with real or constructive knowledge over protected health information. The definition specifically calls out business associates, healthcare payers, governmental entities, information/computer management entities, schools, health researchers, healthcare facilities/clinics/providers, person who maintains an Internet site, or any employee, agents, or contractors that create, receive, obtain, maintain, use, or transmit protected health information.

Texas regulations also expanded the definition of protected health information to mean any information that reflects an individual receiving healthcare from a covered entity and is not considered public information (or subject to disclosures required by law). Furthermore, personal identifying information is defined, under identity theft regulation, as information alone or in conjunction with the following:

- Name, Social Security number, date of birth, or government issued identification number
- Mother's maiden name

- Unique biometric data (including fingerprint, voice print, and retina/iris image)
- Unique electronic identification number, address, or routing code
- Telecommunication access device

Sensitive personal information is further defined as an individual's first name or first initial and last name in combination of any one or more of the following data elements that are not encrypted:

- Social Security number
- Driver's license number (or government-issued identification number)
- Account number or credit/debit card number in combination with code that would permit access to the account
- Information that identifies an individual related to
  - Physical, mental health, or condition of the individual
  - Provision of healthcare
  - Payment of healthcare

A covered entity is required to provide training to employees over regulations governing protected health information no later than ninety (90) after the date of hire and for any material changes, within a reasonable period and no later than with the first anniversary of the date of the change. Employees must sign off on training and records of training must be kept for six (6) years from the date of signing the statement.

In basic terms, it is a violation for any person to reidentify or attempt to reidentify an individual subject to any protected health information without the individual's authorization or consent. For violating this regulation, the State Attorney General of Texas can bring injunctive and civil penalties against a person/entity as shown in Table 5.3.

If the Texas Health and Human Services Commission has evidence that a covered entity is committing violations that constitute a pattern, they could require the covered entity to submit the results of a risk analysis as required by the federal HIPAA regulations or if licensed by the state, require the licensing agency to perform an audit of the covered entity.

It is considered a violation of deceptive trade practices for an entity to obtain, possess, transfer, or use personal identifying information of another person without the person's consent and with the intent of

Table 5.3   Texas State Civil Penalties for Violating Reidentification Statue

VIOLATION	CIVIL PENALTY
Committed negligently	Not to exceed $5,000 per violation (occurs in 1 year)
Committed knowingly or intentionally	Not to exceed $25,000 per violation (occurs in year)
Used for financial gain	Not to exceed $250,000 per violation
If information disclosed was encrypted, recipient did not use/release, or at time of disclosure—developed, implement, maintain security policies (including training)	Not to exceed $250,000 annually for disclosure made to another covered entity
If a pattern of violations took place	Not to exceed $1.5 million annually

Source: Texas State Legislature, Health and safety code: Title 2, subtitle 1, chapter 181 medical records privacy, Retrieved from Texas State Regulations, http://www.statutes.legis.state.tx.us/Docs/HS/htm/HS.181.htm#181.001, February 25, 2016.

Note: Other disciplinary actions can be enforced such as probation, suspension, or revocation of licenses.

utilizing this information for financial gain. An entity that collects or maintains sensitive information is obligated to implement reasonable procedures and take corrective actions to protect the information from unlawful use or disclosure. The entity shall destroy customer records containing sensitive personal information by shredding, erasing, or otherwise making the information unreadable.

A company conducting business in the State of Texas must notify individuals as quickly as possible upon discovery of a breach or unauthorized acquisition of computerized data that compromises the security, confidentiality, or integrity of sensitive personal information. If the breach includes records of more than ten thousand (10,000) persons, the company should make notification to each consumer reporting agency.

Unlike other states, Texas provides for the ability of an individual who has fallen victim to identity theft to file an application with a district court for the issuance of an order declaring that individual a "victim of identity theft" regardless of whether the individual can identify the criminal. A person that violates laws related to identity theft in the State of Texas can face civil penalties between two thousand dollars ($2,000) and fifty thousand dollars ($50,000) for each violation. The State Attorney General can bring action for recovery of the penalties. In addition, an entity that fails to comply with the breach notification requirements can be subjected to civil penalties of not more than one hundred dollars ($100) for *each individual* to whom notification is supposed to be made for *each consecutive day* that the entity fails to comply not to exceed $250,000 for all individuals whom notification is due. The State Attorney General is further entitled to attorney fees, court costs, and investigation costs.

Privacy Culture; Not a Security Culture*

If you were to ask any physician you encountered in the halls of a modern hospital in America, you would find that most, if not all, would state that they had taken the Hippocratic Oath as part of their rite of passage in becoming a physician. While this Oath has changed since it was first created more than 2400 years ago, the concept that protecting the privacy of a patient is still a sacred trust. So, *why do we see such a struggle between the sacred trust of protecting a patient's privacy and the adoption of security controls to do so in modern healthcare?*

Recently, I was invited by a friend of mine who was teaching a graduate level class in information security at Penn State to speak on some of the challenges facing the security community. As part of the discussion, I asked the question, *"Can someone tell me the difference between Privacy and Security?"* It sounded like an easy question, but after a few minutes, it became obvious that while everyone knew there was a difference, articulating what it was could be a bit tricky. It's at this point I offered up my explanation for consideration. I often use this explanation at management meetings, classes, and etc. to show the difference as well as the relationship in just two sentences.

Privacy answers the question: "Is it OK to share the information?"

Security answers the question: "How are you going to share the information and demonstrate that you did?"

It's not a perfect answer, but it does tend to illustrate a significant difference that can cause some interesting "dynamic tension." One example that I often recall of this dynamic tension involves a conversation I had early in my career where I was chastised by a senior physician because I wanted to set some basic complexity and rotation requirements. Specifically I was told:

---

* This section was provided with permission from contributing author, Ramon Balut.

Young man, I am a doctor and I took the Hippocratic Oath, do you know what that is? I don't need to change my password as I wouldn't ever share it.

This statement sums up the disconnect that occurs when talking about privacy and security in a healthcare setting. The idea that information related to a patient should only be shared appropriately has long been ingrained in the healthcare culture and is considered part of "caring for the patient." Unfortunately, healthcare has yet to adopt security into its everyday processes. While every organization will say that it values security, there still exists a wide gap between what organizations say they *do* versus what *actually occurs.*

In fairness, the idea of protecting privacy has had a millennium to work its way into the culture. In the days of Hippocrates, looking around to ensure that no one could overhear a discussion with a patient was probably an adequate security control. Conversely, Hippocrates could never have imagined things like "shoulder surfing," remote access trojans, or Ransomware. All of the actions required to prevent inappropriate disclosure from these types of attacks have really only come into being in the last few years.

Illustrative of how new the idea is to many healthcare organizations, about a year after having assumed my first role as a chief information security officer (CISO) in the late 1990s, I was talking with the chief information officer (CIO) of my organization, John Hummel. During the conversation I said, "John, I have to admit, I was a little surprised you picked me for the role. I really didn't think I had the experience you were looking for."

He chuckled and replied, "Ray, you were the first guy who, when we advertised for the role of data security officer, didn't show up with a crew cut and a baton. You knew what we meant."

Sobering thought indeed. Ask anyone, including most senior leadership, in a hospital twenty (20) years ago what IT Security meant and I would bet a month's pay that they would have directed you to the office of physical security. Now, twenty (20) years later, IT Security is a dynamic and vital part of the business of providing care and can't be considered a hindrance to caring for patients. IT Security is a vital part of not only protecting patient privacy, but keeping the very systems that make care possible at all, up and running. Unfortunately, while the healthcare community has had centuries to ingrain privacy as part of its culture, we have just begun to scratch the surface of integrating the actions necessary to maintain privacy in this bold new electronic world.

At a high level, it will take several things working together to enable security to become an accepted part of the healthcare culture. The first is real support from senior leadership. Security is not something you can "grass-roots" in an organization. It won't come from the bottom up and it won't find many champions in the treatment rooms or business offices. To make security work, it will require leaders who are "steely-eyed missile men" and willing to drive what will often be, at least temporarily, unpopular change. Leadership will have to walk the walk and live by their policies and standards. Nothing will cause the culture change to fail faster than C-suite leadership asking for an exception before the very ink is dry on the policy they just signed.

The second thing is education. Over the past twenty (20) years, I have time and time again seen that people are not trying to thwart security as much as they are trying to get their job done. For that to happen, organizations need to support their people with the right tools and education to allow them to do their jobs securely. The organization needs to train their people on how the security controls work and what is expected of them. This education must be on-going and refreshed to keep pace with the rapid changes in security threats.

The third element is accountability. Most organizations have adopted a low or even zero tolerance for deliberate, inappropriate access to protected health information and other sensitive data, as well as other activities such as bypassing established security controls. The application of these policies, however, must be applied equally to "high and low" within the organization. Allowing senior managers, physicians, and other senior level individuals to slide by with a warning for a security violation while firing a nurse for the same offense will always undermine the integrity of security and slow its adoption as a cultural norm.

Beyond the threat of disciplinary action, organizations should look for opportunities to incentivize those who do work toward a more secure environment. Rewarding those who do well in training related to security, make the "good catch," and report an event that results in preventing a possible incident from occurring are all good examples of instilling the value of security and speeding its adoption into the culture.

All Stick and No Carrot*

In February of 2013, President Obama issued *Executive Order 13636: Improving Critical Infrastructure Cybersecurity.* The result of this order was to establish a set of existing standards, guidelines, and practices to help organizations manage cyber risks. Sadly, as an information system security professional with years of experience, I feel confident that I know what needs to be done and even have some pretty good ideas on how to do it. What's lacking isn't more guidance, but resources to actually make things happen.

The *2015 Global Study on IT Security Spending & Investments* conducted by the Ponemon Institute indicates the following:

- Respondents have a lack of confidence in their organizations' ability to achieve compliance with regulations and security standards because of a lack of sufficient resources, such as experienced personnel and technologies.
- An inadequate budget and lack of support from their organizations' leadership makes it difficult to acquire state-of-the-art technologies. Fifty percent (50%) of respondents say their budgets are flat or actually declining in the next two (2) years.

Simply put, most IT security professionals in healthcare will tell you that in a world of decreasing budgets, security requests are being left on the "budget room" floor. To date, any move toward security has primarily been driven not by the carrot, but by the stick. The threat of penalties has been essentially the only motivator for organizations to take action and those penalties, for the most part, have only been realized as a result of breach investigations.

For better or worse, the move toward the use of electronic health records progressed to where it is today as a result, in large part, to the prospect of incentive dollars and conversely, the threat of reduced federal reimbursements. These reimbursements are going to be enforced, not as a result of a particular audit or incident, but by failure on the part of a provider or hospital to submit *proof of compliance.*

It is not hard to see where a similar program focused on security might provide comparable results. A program that specifically

---

* This section was provided with permission from contributing author, Ramon Balut.

incentivizes the implementation of security controls and requires demonstration that the controls were appropriately applied would likely motivate providers and hospitals to focus on security just as they did for the use of electronic healthcare records. Some may ask, "Didn't this Meaningful Use incentive program include requirements around security? Wouldn't that be incentive enough?"

True. The Meaningful Use incentive program that we'll discuss in detail later did include some very basic security requirements as part of the overall list of criteria objectives; however, these were a relatively minor part of the overall Meaningful Use requirements. These security requirements primarily focused on the medical record solution itself rather than the overall organizational or technical environment. At the end of the day, the incentive program was designed to encourage the implementation of an electronic healthcare record, not secure the organization.

In order for a security incentive program to work, it must

1. Be focused exclusively on security so that the funds are diluted as part of a larger initiative
2. Set reasonable requirements supporting a framework such as the NIST's Cybersecurity Framework that we'll go further into detail on later
3. Require that providers and hospitals demonstrate the actual effective implementation of the controls that the program incentivizes.

Steps 2 and 3 are key. As without some basic requirements /expectations from the program and with no requirement to demonstrate proof that controls were implemented, it is very likely that the only groups that will benefit from such as program would be security vendors selling products attempting to cash in on their share of the program dollars.

*****

Resource Availability

Besides the increase of cybersecurity threats the healthcare industry is facing and the lack of funding, another major issue is the lack of experienced and qualified cybersecurity professionals available to fill open positions. The nonprofit, independent professional certification association, *ISACA* (formerly known as the *Information Systems Audit and Control Association*), recently developed an informational graphic titled, "2016 Cybersecurity Skills Gap," pointing out the major shortage of cybersecurity professionals. By 2019, it is predicted that there will be a global shortage of cybersecurity professionals of two (2) million. Even though a majority of consumers [eighty-nine percent (89%)] feel that it is important for companies to have certified cybersecurity individuals working for them, companies are having a hard time finding qualified candidates. Eighty-four percent (84%) of companies with open positions believe that fewer than half are qualified and it appears that schools are not pushing cybersecurity as a possible career choice even though between 2010 and 2014, cybersecurity job growth, overall, was three (3) times that of other information technology–related jobs.*

These statistics are being echoed by executive recruiters that are assisting companies in finding cybersecurity talent. Companies are looking for individuals that are not only experienced in technology, but also experienced in other parts of a business. Unfortunately, there appears to be a lack of strong career paths for cybersecurity leaders to gain this well-rounded experience. Hunt Scanlon Media, a research firm that provides recruitment market intelligence, indicated that they are seeing a large demand for risk and security executives at the C-suite level due to the leadership need caused by a lot of recent breaches. "Bringing cyber security leadership expertise to the highest levels of management and into the boardroom is therefore a strategic imperative for every company," Scott A. Scanlon, founding chairman and CEO of Hunt Scanlon Media, writes in his article *The Hunt for Cyber Security Leadership Intensifies* (Scanlon, 2016). Hunt Scanlon reports, there is a "high demand and a short talent supply [that] is leading to a 'bidding war for talent' throughout the security sector" (Scanlon, 2016). Table 5.4 shows some of the demand for talent across the different industries.

In an attempt to assist organizations, Hunt Scanlon has published its first listings of the top twenty (20) search firms that are dedicated to cybersecurity talent. The firms that have made the list are given in Table 5.5.

---

* From ISACA (2016).

Table 5.4   Talent Demand across Industry Sectors

MOST DEMAND	OTHER DEMAND	INDUSTRIES
Chief information security officers (CISO)	Infrastructure/monitoring Specialists/leaders	Financial/banking/hedge funds
Information security directors	Cloud security vice presidents	Healthcare/pharmaceuticals/insurance
Chief technology officers (CTO)	Risk leaders	Entertainment
IT leaders	Cyber/incident response	Utilities
	Investigation specialists	Retail
	Compliance/privacy officers	Manufacturing
		Government

Source: Scanlon, S.A., The hunt for cyber security leadership intensifies, Retrieved from LinkedIn, https://www.linkedin.com/pulse/hunt-cyber-security-leadership-intensifies-scott-a-scanlon, February 26, 2016.

Table 5.5   Top Twenty (20) Cybersecurity Recruiting Firms

TOP TWENTY (20) CYBERSECURITY RECRUITING FIRMS	
680 Partners	JM Search
Alta Associates	Kaye/Bassman International
Benchmark Executive Search	Korn Ferry
Bridgen Group Inc.	Russell Reynolds Associates
Caldwell Partners	SI Placement
DHR International	Spencer Stuart
Diversified Search	SPMB
Egon Zehnder	TD Madison
Heidrick & Struggles	Work & Partners
Indigo Partners	ZRG Partners

Source: HuntScanlon, Cyber 20, Retrieved from Hunt Scanlon, http://huntscanlon.com/cyber-20/, February 26, 2016.

Lockheed, Boeing, Raytheon, General Dynamics, and Northrop Grumman, we probably all heard of these companies since they are some of the biggest defense contractors in the aerospace and intelligence sectors. They are on point when it comes to assisting federal agencies with their cyber threats; however, for the Fortune 500s and other corporations, this is a different matter. Although the 2015 cybersecurity market worldwide is around $75 billion and expected to reach $175 billion by 2020, Lockheed Martin recently announced that it is trying to sell its $4 billion government IT business that includes its cybersecurity unit. Since governmental standards are usually more demanding than the commercial sector, one would think that these contractors would be well positioned to fill this demand; however, as Dan Nelson, vice president of Corporate Communications at Lockheed Martin, explains, many factors such as "changing market dynamics, shifting government priorities, increased competition and industry trends" were involved in their decision leading to the belief that it is better their IT and cybersecurity business operates "outside of Lockheed Martin" (Morgan, 2016).

According to a recent report from *Markets and Markets*, the security analytics sector alone is estimated to grow from $2.1 billion to $7.1 billion over the next five (5) years. With cybercrime rising and the shortage of personnel, Symantec hired some of the staff from Narus, a cybersecurity analytics subsidiary of Boeing, about a year ago. Narus retained their software rights and customers, but Andrew Lee, senior manager and division communications lead, Electronic & Information Solutions at Boeing, reported, "It is correct that with the divesture of Narus, we are not focusing on commercial cybersecurity for the time being" (Morgan, 2016).

Raytheon Company basically carved out their cybersecurity products and joined forces with Vista Equity Partners to establish a new company called Forcepoint. General Dynamics sold its Fidelis cybersecurity business to Marlin Equity Partners. Initially cybersecurity was under General Dynamics' Information Systems and Technology business, but as Lucy Ryan, a spokesperson for General Dynamics, stated, Fidelis "serves a commercial customer base, not in our core, and is better served with a commercially focused owner" (Morgan, 2016). Finally, Northrup Grumman created Acuity Solutions Corporation in 2015 that looks like its own company. It appears that even these big contractors know the challenges that the commercial space face and saw better routes to take for their companies.

Cybersecurity or information security is a fairly new career area, but individuals working in this industry tend to protect some of the major critical infrastructures of our country. Although there are many organizations that provide credentialing opportunities to assist candidates in demonstrating their competencies, there have also been some suggestions to license cybersecurity or information security professionals. As one of these professionals, I'm not necessarily opposed to these licensing requirements. I believe, if done correctly, it could assist in raising the bar in the profession. Ensuring that these professionals have clean records, requisite qualifications, experience, and expertise and providing some oversight into their actions could lend credence to the work these individuals dedicate themselves to every day. This licensing could also assist in developing curriculum and minimum standards to establish educational tracks for new candidates interested in this field of study. Career paths could be established in the cybersecurity industry a lot like other trades, for example, electricians, lawyers, doctors, and accountants.

Excuses

"The problem with healthcare is that it's all complex. If people want to find an excuse not to do something, they can find one" (Lynn, 2016c). This was a quote from an unknown source written in an article by John Lynn titled *The Biggest Challenge in Healthcare: Excuses*. From my experience, I can't agree enough with Lynn that this quote is "spot on." If I only had a dollar for every time I received an excuse why a healthcare company wasn't able to do something that I recommended to strengthen their security posture, well, you could estimate how rich I would be by now.

My all-time favorite excuse is related to the rationale behind not having a password-protected screensaver. As a point of reference, it is generally good security practice to lock your workstation when you are not in the vicinity. A group policy should be set on the workstation to lock the system after a certain amount of time [generally within fifteen (15) minutes] when the system determines that it is inactive. A user should be required to enter their credentials to resume using the system. The most common excuse I get from this recommendation is that it takes too long to have to re-enter the credentials each time the system "goes to sleep." Instead, it makes more sense to leave the systems unlocked when not in use, *right*? I can't even count the number of times I've inspected healthcare facilities and found systems in hallways completely open with patient information on the screen for anyone that walks by could see.

My friends and family know what I do for a living and they often hear some of the adventure stories I tell of previous assessments or "hacks" I performed on my clients. *Don't worry, I always leave information out or change names to protect the innocent.* My friends and family become more "security aware" after sharing these tales and I always hear back from them about situations that they observe. The best is when they visit a doctor's office and they are left alone in the patient room with a computer unlocked, with patient information on the screen. *They refer to these incidents affectionately as "another Jay story."* When it only takes two (2) key strokes, known as the "two finger salute" (holding down the Windows key ⊞ and the "L" key) to lock the system, *why does staff feel that it is OK to leave these sensitive systems available to anyone in the area*? Again, it only takes a few seconds to re-enter the credentials to turn the system "back on."

Another one of my favorite excuses is that "we can't use long or complex passwords." This is usually followed by accusing doctors that they can't remember these passwords. If a doctor can't remember an eight (8) character password, I may question their ability to diagnose my illness or to provide me adequate healthcare treatment. Doctors are generally known to be intelligent and have gone through several years of higher learning before they are able to practice medicine. They had to pass rigorous tests and remember a ton more information than a password throughout their careers. The logic around this excuse I find just utterly incredible. As Lynn states, "Doctors['] principle of 'first do no harm' is very real in healthcare…but it can also be invoked easily to say no to anything you don't want to do" (Lynn, 2016c).

"We don't have the money for that." Although this may appear to be a legitimate reason why certain security systems weren't in place, I always took this into consideration when providing recommendations to my clients. I normally based my recommendations on knowing my clients' needs and resources allowing for multiple possibilities to mitigate risks. In most cases, the client would need to spend little to no money to implement a solution that would make them more secure. In some cases, the client would already have a solution in place, but it wasn't configured properly or being appropriately utilized. In other cases, it just came down to the fact that security was an inconvenience or cut into their bottom line. Unfortunately, as a company that maintains sensitive information, security is not optional; *it is the cost of doing business*. As Lynn concludes, "After all, the very best things in life are challenging and difficult. Let's embrace the challenging and difficult instead of using it as an excuse for inaction" (Lynn, 2016c).

According to a survey conducted by Cisco, seventy-one percent (71%) of one thousand (1000) chief executives believe commerce is slowed down by efforts put into enhancing IT defenses. For this reason, Craig Williams, a senior technical leader at Cisco's security business, Talos, believes some individuals in computer security won't be there in five (5) years, "I think security has moved away from being something that involves configuring a firewall to something that is more data and analytic driven. A large percentage of engineers out there will probably be doing something else" (Hall, 2016a). Adam Philpott, director of cybersecurity at Cisco EMEA, agrees that security jobs are changing and there is an increase in automation that "free people up to do more intellectual activities, so to speak" (Hall, 2016a). Security may appear to be a hindrance to operations, but it is an essential element to keep an organization's data private.

Security may have a hard time demonstrating any return on investment. I believe the metrics we utilize in these efforts tend to be the wrong measurements when it comes to determining effectiveness. I see where we attempt to *quantify* security by counting the number of attacks or the number of phishing e-mails, for example, rather than *qualifying* security efforts. This goes back to the analytics of the security data produced. Determining where the threat actors are coming from, what they are doing, and trending cybersecurity activities to allow organizations to respond to these risks in almost real time is where the "tire meets the road."

A Funny Thing Happened on the Way to Security…Nothing*

In April of 2003, the HIPAA Privacy Rule went into effect. That same year, the HIPAA Security Rule was published and ultimately became effective two (2) years later in April 2005. The publishing of the Security Rule initiated the single most significant event to impact the issue of information security in healthcare to date.

Working as a CISO in healthcare at the time, I, as well as many of my colleagues, scrambled to determine what the regulations meant. Of course privacy had been center stage for years, but in 2003 the race was now on to answer questions such as: *How we were going to*

---

* This section was provided with permission from contributing author, Ramon Balut.

ensure confidentiality, integrity, and availability? What were acceptable standards? What technologies will the Department of Health and Human Services (HHS) expect us to use?

Much like the preparation for privacy and in the tradition of getting ready for any new regulatory requirement, we formed workgroups, committees, and scoured the Internet for any glimmers of guidance that would help us interpret and prepare. After two (2) years of acquiring budget, developing policies, training staff, and other activities, we stood as ready as we probably ever would be to be audited by the OCR in the fine traditions of the Joint Commission on Accreditation of Healthcare Organizations (JCAHO) and other regulatory/accrediting bodies. We waited, and waited, and then waited some more, but in the end, we discovered that we were all "dressed up"; no one was coming to the party.

In 2013, the Department of Health and Human Services' Office of Inspector General criticized their own OCR responsible for providing oversight with regards to compliance with the Security Rule. Specifically from the *November 2013 Department of Health and Human Services' Office of Inspector General: The Office for Civil Rights Did Not Meet All Federal Requirements in Its Oversight and Enforcement of the Health Insurance Portability and Accountability Act Security Rule report*, the OIG stated:

(Direct Excerpt from the Report)
OCR did not meet other Federal requirements critical to the oversight and enforcement of the Security Rule:

- *Although OCR made available to covered entities guidance that promoted compliance with the Security Rule, it had not assessed the risks, established priorities, or implemented controls for its HITECH requirement to provide for periodic audits of covered entities to ensure their compliance with Security Rule requirements. As a result, OCR had limited assurance that covered entities complied with the Security Rule and missed opportunities to encourage those entities to strengthen their security over ePHI.*
- *Although OCR established an investigation process for responding to reported violations of the Security Rule, its Security Rule investigation files did not contain required documentation supporting key*

decisions because its staff did not consistently follow OCR investi-
gation procedures by sufficiently reviewing investigation case docu-
mentation. OCR had not implemented sufficient controls, including
supervisory review and documentation retention, to ensure investi-
gators follow investigation policies and procedures for properly ini-
tiating, processing, and closing Security Rule investigations (Office
of Inspector General, 2013).

In response, the OCR made the following comment: "no funds had
been appropriated for it to maintain a permanent audit program and
that funds used to support audit activities previously conducted were
no longer available" (Office of Inspector General, 2013).

While at the present time, efforts have been renewed to establish
an audit program, the damage has already been done. In short, healthcare is an industry that is highly compliance driven. Given limited
resources and hundreds of other compliance issues to address, if no
one was willing to come out and inspect us on the issue of security,
then beating the drum to remain vigilant becomes harder and harder.
Over the course of a decade, the "compliance driver" faded and along
with it, many programs.

Beyond mere compliance, another ironic, but major blow to healthcare security programs was that the "hacks" we all braced for hardly
materialized. A review of the Department of Health and Human
Services' "Wall of Shame" shows that losses were overwhelmingly due
to the theft or loss of devices, paper, and media especially in the early
years of reporting.

It was almost prophetic when, in April of 2014 the Federal Bureau
of Investigations (FBI) Cyber Division issued a Private Industry
Notification (PIN#: 140408-009) to the healthcare sector warning:
"The healthcare industry is not as resilient to cyber intrusions compared to
the financial and retail sectors, therefore the possibility of increased cyber
intrusions is likely" (Federal Bureau of Investigations, 2016).

This understatement didn't bode well since financial and retail
breaches were becoming more commonplace and the public was
effectively becoming desensitized to any announcement that another
large-scale credit card breach had occurred. If financial and retail
organizations were having such a rough time and healthcare was
considered even less "resilient," then we were in a world of hurt.

In that same year, 2014, we began to hear of "sophisticated malware attacks" leading to large-scale breaches such as the Community Health System's breach involving 4.5 million records. Unfortunately, this would be just a precursor to 2015 in which three (3) of the seven (7) largest breaches that year belonged to healthcare organizations including the Anthem breach, which resulted in a staggering 80 million lost records. With this flurry of heavy blows, boards of directors and senior leadership turned to their security staff (if they had them) and asked, *"Can this happen to us and what are we doing to prevent this?"*

Due to the lack of external compliance follow-up, no real-world tests of security (in the form of significant targeted attacks), lack of tools, lack of techniques, and outdated security designs, for most organizations the reality was the answer to this question was a resounding "YES, it could happen to us." Because nothing really happened over the course of a decade, maintaining and updating tools, standards, response techniques, and other security best practices simply didn't occur, and many organizations found themselves horribly outmatched.

Fortunately, as former White House chief of staff, Rahm Emanuel, famously stated, *"You never let a serious crisis go to waste. And what I mean by that it's an opportunity to do things you think you could not do before."* Healthcare organizations are now waking up to the new reality of the security landscape. To successfully close this gap, organizations will need to start at the beginning, just as we did in 2012, but this time, the focus will need to shift from wondering, *"What will it take to be HIPAA Compliant"* to *"What will it take to defend against motivated, organized, and skilled attackers whom are profit (or national interest) motivated and whom, in a very real way, have shown us just how successful they can be at compromising our security?"*

6

Enforcement

The culture of any organization is shaped by the worst behavior the leader is willing to tolerate.

—Steve Gruenter and Todd Whitaker, *Education Experts and Authors*

OCR

The Office for Civil Rights (OCR) is the enforcement arm of the Department of Health and Human Services (HHS) when it comes to compliance over Health Insurance Portability and Accountability Act (HIPAA), Health Information Technology for Clinical and Economic Health (HITECH), and breach notification as well as receiving/investigating complaints over privacy/security violations related to these regulations. The OCR can levy fines (or what they term civil money penalty [CMP]) and turn over cases to the Department of Justice (DOJ) for criminal actions.

CMP is broken down into four (4) categories as shown in Table 6.1.

It is important to also include some definitions of the terms used within the categories for clarity, as per 45 Code of Federal Regulations (CFR) § 160.401 of the HIPAA regulations:

- *Reasonable cause*—means an act or omission in which a covered entity or business associate knew, or by exercising reasonable diligence would have known, that the act or omission violated an administrative simplification provision, but in which the covered entity or business associate did not act with willful neglect.
- *Reasonable diligence*—means the business care and prudence expected from a person seeking to satisfy a legal requirement under similar circumstances.
- *Willful neglect*—means conscious, intentional failure or reckless indifference to the obligation to comply with the administrative simplification provision violated.

Table 6.1 Breakdown of CMP Based on Category of Violations

CATEGORY OF VIOLATIONS	CMP
Did not know and would not have known by exercising reasonable diligence	Per violation: $100 to $50,000 each Or for identical violations during calendar year: Not to exceed $1,500,000
Reasonable cause to know, but no willful neglect	Per violation: $1,000 to $50,000 each Or for identical violations during calendar year: Not to exceed $1,500,000
Willful neglect, but corrected within thirty (30) days	Per violation: $10,000 to $50,000 each Or for identical violations during calendar year: Not to exceed $1,500,000
Willful neglect, failed to correct within thirty (30) days	Per violation: Not to exceed $50,000 each Or for identical violations during calendar year: Not to exceed $1,500,000

Note that penalties are assessed on a "per violation" basis so an organization could be assessed penalties for different kind of violations, which could subject an organization to penalties in excess of the $1.5 million limits.

A perfect example of how these fines are levied was reported by the OCR back in October 2010 when they investigated forty-one (41) individual complaints against Cignet Health regarding patients' rights to access their own medical records. According to the HIPAA Privacy Rules, a patient has a right to get a copy of their medical records within thirty (30) days and no later than sixty (60) days from the time of their request from a covered entity. OCR levied a $1.3 million CMP for these violations. Furthermore, Cignet Health refused to respond to OCR's repeated demands to produce the records and willfully neglected to cooperate with OCR's investigation. OCR levied an additional $3 million CMP bringing the total to $4.3 million. Former OCR Director Georgina Verdugo stated at the time of the Notice of Proposed Determination against Cignet Health, "The U.S. Department of Health and Human Services will continue to investigate and take action against those organizations that knowingly disregard their obligations under these rules [HIPAA]" (HHS, 2016a).

Lincare, Inc., a home healthcare company, is the only other organization that has received a Notice of Proposed Determination of CMP. The action took place after OCR received a complaint from an estranged husband of one of Lincare's managers. The wife moved out of the house, but the husband found records of two hundred seventy-eight (278) patients "under a bed and in a kitchen drawer." Further investigation showed that records were continuously stored in the car and in her home. Lincare also did not have required policies, logging or tracking of protected health information, and did not instruct employees on the proper handling of records. OCR failed to obtain a settlement from the organization and levied a $239,800 penalty for failure to safeguard protected health information, impermissible disclosure, and failing to have policies/procedures in place to ensure compliance. An administrative law judge (ALJ) upheld the fine after Lincare appealed the decision (HHS, 2016b).

As you may have realized by now, organizations settle with the OCR over complaints or violations before an actual CMP is levied. Let's take a look at some of the settlements that occurred between 2014 and 2015 (Table 6.2).

Although Table 6.2 is a good example of enforcement actions taken by the OCR, fines still appear to be rarely delved out. According to a report by *ProPublica*, since October 2009, OCR has received one thousand one hundred forty-two (1142) reports of breaches affecting over five hundred (500) records. OCR also apparently received more than one hundred twenty thousand (120,000) notifications of breaches involving less than five hundred (500) records. "Yet, over that time span, the Office for Civil Rights has fined health care organizations just [twenty-two] 22 times" (Ornstein, 2016). *Is OCR really doing enough to enforce regulatory compliance?* As a comparison, the California Department of Public Health that enforces California's stricter privacy laws has levied twenty-two (22) penalties in 2015 and an additional eight (8) just in the first two (2) months of 2016.

Even after Leon Rodriguez, former director of the U.S. Department of Health and Human Services' Office for Civil Rights warned at a privacy/security forum back in December 2012, "We've now moved into an area of more assertive enforcement" (Ornstein, 2016), it appears that OCR goes after "high-impact cases that send strong enforcement messages about important compliance issues" or those that "have involved systemic and/or long-standing" concerns per an OCR statement provided to *ProPublica* on the topic (Ornstein, 2016).

One of the reasons pointed out by some security experts for the lack of enforcement by OCR is that OCR has fewer than two hundred (200) staff members with a budget of just thirty-nine ($39) million.

Table 6.2   Review of 2014–2015 HIPAA Enforcement Actions

DATE	ORGANIZATION	MAIN VIOLATION	ADDITIONAL NOTES	SETTLEMENT	NOTICE
11/30/2015	Triple-S Management Corporation	Security risk assessment	OCR received five breach notices; failed to implement safeguards; minimum necessary use not followed; no risk analysis; no security measures implemented to reduce risks; no access termination procedures; and impermissible disclosure to vendor—no business associate agreement in place.	$3.5 million and 3-year corrective action plan (CAP)	http://www.hhs.gov/about/news/2015/11/30/triple-s-management-corporation-settles-hhs-charges.html#
8/31/2015	Cancer Care Group, P.C.	Device encryption/controls	Breach report made when unencrypted laptop stolen (55,000 records); no policies/procedures for receipt/removal of hardware/media containing ePHI	$750,000 and 3-year CAP	http://www.hhs.gov/about/news/2015/09/02/750%2C000-dollar-hipaa-settlement-emphasizes-the-importance-of-risk-analysis-and-device-and-media-control-policies.html
4/22/2014	Concentra Health Services	Device encryption/controls	Breach report made when unencrypted laptop stolen (unknown # of records); no policies/procedures for remediation efforts based on risk assessment	$1,725,220 and 2-year CAP	http://www.hhs.gov/about/news/2014/04/22/stolen-laptops-lead-to-important-hipaa-settlements.html
4/22/2014	QCA Health Plan, Inc.	Device encryption/controls	Breach report made when unencrypted laptop stolen (148 records); no security risk analysis performed	$250,000 and 2-yearCAP	http://www.hhs.gov/about/news/2014/04/22/stolen-laptops-lead-to-important-hipaa-settlements.html

(Continued)

Table 6.2 (*Continued*) Review of 2014–2015 HIPAA Enforcement Actions

DATE	ORGANIZATION	MAIN VIOLATION	ADDITIONAL NOTES	SETTLEMENT	NOTICE
5/7/2014	New York-Presbyterian Hospital & Trustees of Columbia University	Data access controls	Breach report made when 6,800 records were accessible through Internet search engine; no security risk assessment performed; failed to comply with data security policies/procedures	$3,300,000 by NYP; $1,500,000 by Columbia; 3-year CAPs	http://www.hhs.gov/about/news/2014/05/07/data-breach-results-48-million-hipaa-settlements.html
3/7/2014	Skagit County, Washington	Data access controls	Breach report made when 1,581 records moved to publicly accessible server; widespread noncompliance of rules	$215,000 and 3-year CAP	http://www.hhs.gov/about/news/2014/03/07/county-government-settles-potential-hipaa-violations.html
12/2/2014	Anchorage Community Mental Health Services, Inc.	Malware protection	Breach report made regarding malware compromising systems (27,430 records compromised); failed to perform risk assessment; failed to install patches/updates	$150,000 and 2-year CAP	http://www.hhs.gov/sites/default/files/ocr/privacy/hipaa/enforcement/examples/acmhs/acmhsbulletin.pdf
6/10/2015	Elizabeth's Medical Center	File-sharing applications	Complaint over Internet-based file sharing application storing documents (at least 498 records involved); separate breach report made for unsecured ePHI on personal laptop and USB drive (595 records involved); failed to identify/respond to incident; failed to mitigate effects of incident and document incident and results	$218,400 and 1-year CAP	http://www.hhs.gov/sites/default/files/bulletin.pdf

(Continued)

Table 6.2 (*Continued*) Review of 2014–2015 HIPAA Enforcement Actions

DATE	ORGANIZATION	MAIN VIOLATION	ADDITIONAL NOTES	SETTLEMENT	NOTICE
12/14/2015	University of Washington Medicine	Social engineering	Breach report over employee opening phishing email (90,000 records compromised); although policies required affiliates/partners to perform risk assessments, failed to ensure affiliates were performing these assessments and responding to risks	$750,000 and 2-year CAP	http://www.hhs.gov/about/news/2015/12/14/750000-hipaa-settlement-underscores-need-for-organization-wide-risk-analysis.html
11/24/2015	Lahey Hospital and Medical Center	Physical security	Breach report made when laptop attached to CT scanner stolen from unlocked room (599 records breached); failed to perform risk assessment; failed to safeguard workstation; no unique user names utilized; no documentation of workstation activity	$850,000 and 3-year CAP	http://www.hhs.gov/about/news/2015/11/25/hipaa-settlement-reinforces-lessons-users-medical-devices.html
April 2015	Cornell Prescription Pharmacy	Paper records	Disposal of unsecured documents in an unlocked, open container (1,610 records involved); OCR discovered through a local news report	$125,000 and 2-year CAP	http://www.hhs.gov/hipaa/for-professionals/compliance-enforcement/examples/cornell/cornell-press-release/index.html
6/23/2014	Parkview Health System	Paper records	Unsecure handling of paper records	$800,000 and CAP	http://www.hhs.gov/about/news/2014/06/23/800000-hipaa-settlement-in-medical-records-dumping-case.html

Source: Hiser, D.C., HIPAA Compliance: Another year older, but hopefully not deeper in debt, Retrieved from Lexology, http://www.lexology.com/library/detail.aspx?g=929b0b7a-a5a3-42b9-b38e-dadb3a100222, February 14, 2016.

Although the agency gets to keep fines imposed for enforcement to continue to improve compliance activities, Figure 6.1 demonstrates some of the other duties the OCR is responsible for.

The number of privacy complaints has been rising as seen in Figure 6.2. It is of importance to note that OCR has seen a dramatic increase in the last few years as they made it easier to report a

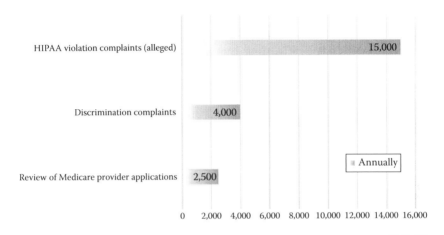

Figure 6.1   OCR's responsibilities by the numbers (per year). (From Ornstein, D.C., Fines remain rare even as health data breaches multiply, Retrieved from ProPublica, http://www.propublica.org/article/fines-remain-rare-even-as-health-data-breaches-multiply, February 15, 2016.)

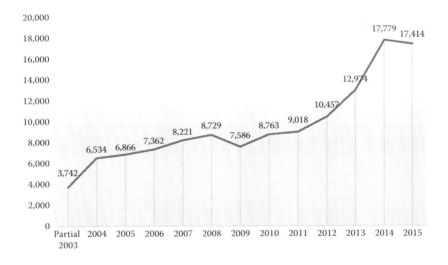

Figure 6.2   Increase in privacy complaints. (From HHS Office for Civil Rights, OCR, 2016a.)

complaint utilizing an online complaint portal located here: https://ocrportal.hhs.gov/ocr/smartscreen/main.jsf.

In addition, OCR indicated that it resolved ninety-six percent (96%) of the 125,445 complaints received. Of the 34,975 investigated, there were thirty-one percent (31%) that resulted in "no violation." The other sixty-nine percent (69%) or 24,047 were resolved with corrective action. "To date [as of December 31, 2015], OCR has settled 29 such cases resulting in a total dollar amount of $27,974,400.00" (OCR, 2016b; Figure 6.3).

There are multiple healthcare organizations that have multiple reports of violations; however, analysis performed by *ProPublica* indicates that there is lax enforcement. According to Joy Pritts, former chief privacy officer for HHS' Office of the National Coordinator for Healthcare Information Technology, "The patterns you've [ProPublica] identified makes a person wonder how far a company has to go before HHS recognizes a pattern of noncompliance," even though a prior track record is a determining factor, "you have to ask whether that's happening" (Waldman, 2016).

As an example, ProPublica points to the repeated violations at the Veteran Affairs (VA) since they have the highest number of complaints. From 2011 to 2014, there were two hundred twenty (220) violations reported. Violations were considered complaints that resulted in corrective actions or "technical assistance." These violations could include such activities as employees looking into each

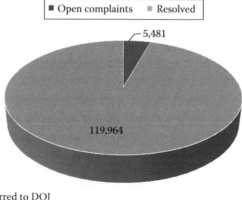

*566 referred to DOJ

Figure 6.3 Complaint resolution by OCR. (From HHS Office for Civil Rights, OCR, 2016c.)

other's medical records, records of patients they weren't directly treating, records of family members, posting details of such records on Facebook, or improperly sharing records. OCR has not once sanctioned the VA for their repeated offenses and has never publicly called them out for these violations. One of the problems that OCR is facing that was pointed out by the HHS inspector general in two separate reports is the lack of a tracking system to account for repeat offenders.

As a former law enforcement officer, I can relate to some security experts that believe regulators should enforce compliance by imposing fines for violations. These actions send a clear message to everyone in the industry that lax of privacy or security will not be tolerated. Bruce Schneier, a computer expert and blogger, provides a good analogy to pollution: "if the cost of polluting is zero, companies will pollute … If your CEO said we're going to spend four times as much money not to pollute, he would be fired" (Ornstein, 2016). Schneier urges that security has to be rational. If I pulled you over for speeding and I gave you a ticket, you hopefully will slow it down next time. I lived in an area that had what everyone referred to as a "speed trap." Police constantly patrolled the area and picked up violators left and right. Recently, the town disbanded the police and now, with the lack of enforcement, the speed of traffic has increased on this stretch of highway. It is the same with healthcare security, as I keep iterating—if there is no enforcement, there is no compliance.

In addition to the CMP that are assessed against an organization, violation of the HIPAA Privacy Rules could result in personal fines and jail time. Under U.S. Code Title 42 Chapter 7—1320d-6, it is unlawful to wrongfully disclose individually identifiable health information. A person who knowingly uses or causes to be used a unique health identifier, obtains individually identifiable health information relating to an individual, or discloses individually identifiable health information to another person could be subjected to the punishment specified in Table 6.3.

As you may have noted in Figure 6.3, five hundred sixty-six (566) individuals have been referred to the DOJ for possible criminal charges related to privacy violations. The first individual reported to have been sentenced to prison for violating a patient's privacy was Huping Zhou, a researcher with the UCLA School of Medicine. Zhou plead guilty

Table 6.3 Criminal Offense for Disclosing Individually Identifiable Health Information

CATEGORY	PER VIOLATION
Knowingly or with reasonable cause	Maximum $50,000 and/or maximum of one (1) year incarceration
Under false pretenses	Maximum $100,000 and/or maximum of five (5) years incarceration
With intent to sell, transfer, or use for commercial advantage, personal gain, or malicious harm	Maximum $250,000 and/or maximum of ten (10) years incarceration

to four (4) misdemeanor counts of accessing medical records without proper authorization in January 2010. The incident took place back in October 2003 when Zhou received notice of termination, but used his access to the UCLA record systems to view records of his boss and other coworkers. Over the next three (3) weeks, he accessed the system three hundred twenty-three (323) times and viewed records of some celebrities. Zhou was sentenced to four (4) months in prison and a fine of $2000 (Dimick, 2016).

Here is a list of other individuals that have been unfortunate enough to violate the HIPAA regulations and have been sentenced for their activities (Table 6.4).

OCR performed a Phase 1 "pilot" audit program on one hundred fifteen (115) covered entities between 2011 and 2012. Based on the results of this audit, OCR plans to conduct Phase 2 audits starting with a survey issued to a random pool of up to eight hundred (800) covered entities. From the survey results, OCR has indicated that "it will select approximately three hundred fifty (350) covered entities, including two hundred thirty-two (232) health care providers, one hundred nine (109) health plans and nine (9) health care clearinghouses" (Gottlieb et al., 2016).

The Phase 2 audits will primarily be a "desk audit" whereby the organization under review will have two (2) weeks to respond to requested information from the OCR. The organization will be referred to the regional OCR office for a compliance review (and possible enforcement activities) if the organization fails to appropriately respond to the requests. This next round of audits will focus on specific areas of most frequent noncompliance security-related issues such as risk analysis/management, training, device/media controls, and transmission security. It will also focus on privacy issues such as requirements around the notice of privacy practices, individual access, and

Table 6.4 Other Individuals Sentenced for Privacy Violations

DATE	NAME	CRIME	OTHER COMMENTS	PENALTY
August 2014	Joshua Hippler	Plead guilty to wrongful disclosure of individually identifiable health information	Former employee of an East Texas Hospital (unknown); intended to use information for personal gain; found in possession of records in Georgia after an arrest	Eighteen (18) months prison term; three (3) years supervised release; $12,152 in restitution
October 2013	Denetria Barnes	Plead guilty to several federal offenses (along with conspiracy to defraud and wrongful disclosure)	Former nursing assistant at a Florida assisted living facility	Thirty-seven (37) months prison term
October 2013	Christopher R. Lykes, Jr.	Plead guilty to four (4) felony counts willful examination of records and one (1) felony count of criminal conspiracy (Toshia Yvette Latimer-Addison) was also charged with one (1) count of criminal conspiracy	Former state employee of South Carolina, sent 228,000 Medicaid records to personal e-mail	Three (3) years of probation; three hundred (300) hours community service
April 2013	Helene Michel	Found guilty of $10.7 million in Medicare fraud along with criminal HIPAA violations	Former owner of a medical supply company in Long Island, NY	Twelve (12) years prison term

Source: McGee, M.K., Prison term in HIPAA violation case, Retrieved from InfoRisk Today, http://www.inforisktoday.com/prison-term-in-hipaa-violation-case-a-7938/op-1, February 16, 2016e; McGee, M.K., Sentencing in S.C. Medicaid Breach Case, Retrieved from HealthcareInfoSecurity, http://www.healthcareinfosecurity.com/sentencing-in-sc-medicaid-breach-case-a-7546, February 16, 2016h.

the administrative safeguard requirements. In addition, breach notification requirements such as content and timeliness will be included. These audits are expected to run over the next three (3) years.

To ensure the HIPAA compliance audits take place, OCR is seeking an increase of ten percent (10%) from $39 to $43 million in their upcoming fiscal year 2017 budget. From a current staff of one hundred eighty (180), OCR is proposing to add eighteen (18) full-time employees (McGee, 2016d). In a budget note, HHS states, "Audits are a proactive approach to evaluating and ensuring HIPAA privacy and security compliance. The audit program will offer a new tool to help ensure HIPAA compliance by covered entities and business associates while also informing OCR on areas in which to direct its enforcement and technical assistance" (McGee, 2016d).

Furthermore, the additional funds request, based on another budgetary note, would enable OCR to "modernize HIPAA protections, support innovation in healthcare, ensure adequate protections in new programs and technologies, streamline requirements to make them less burdensome, and evaluate new areas where HIPAA does not currently apply" (McGee, 2016d). Unfortunately, OCR requested additional funding for fiscal year 2016; however, Congress didn't approve this increase. This may explain one of the reasons why we have not seen the OCR published audit protocols updated to this point.

Omnibus Rule

The HHS published the final Omnibus Rule on March 26, 2013 ensuring that all covered entities and business associates are directly liable for compliance over the HIPAA Security Rules and applicable HIPAA Privacy Rules. In basic terms, anyone that creates, receives, maintains, or transmits protected health information on behalf of a covered entity (or business associate) is responsible for compliance. This also includes organizations that store electronic-protected health information. Furthermore, those subcontractors that create, receive, maintain, or transmit protected health information (PHI) on behalf of business associates fall under this liability since they are now considered business associates themselves.

Covered entities are defined as healthcare providers that transmit any health information in electronic form in connection with a covered transaction, health plans, and healthcare clearinghouses. Whereas, specific business associates include health information organizations, e-prescribing gateways, or other persons that provide data transmission services with respect to PHI and requires access to the PHI on a routine basis. Business associates also include persons that offer personal health records to individuals on behalf of a covered entity.

There is a narrow exemption for organizations that may be considered as conduits. Examples of a conduit include Internet service providers and mail service providers like FedEx or UPS that merely "transmit" protected health information. HHS has made it clear that the test for determining if an entity is considered a business associate (or subcontractor of a business associate) is the *persistence of custody* and not the degree of access, if any, over the PHI. For example, cloud service or hosting providers that store PHI attempted to claim that they were conduits and exempt from complying with the HIPAA regulations since they had no access (or may only have access on a random or incidental basis) to the data. The regulators have reiterated that even if this is the case, they are considered business associates or subcontractors of business associates through their persistence of custody over the PHI and must demonstrate their compliance over the HIPAA administrative, physical, and technical requirements. These service providers are subject to criminal and civil penalties if they are not in compliance with the law.

Business Associate Agreements

To obtain satisfactory assurance of compliance, it is necessary that a covered entity and business associate sign a business associate agreement or similar agreement that meets the minimum statutory requirements for a business associate agreement. This business associate agreement is a binding, legal document that defines, at a minimum, the following requirements:

- The permitted or required uses and disclosures of PHI
- Applying appropriate safeguards and preventing the unauthorized use or disclosure of PHI
- Termination of contract for a breaching or violating the terms of the agreement

- Ensuring that subcontractors agree to comply with the same applicable requirements of the agreement
- Report any security incident, including breaches of unsecured PHI, to the covered entity (or business associate)
- Make PHI available, as may be required, to the individual, for amendments, for accounting of disclosures, to meet the covered entity (or business associates) other obligations, and available to the secretary of HHS for the purpose of compliance
- Return or destruction of PHI at the termination of a contract or when it is no longer needed by the business associate/subcontractor

As was the case for Triple-S Management Corporation being fined $3.5 million, it is a violation for a covered entity or business associate to transmit and for a business associate or subcontractor to receive PHI without a written, compliant business associate agreement being executed between the two parties. "A Business Associate Agreement may be a software license agreement, a data storage agreement, an outsourcing agreement, an insurance policy, a medical center's IT maintenance or billing services agreement, a HMO services or employment agreement or any of many other types of contract," as indicated by Owens Kurtin, attorney at Kurtin PLLC (Kurtin, 2016b). Kurtin reiterates the warnings on the website by OCR regarding the sample business associate agreement by indicating the "HIPAA Omnibus Rule Sample Terms" (as he refers to them) addresses only the requirements set forth in the regulations (Kurtin, 2016b). "They do not include many formalities and substantive provisions that may be required or typically included in a valid contract. Reliance on this sample may not be sufficient for compliance with State law, and does not replace consultation with a lawyer or negotiations between the parties to the contract" (U.S. Department of Health & Human Services, 2016).

In another very recent case, North Memorial Health Care of Minnesota agreed to a $1,550,000 settlement with OCR over alleged violations of the HIPAA Security Rules. As per a press release from HHS OCR, Director Jocelyn Samuels stated, "Two major cornerstones of the HIPAA Rules were overlooked by this entity [North Memorial

Health Care]: Organizations must have in place compliant business associate agreements as well as an accurate and thorough risk analysis that addresses their enterprise-wide IT infrastructure" (OCR, 2016d). The incident that started the investigation was a report of a breach back in September 2011 where 9497 individuals were affected by the theft of an unencrypted laptop by a business associate's employee. Upon investigation, it was determined that North Memorial Health Care did not have a business associate agreement in place with Accretive Health, Inc. that performed payment (and other healthcare operational activities) for North Memorial. Furthermore, North Memorial did not perform an organization-wide risk analysis over all of the ePHI it maintains, accesses, or transmits to include "all applications, software, databases, servers, workstations, mobile devices and electronic media, network administration and security devices, and associated business processes" (OCR, 2016d).

ONC

The Office of the National Coordinator for Health Information Technology (ONC) was created by Executive Order in 2004, but was then mandated by legislation in 2009 under the Health Information Technology for Economic and Clinical Health Act. ONC is organized under the Office of the Secretary of HHS and leads the charge in health IT efforts along with promoting the nationwide health information exchange.

Figure 6.4 shows the organizational structure of the ONC.

The National Coordinator is charged with the following responsibilities as it relates to the mission and functions of the ONC paraphrased here:

- Ensure key health information technology initiatives are coordinated across HHS.
- To avoid duplications and assist agencies to concentrate their efforts in areas of their expertise/technical capabilities, ensure policies/programs of HHS related to health information technology are coordinated with other relevant executive branch agencies (including federal commissions and advisory committees).

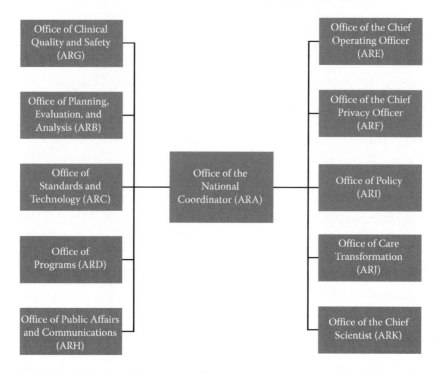

Figure 6.4 ONC organizational structure. (From Health and Human Services, Statement of organization, functions, and delegations of authority, Office of the National Coordinator for Health Information Technology, Retrieved from *Federal Register*, https://www.federalregister. gov/articles/2014/06/03/2014-12981/statement-of-organization-functions-and-delegations-of-authority-office-of-the-national-coordinator, March 19, 2016b.)

- Review health IT investments and ensure programs are meeting objectives under *Executive Order 13335* in creating a nationwide interoperable health IT infrastructure.
- Provide advice regarding specific federal health IT programs per the request of the Office of Management and Budget (OMB).
- Within HHS and other executive branch agencies—develop, maintain, and report on measurable outcomes for health IT to assess progress; for the private sector—develop and implement a nationwide interoperable health infrastructure (HIE coordination).
- ONC federal health architecture oversight.
- Fulfill administrative, reporting, program management, legislative affairs, infrastructure, and budget support needs of the office.

ENFORCEMENT   177

   As can be seen by the number of offices and breadth of the ONC's
responsibilities, ONC maintains a larger budget than the OCR. Due
to its complexity and role in establishing an infrastructure for health
information exchange, ONC has proposed to increase its funding by
thirty-six percent (36%) from $60 to $82 million for fiscal year 2017.
Although ONC doesn't necessarily perform enforcement activities, it
does play a major role in health IT. As per budget notes, the requested
funds "provides continued investments to achieve secure, seamless
data interoperability in order to better serve caregivers, providers, payers, public health officials, scientists, and ultimately enhance health
for all Americans" (McGee, 2016d). When it comes to privacy and
security, the requested funds will provide for "a coordinated approach
to explicitly prohibit [inappropriate] information blocking and investigate and impose appropriate sanctions for offenders" (McGee,
2016d). The budget increase indicates that the ONC is seeking new
authorities and to ensure health record vendors don't prevent the
secure exchange of health information. ONC has been working with
the Federal Trade Commission (FTC) on best practices for health IT
and application developers.

Office of Inspector General (OIG)

With a staff of approximately sixteen hundred (1600), the HHS OIG
is the largest inspector general's office within the U.S. government
dedicated to investigating fraud, waste, and abuse primarily within
the Medicare/Medicaid programs along with improving efficiency
of more than one hundred (100) other HHS programs. The OIG's
mission is to protect the integrity of HHS's programs as well as the
health and welfare of program beneficiaries. The OIG has broad
authority to seek civil monetary penalties for a wide variety of prohibited activity. Table 6.5 provides an example of some of the recent
enforcement actions taken by the OIG.

   As an important note, the OIG maintains an exclusion database
located here: https://exclusions.oig.hhs.gov. It is important that a
healthcare provider that participates in federal healthcare programs
check this exclusion list for individuals or companies that are on
this list. The provider should not be utilizing or employing any of
these individuals or companies or they may be subject to penalties

Table 6.5 OIG Enforcement Actions

DATE	ENTITY	VIOLATION	ENFORCEMENT ACTIONS
2/5/2016	Illinois Pharmacist and owner of durable medical equipment supply company	Individual offered, paid kickbacks, and bribed hospitals/nursing homes to order items from his company where payments were made under Medicare.	Three (3) years exclusion from participating in federal healthcare programs
1/27/2016	Lifeline Ambulance Service, LLC	Billed transportation to skilled nursing facilities and patient residence under emergency rates as opposed to the lower nonemergency rates.	$74,414.66 settlement agreement
1/7/2016	CardioSpecialists Group, Ltd.	Employed an excluded medical biller to provide services that were billed to federal healthcare programs.	$274,721.40 settlement agreement
12/23/2015	City of Barre, Vermont	Billed basic/advanced life support (emergency) ambulance transportation claims that did not meet Medicare requirements for emergency transportation and should have been billed at lower nonemergency rates.	$127,669.90 settlement agreement
12/21/2015	South Central Regional Medical Center	Billed transportation to skilled nursing facilities and patient residence under emergency rates as opposed to the lower nonemergency rates.	$318,885.62 settlement agreement
12/21/2015	Pennsylvania chiropractor	Submitted false/fraudulent claims to Medicare even after being excluded from participating in a federal healthcare program.	Twenty-five (25) years exclusion from participating in federal healthcare programs

Sources: Office of Inspector General, Civil monetary penalties and affirmative exclusions, Retrieved from Office of Inspector General—U.S. Department of Health & Human Services, http://oig.hhs.gov/fraud/enforcement/cmp/index.asp, February 28, 2016a; Office of Inspector General, *Work Plan Fiscal Year 2016*, U.S. Department of Health and Human Services, Washington, DC, 2016b.

as seen from these enforcement activities. For fiscal year 2015 alone, OIG reported expected recoveries of more than $3 billion along with 4112 individuals/entities being added to the exclusion list. In addition, there were 925 criminal actions taken and 682 civil actions that included false claims and unjust-enrichments (Office of Inspector General, 2016a).

The OIG develops *Work Plans* that address certain areas that they will be concentrating on during the upcoming fiscal year. In their *Work Plans for Fiscal Year 2016*, as it relates to the topic of privacy and security, OIG will perform reviews of State-based marketplaces to assess whether information security controls have been properly implemented in accordance with federal requirements and industry best practices. In addition, they will be conducting vulnerability scans of web-based systems with automated tools and review previous assessments to determine if vulnerabilities identified were remediated in a timely manner. OIG will monitor cybersecurity threats through coordination with other law enforcement partners and continue to promote awareness with consumers about fraud, identity theft, and other activity related to protecting consumers' personal information (Office of Inspector General, 2016a).

OIG plans to review various operating divisions within HHS to determine their compliance with the Federal Information Security Modernization Act of 2014 (FISMA). FISMA requires governmental agencies with systems and applications that collect, process, transmit, store, or disseminate information maintain adequate security programs. Due to an increase in computer hacking activities especially on government systems, OIG will be conducting network and Web application penetration testing.

OCR, as previously mentioned, is responsible for security oversight of electronic protected health information (ePHI) maintained by covered entities and business associates. According to prior audits performed by OIG, "OCR had not assessed the risks, established priorities, or implemented controls for its HITECH Act requirement to provide for periodic audits of covered entities and business associates" (Office of Inspector General, 2016a). OIG reported that OCR "had limited assurance" that ePHI is being protected due to the lack of compliance covered entities and business associates had with the HITECH Act and HIPAA Rule requirements (Office of Inspector

General, 2016a). "Prior OIG audits have also summarized numerous vulnerabilities in the systems and controls to protect ePHI at selected covered entities" (Office of Inspector General, 2016a).

The HIPAA Security Rule requires a contingency plan be established to respond to emergencies or other situations that could cause damage to systems that contain protected health information. Therefore, OIG will review hospital's contingency plans to determine if they meet requirements of HIPAA and compare them with recommended practices from the government and other industries.

Under federal law, Medicare Administrative Contractors (MACs) must have an independent evaluation of their security programs. OIG is required to assess these evaluations and make an annual report to Congress on the results of these independent evaluations.

As a new review for 2016, OIG will be examining the Food and Drug Administration's (FDA) oversight of medical devices that are integrated into a hospital's network and a hospital's electronic medical records (EMRs). As a note of reference, Manufacturer Disclosure Statement for Medical Device Security (MDS2) forms are supposed to be provided by the device manufacturer to assist providers in determining their risks associated with information being transmitted or maintained by a device. OIG will determine if the FDA's oversight is effective to protect information and ensure safety due to the growing threat that medical devices pose to security and privacy of protected health information. These threats are not only growing from medical devices, and as indicated in the *Work Plan for Fiscal Year 2016*, "OIG expects to broaden its portfolio regarding information privacy and security, including issues that arise from the continuing expansion of the Internet of Things" (Office of Inspector General, 2016a).

Finally, as it relates to incentive payments provided under the Meaningful Use program for the use of electronic medical records, OIG will perform audits on various covered entities that have received payments from the Center of Medicare & Medicaid Services (CMS) to ensure that they are adequately protecting electronic health information created or maintained by certified electronic health records solutions. This is one of the core objectives of meaningful use to ensure protection of this information by implementing appropriate technical controls. To meet this objective, eligible providers and hospitals must conduct a security risk analysis of the solutions along with ensuring the security capabilities of the certified electronic health record (EHR) technology solution are being utilized.

State Attorney General

To increase enforcement and to give the HIPAA Privacy and Security Rules more "teeth," the State Attorney General from each state has the authority to bring actions on behalf of their state's residents. This came about through the passage of the (HITECH) Act, under section 13410(e), which was part of the American Recovery and Reinvestment Act (ARRA) of 2009. Unfortunately, there appears to be a limited number of actual civil actions taken by State Attorney Generals under this new authority.

The first reported action taken by the Attorney General of Connecticut was back in January 2010. This occurred after a health insurer lost a disk drive containing unsecured protected health information for almost 500,000 Connecticut residents. The lawsuit was settled in July 2010 requiring the insurer to pay statutory damages of $250,000 along with a contingent payment if the drive was later compromised and information was used in the amount of $500,000. There was also a Corrective Action Plan requiring the insurer to provide identity theft protection, enhance controls, manage oversight, train employees, and improve monitoring/reporting (Metzger, 2016).

The second reported action came from Vermont. The Vermont Attorney General brought action against a health insurer that lost an unencrypted hard drive containing information on five hundred twenty-five (525) residents of Vermont. On top of this, the insurer took six (6) months to notify affected individuals. The settlement required the insurer to pay $55,000 to the state of Vermont and submit to audits of their data security. They also had to report on their information security program for two (2) years to the State.

Although the State Attorney General has the power under federal regulations, it appears as the states individually pass more stringent regulations at the state level compared to federal regulations, the State Attorney Generals will take enforcement actions under their own state laws as opposed to the federal HIPAA regulations.

This could get very complicated for organizations that work or maintain information of residents in multiple states. These organizations will need to ensure that they are abiding by each of the states' own privacy and security laws or they may be subject to enforcement actions by these states.

FTC

FTC is a U.S. federal, independent law enforcement agency with the primary responsibility of protecting consumers. Under Section 5 of the Federal Trade Commission Act set back in 1914, the FTC has authority to prohibit unfair or deceptive trade practices. The FTC also has specific enforcement authority under a variety of laws such as

- The Truth in Lending Act
- The CAN-SPAM Act
- The Children's Online Privacy Protection Act
- The Equal Credit Opportunity Act
- The Fair Credit Reporting Act
- The Fair Debt Collection Practices Act
- The Telemarketing and Consumer Fraud and Abuse Prevention Act

As you can see, the FTC has broad authority over a variety of areas to protect consumers. For our course of discussion, we are going to limit the scope of FTC enforcement to the areas of privacy and data security.

Under FTC's goal to protect consumers' personal information, the FTC has brought numerous enforcement actions against businesses to stop violations and to take remediation steps toward unlawful behavior. Some of these steps include companies developing comprehensive privacy and security programs, perform independent assessments, enforcing the deletion of information obtained illegally, providing privacy notices, enhancing choices consumers have over the use of their information, and financial redress to consumers for violations. The FTC can obtain civil monetary penalties from companies that violate certain privacy regulations.

Although laws are sparse when it comes to the area of cybersecurity, the FTC has been successful in filling this void. In June 2012, the FTC sued Wyndham Worldwide Corporation that include brands such as the Days Inn, Howard Johnson, Ramada, Super 8 and Travelodge, claiming their computer systems "unreasonably and unnecessarily" exposed their customers' data. The suit followed after three (3) breaches occurred in 2008 and 2009 when hackers compromised the systems stealing credit card and other personal data from 619,000 customers that lead to over $10.6 million in fraudulent charges (Stempel, 2016). In August 2015, the third U.S. Circuit Court of Appeals in Philadelphia upheld a lower court's ruling in a 3-0 decision that the case could proceed and that the FTC has grounds for enforcement over companies that fail to secure personal information.

The FTC has indicated that it has handled over one hundred thirty (130) spam/spyware type cases along with more than fifty (50) general privacy lawsuits. The FTC provided an indication of examples of privacy cases it handled in 2015 as shown in Table 6.6.

The FTC has indicated that it has brought almost sixty (60) cases since 2002 involving unfair or deceptive practices against companies that put consumers' data at risk. The FTC provided an indication of examples of data security cases it handled in 2015 (Table 6.7).

Due to the recent rash of breaches involving credit card information, the FTC is assessing the Payment Card Industry Data Security Standards (PCI DSS) audit program. Businesses that process more than one (1) million card transactions per year are required by the major payment card issuing companies to perform a PCI DSS audit. These audits are performed by approved assessor firms. The FTC has issued orders to require nine (9) of these firms to supply information on how they perform these assessments. Information requested includes how assessors and clients interact, examples of assessments, and information on additional services these assessing firms offer. The following companies are being ordered to provide this type of information to the FTC: Foresite MSP, LLC; Freed Maxick CPAs, P.C.; GuidePoint Security, LLC; Mandiant; NDB LLP; PricewaterhouseCoopers LLP; SecurityMetrics; Sword and Shield Enterprise Security, Inc.; and Verizon Enterprise Solutions (also known as CyberTrust) (PPAI Publications, 2016).

When it comes to healthcare, the FTC enforces its own rules for data breaches for nonprovider health industry entities involving

Table 6.6   FTC General Privacy Cases for 2015

DEFENDANT/COMPANY	VIOLATION	ENFORCEMENT ACTIVITY
Craig Brittain, "revenge porn" website operator	Deceptive practices to obtain intimate images of women; told victims they could remove pictures for a price	Settlement agreement banning him from sharing images without consent; destroy all images and information collected
Operators of Jerk.com, "antisocial network"	Misled consumers by claiming content posted on site by other users (most of content came from Facebook profiles); also misrepresented paid membership benefits allowing users to update information (users unable to correct information and received nothing of value)	Granted summary judgment
Nomi Technologies, retail tracking of consumers movements through store	Consumers misled about opt-out mechanisms and notification when they were being tracked	Settlement agreement prohibiting misrepresentation of options and notification practices
TRUSTe, Inc., privacy certification provider	Company failed to conduct recertifications of companies holding TRUSTe seals in over 1,000 incidences, despite indicating they receive annual recerts	Settlement to prohibit misrepresentation of certification process and must restrict the means of other companies to represent themselves of the certification; under Children's Online Privacy Protection Act of 1998 (COPPA)—must make annual filings, maintain comprehensive records for 10 years, and pay $200,000 settlement
PyamentsMD, LLC, health billing company and former CEO Michael C. Hughes	Misled thousands of consumers that signed up for online bill portal—didn't inform that they sought detailed medical information from other health organizations (pharmacies, labs, insurance)	Settlement must destroy information collected; banned from misleading consumers about information collected; must obtain express consent from consumers
Sequoia One, data broker	Bought payday loan applications, sold them to scam operators that charged financial accounts without consent (affected more than 500,00 consumers and at least $7.1 million)	A few of the defendants are under settlement agreements; one has a $7.1 million judgment that will be suspended when $15,000 is paid; other has $3.7 million—suspended to inability to pay; if defendants found to misrepresent financial condition—full judgment due; litigation still pending on others

(Continued)

Table 6.6 (*Continued*)   FTC General Privacy Cases for 2015

DEFENDANT/COMPANY	VIOLATION	ENFORCEMENT ACTIVITY
Bayview Solutions and Cornerstone and Company, data brokers	Exposed sensitive information about consumers that allegedly owned debts (about tens of thousands affected when consumer debt portfolios were sold on public website)	Agreement requires them to abide by strict protection requirements; take down website; inform consumers affected and steps to take to protect themselves; must have security program evaluated every 2 years by certified third party
CWB Services, LLC, operators of payday lending scheme	Used personal financial information bought from data brokers; made unauthorized deposits into consumer accounts; withdrew biweekly payments for "finance charges" without loan principal reducing; call to advise consumer of obligation even though consumers never asked for loan and misrepresented true costs of loan	Banned from consumer lending business
Pairsys, Inc., tech support scam	Tricked customers into providing financial information to pay hundreds of dollars for tech support they didn't need and for other freely available software	Required to surrender multiple real estate properties, bank accounts, and leases on 2 luxury cars
Click4Support, LLC, tech support scam	Obtained more than $17 million pretending to represent major tech companies; using advertisements to trick consumers into calling than misleading them into thinking computers were infected with malware; provided sales pitch to obtain hundreds/thousands of dollars in unnecessary tech repair services	Obtained preliminary injunction
Prized mobile app	Consumers misled into thinking they can earn points for playing games or downloading affiliated apps; points could be used for other items; promised downloads were free of malware, unfortunately not the case—apps were mining virtual currency for defendant	Banned from creating/distributing malicious software; must destroy all information collected; also $50,000 judgment suspended upon payment of $5,200

Source: Federal Trade Commission, Privacy & data security update (2015). Retrieved from Federal Trace Commission, https://www.ftc.gov/reports/privacy-data-security-update-2015, March 5, 2016.

Table 6.7 FTC Data Security Cases for 2015

DEFENDANT/ COMPANY	VIOLATION	ENFORCEMENT ACTIVITY
Oracle	Alleged Oracle promised consumers that installing new version of updates to its Java platform that it would protect system from known vulnerabilities within the platform; however, updates only affected the recent prior version and earlier versions may still have been installed	Required to notify consumers of older version installed, provide consumers the ability to uninstall insecure versions; and provide broad notice of settlement along with instructions to remove older versions
Wyndham Hotels and Resorts	Security practices exposed payment card information; comes after 3 separate data breaches	As described, Third Circuit affirmed FTC's authority; must establish comprehensive information security program; required to conduct annual audit and maintain safeguards
Lifelock	Continued to make deceptive claims about identity theft protection; failed to protect users' data	Agreed to pay $100 million to settle contempt charges for violating a 2010 settlement requiring maintaining a comprehensive information security program; falsely advertising sensitive data protected at same level of financial institutions; failing to meet recordkeeping requirements
Morgan Stanley	Alleged failure to secure information in a reasonable and appropriate manner	Letter sent in reference to closing investigation; FTC staff indicated Morgan Stanley implemented comprehensive policies to protect against insider theft

Source: Federal Trade Commission, Privacy & data security update (2015), Retrieved from Federal Trace Commission, https://www.ftc.gov/reports/privacy-data-security-update-2015, March 5, 2016.

vendors of personal health records (PHR). Some of these rules include the following:

- Breaches involving less than five hundred (500) records— Entity is required to notify the FTC within sixty (60) calendar days following the applicable calendar year.
- Breaches involving more than five hundred (500) records— Entity is required to notify individuals within ten (10) days of discovery.

- Breach affects at least five hundred (500) residents of a given state—Entity is required to notify the media within sixty (60) days of discovery.

Further information on complying with the FTC's Health Breach Notification Rule can be found on their website: https://www.ftc.gov/tips-advice/business-center/guidance/complying-ftcs-health-breach-notification-rule.

Beyond enforcement activities, FTC provides several outreach and educational programs such as introducing *IdentityTheft.gov* website to provide resources to help victims of identity theft. FTC also launched its *Start with Security* campaign to provide more information to business to assist them in protecting the information they maintain on consumers. The FTC provides guidance, conferences, videos, and websites to assist both consumers and business with data security and privacy.

In an ironic turn of events, however, the FTC hosting a day-long privacy conference accidently sent an e-mail to more than six hundred (600) attendees that included the e-mail information of these individuals within the "cc" function of the e-mail (as opposed to the "bcc" function). This made the list of all attendees available to everyone else on the list. FTC responded with a follow-up email apologizing for the oversight and explaining, "We are assessing how this happened and will work to ensure that this does not occur in the future" (Hautala, 2016). This just goes to show that even the regulators that are supposed to enforce privacy can also have lapses from time to time.

In a paper written by Hartzog, Woodrow and Solove, Daniel J., *The Scope and Potential of FTC Data Protection* (November 1, 2015). 83 George Washington Law Review 2230 (2015); GWU Law School Public Law Research Paper No. 2014-40; GWU Legal Studies Research Paper No. 2014-40. Available at SSRN: http://ssrn.com/abstract=2461096, Hartzog and Solove provide some recommendations on what the FTC could do to improve their enforcement efforts. One of these suggestions is the FTC could be more transparent about their investigations. Companies can learn a tremendous amount about what is expected of them under fair trade practices when results of investigations related to privacy complaints are publicly available.

The FTC may send closing letters to a company that was investigated. These closing letters oftentimes will provide significant insight into how the investigations were handled, what factors the FTC may have looked at in making a decision to enforce or not enforce their regulatory authority, and may also contain suggestions or recommendations for continued improvements.

Hartzog and Solove further suggest that the FTC should be more flexible when to enforcement actions. Hartzog and Solove contend, "In its consent decrees, the FTC has not done enough to adjust the audit period or other measures to reward good practices when there is good mixed with bad" (Hartzog, 2015). In addition, it is recommended that FTC should lead first through training when new technologies are introduced or risks are identified. After providing a training period with guidance for companies to follow, the FTC could then switch to stricter enforcement.

Finally, Hartzog and Solove state "privacy and data security are complex issues that depend heavily on context" (Hartzog, 2015). Although the FTC could develop specific rules for certain actions, they need to be somewhat flexible. Hartzog and Solove recommend that a "case-by-case approach should remain a key feature of the system" (Hartzog, 2015). The FTC has a wide enforcement area over data protection and with their broad authority, Hartzog and Solove argue that the FTC "is in the ideal position to take center stage and take U.S. data protection law to a new level" (Hartzog, 2015).

Solove had the opportunity to interview Chris Hoofnagle, a professor of Berkeley Law School, about Hoofnagle's new book titled *Federal Trade Commission Privacy Law and Policy* (Cambridge University Press, February, 2016). Solove recommends "that all privacy and cybersecurity lawyers should have [this book] on their shelves" (Solove, 2016a). Providing a response to the question of the five (5) most important things that privacy/security professionals may not know about the FTC, but should know, Hoofnagle indicated the following, paraphrased here:

1. FTC's staff attorneys have autonomy to make a lot of decisions about investigating certain cases or not. The Commission has veto powers; however, a single commissioner doesn't have the authority to decide a case and once a case reaches the

Commission level, it may be too late to do much about it. Staff at the FTC may be long-term employees while commissioners have a limited time of service.

2. FTC has internal politics with each division having different criteria for taking up cases. The FTC is looking for major policy-setting cases, so if a company understands the issues and is willing to do right by their customers, the FTC may move on to other cases as opposed to making the company an example.

3. The FTC has been around for a long time and even the richest companies have lost to the FTC. It may be better to concede than to go to war with the FTC.

4. As it relates to privacy, the FTC leverages other cases and activities from different divisions such as advertising. As previously mentioned, the FTC has broad authority.

5. In most cases, the FTC doesn't even utilize its full powers in investigating unfair trade practices. It can perform inspections in-person or even leverage a company's purchase of "keywords" in their advertising to demonstrate deceptive practices. In other words, if an investigation occurs, the FTC could find other multiple issues; therefore, most companies settle up front (Solove, 2016a).

When asked about the FTC's biggest failure, Hoofnagle points out the issues with enforcing privacy around data brokers. Hoofnagle suggests the FTC "struggles to articulate how data brokers' systemic undermining of privacy rights creates marketplace harms" (Solove, 2016a). Hoofnagle indicates that he provides recommendations in his book to overcome these obstacles by "drawing upon how the FTC overcame similar challenges in false advertising cases" (Solove, 2016a).

CMS

On February 17, 2009, ARRA was signed into law by President Barack Obama. A key part of that act was the HITECH Act that allocated billions in incentives to motivate healthcare providers away from paper-based records and into electronic healthcare record systems.

The Center for Medicare and Medicaid Services (CMS) manages the EHR Incentive Programs. In general, it was thought that EMRs would improve the delivery of healthcare, drive better clinical outcomes, improve care coordination, engage patients and families, and do so while improving the level of privacy and security of data.

Beginning in 2011, incentive funds were available to eligible professionals, eligible hospitals, and critical access hospitals to encourage the adoption, implementation, upgrade, and demonstration of "meaningful use" of certified EHR technologies. Although it was presented as an "incentive," conversely, beginning in 2015, eligible professionals and hospitals who did not keep pace through the various stages of compliance would find themselves penalized by reduction in reimbursements with the amount of penalization starting at one percent (1%) and increasing each year of noncompliance to a maximum of five percent (5%) of Medicare Part B reimbursements. Incentive payments are paid over three (3) stages. Each stage has increased criteria or metrics that these organizations must meet in order to receive payments as it relates to the meaningful use of the technology.

Since the payments provided for this incentive program are federal funds, that come with stipulations. Depending on the stage in which the organization is attesting to the meaningful use will determine the specific criteria that must be met. CMS also has the authority to audit organizations to ensure that these requirements are being met. CMS has the authority to take back money paid and since individuals of an organization "self-attest" to the facts that they meet certain standards under penalty of law, these individuals could face criminal charges if they were found to have misrepresented the information provided to CMS.

Currently, there is a great deal of discussion as to whether this incentive program is working as intended and achieving its goals of better care. From an IT perspective, however, the effort to move hospitals and physician practices out of the "dark ages" of paper records and into the world of the EMRs has certainly been brisk and, at least to some degree, successful. Some were incentivized by additional dollars while others capitulated in the face of looming penalties, but whatever the motivation, many physicians and hospitals have made the move.

At a J.P. Morgan Healthcare Conference held in San Francisco on January 12, 2016, acting CMS administrator, Andy Slavitt, announced "The Meaningful Use program as it has existed, will now be effectively over and replaced with something better" (Powderly, 2016). This new path follows the Medicare Access and CHIP Reauthorization Act of 2015 (MACRA) that was signed into law that changes existing Medicare fee-for-service to a Merit-Based Incentive Payment System. As Slavitt indicates, "focus will move away from rewarding providers for the use of technology and towards the outcome they achieve with their patients" (Powderly, 2016).

Slavitt also indicated that there will be more ways providers and technology companies can work together to improve solutions for their specific practices along with making it easier for start-ups to enter the market space. This will be achieved by requiring open application program interfaces (APIs) to allow for additional application development, analytics, and connectivity. Finally, Slavitt "laid down the law" by reiterating CMS's priority over interoperability, "technology companies that look for ways to practice 'data blocking' in opposition to new regulations will find that it won't be tolerated" (Powderly, 2016).

The federal government has provided almost $32 billion in incentive payments to date. Slavitt's comments raise a lot of uncertainty around the program and the future state of EHR technology. I've been a big proponent of ensuring that this technology is validated or certified to ensure that it meets security standards. It is my belief that any system that comes in contact with (ePHI) is scrutinized and vetted with required security safeguards in place.

As Margalit Gur-Arie posted in a blog, *Meaningful Use Is Dead. Long Live Something Better!* "Meaningful Use… is the enabler of data collection which fuels all other investment opportunities" (Gur-Arie, 2016). Gur-Arie goes on to point out Slavitt's use of the words "moving to a new regime" in his speech and states, "of course all sorts of new technologies to better transfer all medical data into places where J.P. Morgan clientele can monetize them" (Gur-Arie, 2016). Gur-Arie brings attention to the American Medical Association (AMA) announcing their investment of $15 million to become a founding partner in Health2047, Inc. on the same day as Slavitt's speech at the J.P. Morgan conference (American Medical Association, 2016). *Coincidence?*

Per Health2047's website, they are "an integrated innovation company whose mission is to develop, guide, and commercialize disruptive ideas that enhance—at the system level—the practice of health care" (Health2047, 2016). Although the post may be a little "conspiracy theory" in nature, Gur-Arie suggests that providers may now be forced to buy new applications even after billions of dollars have been spent on EHR technology opening the door to the $3 trillion healthcare market by new companies. *Why?* Gur-Arie answers—"planned obsolescence"—"Because the next app is sure to fix health care in America…There is always 'something better' you can buy" (Gur-Arie, 2016).

FCC

The Federal Communications Commission (FCC) is charged with the enforcement of the Communications Act of 1934. As such, cable operators, satellite carriers, telecommunication carriers, and providers of Voice over Internet Protocol (VoIP) services are required to protect their subscribers' privacy. In addition, the FCC is empowered to create other consumer protection requirements over broadband, broadcasting, cable, satellite, wireless, and wired telecommunication services, in essence, the backbone of the Internet.

The FCC and the FTC has entered into a Memorandum of Understanding (MOU) related to consumer protection. In this MOU, the FTC and FCC agreed to "continue to work together to protect consumers from acts and practices that are deceptive, unfair, unjust and/or unreasonable" (FCC and FTC, 2016). Furthermore, "the agencies will engage in joint enforcement actions, when appropriate and consistent with their respective jurisdiction" (FCC and FTC, 2016). The FCC and FTC will share data on complaints through the FTC's Consumer Sentinel Network and meetings will be held between senior officials of the two agencies to effectively exchange information.

As a result of reclassifying broadband services as a Title II common carrier (i.e., telecommunication) service, FCC is in a position to enforce privacy over providers of broadband Internet access services to include wired or mobile telephone, cable, and satellite providers. In basic terms, the "gatekeepers of the Internet" have not had clear direction when it comes to protecting their consumers' privacy in the past.

In a letter to the FCC chairman, Tom Wheeler, about fifty (50) digital rights and consumer protection groups are asking for the FCC to institute rules regarding the protection of consumers' personal data that may be collected or shared by these providers. These groups are requesting that rules be developed to prohibit the sharing of personal data without affirmative consent or for purposes other than providing respective Internet services. They are requesting requirements for notices for a breach, enforcing accountability of providers who fail to protect the data they collect on consumers, and require the disclosure of the service's data collection practices to the consumers (Data Protection—Consumer Groups, 2016).

FCC Chairman Wheeler has issued a Notice of Proposed Rulemaking (NPRM) that will be voted on by the Commission and then, if adopted, would be put out for public comment. In his NPRM, Wheeler proposes that privacy for consumers utilizing broadband services relies on three (3) core principles: choice, transparency, and security. Wheeler asserts that Internet service providers (ISPs) have the ability to view users' activities and even if their network traffic is encrypted, they know what sites they visit along with how long they stay on these sites. By piecing this data together, ISPs can gleam a lot of personal information about their customers.

The proposal stipulates that consumers should be able to maintain privacy over their data. Therefore, service providers can only use customer data to market their own or affiliates communications-related services unless the customer affirmatively opts out. All other uses or sharing of data requires express consent or affirmative opt in. ISPs have a duty to secure customer data. The proposal would require ISPs to take reasonable safeguards and adopt risk management practices to include training, authentication, senior management data security responsibilities, and responsibility over sharing information with third parties. Finally, the proposal calls for breach notification in the event of customer data compromise to include notifying customers within ten (10) days of discovery, notifying the Commission within seven (7) days of discovery, and notifying the FBI and U.S. Secret Services within seven (7) days of discovery if a breach affects more than 5000 customers (Wheeler, 2016).

Although stronger privacy protection may be a good thing, some people, however, believe the FCC may be overstepping their legal authority and may be misinterpreting a certain rule under Title II that prohibited phone companies steeling customers' data from each other. As Mike O'Reilly, an FCC commissioner, objects, "The 'fact' sheet [NPRM] demonstrates that the FCC is doubling down on its misguided and broken Net Neutrality decision by imposing troubling and conflicting 'privacy' rules on Internet companies, as well as freelancing on topics like data security and data breach that are not even mentioned in the statute" (O'Reilly, 2016).

The U.S. Court of Appeals in Washington is already taking up challenges to the changes in the rules that brought broadband service providers under the FCC authority. Some of the major challengers included U.S. Telecom and the Cellular Telecommunications and Internet Association (CTIA). When it comes to wireless Internet access, some strongly believe that the FCC will lose, but for wired connections, it is undecided. Berin Szoka, TechFreedom's president, believes the FCC will lose when it comes to wireless Internet access, but "if the FCC prevails on the Open Internet case regarding the reclassification of broadband, then the FCC can do anything it wants about broadband and consumer protection (Rash, 2016b). Szoka goes on to say, "what begins today as regulation of broadband providers will eventually grow to include other Internet companies, too" (Rash, 2016b).

Since legislation lags behind technology and the need to protect privacy has come into question, federal agencies are left to propose changes that ultimately get decided within the court systems. These agencies may have good intentions, but may lack the authority to make changes leaving decisions in the hands of the judges. For consumers, this means that privacy enforcement activities may not come anytime soon.

Class Action Lawsuits

Organizations that have been involved in a data breach now must worry about the class action lawsuit. Class action lawsuits have been around for some time; however, it is becoming a tool used by some attorneys to ensure companies are taking security seriously. Since most, if not all, data breach-related lawsuits have ended up in settlements, one could see why attorneys might find this avenue to pursue a fairly easy way to generate revenue. Unfortunately, where intents of regulations and reasonable levels of security may be defined by precedents set through litigation, these cases have not been put through the test of trial.

Some examples of data breach settlements are shown in Table 6.8.

Home Depot was involved in a data breach of credit card information of fifty-six (56) million customers. This incident has been dubbed one of the largest data breaches ever recorded. As a result of a class action lawsuit, Home Depot has decided to settle and pay up to $19.5 million; $13 million will be set aside in a fund to reimburse customers for any damages and the remaining amount goes toward legal expenses. Home Depot further indicated that it will improve its data security (Musil, 2016).

Up until now, the courts have blocked several attempts to carry class action cases through to trial due to the grounds that victims may not have definitive proof of damages. This precedent of showing "actual" damages is slowing changing with the courts. The retailer Neiman Marcus fell victim to a cyberattack that claimed the theft

Table 6.8 Examples of Data Breach Settlements

COMPANY	BREACH	SETTLEMENT
LinkedIn	6 million users; usernames and passwords compromised	$1.25 million (only applied to 800,000 premium users)
AvMed	More than 1 million; Social Security numbers and health records	$3.1 million
Target	Over 100 million; credit card numbers, names, addresses, e-mails, phone numbers	$10 million; MasterCard $39 million; Visa $67 million
Stanford University Hospital and Clinics	20,000 patient health records	$4.1 million
Sony PlayStation Network	77 million; names, addresses, credentials, and encrypted credit card numbers	$15 million
Sony Pictures Entertainment	Sensitive employee information	$8 million
Vendini Inc.	Undisclosed number of records; credit cards, e-mails; phone numbers and personally identifiable information	$3 million
Schnuck Markets, Inc.	2.4 million; credit card information	$2.1 million

Source: Eckerson, O.L., Data breach lawsuits indicate a trouble trend for enterprises, Retrieved from Tech Target, http://searchsecurity.techtarget.com/news/4500273340/Data-breach-lawsuits-indicate-a-troubling-trend-for-enterprises, March 6, 2016.

of customers' personal financial information in 2013. A class action lawsuit was filed; however, a U.S. District Court judge threw the case out due to a lack of damages being proven by the plaintiffs. A panel of judges in the Seventh U.S. Circuit Court of Appeals overturned this decision allowing the case to move forward. The court ruled that it is an "objectively reasonable likelihood" that individuals are at risk of identity theft. Even though the plaintiffs would have been reimbursed for any unauthorized credit card charges, this did not protect individuals from other potential injuries (Eckerson, 2016).

This is similar to a recent court case *Walker et al v. Boston Medical Center Corp.*, No. 2015-1733-BLS 1 (Massachusetts Superior Court, November 19, 2015). In this case, a Massachusetts Superior Court judge held plaintiffs' standing that they face a "real and immediate risk" of injury when their medical records were made available to the public inadvertently through a third-party transcription service's online site. Even though the plaintiffs don't allege unauthorized access, the judge ruled that they could proceed with suing for money damage on the mere exposure of the information (Zeidel, 2016).

This case will be interesting to watch unfold since it takes a different interpretation of harm as opposed to previous federal cases such as the Supreme Court's decision in *Clapper v. Amnesty International USA*, 113 S. Ct. 1138 (2013). In this case, the mere fact that private information was exposed is not enough to sue for damages in federal courts. There has to be proven some additional harm or injury. The *Walker* case may also demonstrate that the state courts may not be hindered by some of the precedents set at the federal level and may take into consideration other factors when it comes to class action lawsuits related to data breaches. Fortunately, or unfortunately, the outcome of this case may have limited impact on other cases brought before the courts in other states.

In another court ruling, U.S. District Court Judge Lucy Koh ruled that consumers were harmed due to a breach of their information by the health insurer Anthem under New York's General Business Law. This decision establishes that in the early stages of a breach case, "allegations of a 'concrete and imminent threat of future harm' are enough to establish an injury and standing" (Roberts, 2016). Regardless if misuse of information can be proven, the theft of personal information is harm enough. *Will Anthem be*

one of the next big corporations to follow in settling their breach related
class action lawsuit or will they take their chances through the courts?
Only time will tell.

St. Joseph Health System, on the other hand, decided not to take
their chances in court. They settled their class action lawsuit paying
each of the class members $242, totaling $7.5 million. St. Joseph
Health System also set aside $3 million to pay up to $25,000 for
anyone that may have been victimized by identity theft as a result of
the breach. The lawsuit came about from a breach involving 31,802
patients between 2011 and 2012 where protected health information
such as names, medical data, diagnoses, and demographic information,
primarily from inpatient records, ended up online and was searchable
by Internet search engines (Heath, 2016a).

Examples of enforcement actions along with both pending and
settled class action lawsuits should act as alerts to all healthcare
organizations that they need to take security and privacy very seriously.
Negligence over the handling of personal information and failure to
comply with regulations will no longer be tolerated.

Violation of Privacy

A jury awarded Terry Gene Bollea, professionally known as Hulk
Hogan, $115 million for violation of privacy and other damages
against Gawker Media in the case of *Bollea v. Gawker*. This case
stemmed from Gawker posting a sex video of Bollea without his consent. Bollea spoke about the incident publicly on another entertain-
ment show; however, after repeated attempts and a court order to have
Gawker remove the video from their site, Gawker refused claiming
protection under the First Amendment.

This case is important when it comes to demonstrating liability
over privacy matters when someone releases private information of
another that could be reasonably considered offensive and not of
public concern. The First Amendment has been utilized to protect
against liability cases when private information has been released that
is important to the public; however, a sex video may not be considered as such. As Daniel Solove states in his article, *The Gawker-Hulk*
Hogan Case Shows Not All Truth Has the Same Value, published by *The*
New York Times, "The First Amendment doesn't protect free speech

because it is a source of profit. It protects it as essential to freedom and democracy" (Solove, 2016d).

Unfortunately, judges have thrown out privacy cases due to narrow definitions over privacy and a broad concept of public concerns. Attorneys have not taken on these types of privacy cases due to the low probability of recovery. Individuals may be victimized by another as opposed to a larger media group and if they were successful in court, the defendants may not have any source for recovery. Furthermore, going through a lawsuit may open up victims of privacy to further harm since U.S. courts don't provide a lot of privacy protection in these matters.

A lot of websites have been protected from liability over content or information supplied to them by third parties under the *Communications Decency Act* (47 U.S.C. § 230). This allows individuals to publish personal information of others that could be personally damaging to these victims. These victims could have little recourse and "these cases remain hard to litigate for most people, especially non-celebrities and those without great wealth or power" (Solove, 2016b).

7

PRIVACY...CLEAR...<SHOCK>

Privacy is a right not a preference.

—Privacy Platform of the Electronic Privacy Information Center
(Electronic Privacy Information Center, 2016)

Individual Rights

When it comes to healthcare, patients have a fundamental right to access and obtain a copy of their medical records. Any information contained in the medical record should be available to the patient. As per Dr. Peter Elias, "Nothing should go in the chart [medical record] that the patient does not know about" (Elias, 2016). Responding to critics that say medical records are filled with erroneous information and shouldn't be provided to patients, Dr. Elias further suggests in another post that, "We need to make it easy for the patient to access the record so we can do a better job of making it accurate and usable" (Peter Elias, 2016). Patients rely on this information for many reasons such as monitoring their condition, assist themselves in the healing process, or fix errors that may be in their records.

The Health Insurance Portability and Accountability Act of 1996 (HIPAA) directly addresses the rights of patients over their medical records providing for enforceable actions to ensure patients can access these records. Upon request, you, as a patient, have the right to inspect and/or obtain a copy of information in a designated record set for as long as the information is maintained by the entity. A designated record set is a group of records or any item, collection, or grouping of information including protected health information (PHI) that is maintained, collected, used, or disseminated by/for a covered entity. A designated record set may be medical records, billing records, case or medical management records (such as enrollment, payment, or claims records), or any other record that may be utilized in making a decision about the patient.

These rights are rather broad when it comes to the access of patient records, but there are a couple of exceptions. Patients don't have the right to see psychotherapy notes or the personal notes by a mental health professional documented to analyze a patient during a counseling session that are maintained outside of the patient's medical record. In addition, information around an anticipated civil, criminal, or administrative action is exempt from the right of access.

Request for access to a medical record may be required in writing provided they inform the patient of this and reasonable steps must be taken to verify the identity of the individual making the request. Providers may not put unreasonable barriers to the right of access such as requiring a patient to physically come to the office when the patient requested the information be mailed to them or force patients to use the provider's website to obtain a copy of the medical record if the patient doesn't have Internet access.

The HIPAA Privacy Rules also require a covered entity to make the information requested available in a format that the patient requested, if possible, or an agreed-upon format. For instance, if the individual requests a paper copy then the covered entity is expected to provide these records in paper form. If the patient requests the records in electronic form and the record is in paper form, the covered entity is expected to scan the paper into an electronic format if this is readily producible. If the patient requests the records in electronic form and the records are maintained electronically, the covered entity must provide the records in a format requested by the patient or an agreed-upon alternative format. It is only after a patient refuses to accept the records in this format would a paper copy of these records be acceptable to provide to the patient.

It should be noted that "mail and e-mail are generally considered readily producible by all covered entities" (Health and Human Services, 2016a). Although there may be some risk to sending unencrypted e-mail, if the patient accepts this risk, then a covered entity should e-mail the records to the patient per their request. It is expected that all covered entities can transmit protected health information by mail or e-mail. A covered entity may charge a reasonable, cost-based fee for copies of records. This fee may include labor for copying, supplies for creating the record, postage, or cost to prepare a summary if the patient agrees to this summary.

Individuals have a right to receive their requested information in a timely manner. Under the Privacy Rules, a covered entity has up to thirty (30) days from receipt of request to act on the request. If the individual is notified of a delay in writing within this time, the covered entity may have up to another thirty (30) days. This time span was shortened drastically for covered entities that are utilizing certified electronic medical record technology solutions that have received "meaningful use" funds to implement these solutions. Under Stage 2, eligible professionals must make information available within four (4) business days and for hospitals, within thirty-six (36) hours of discharge. Under Stage 3, information must be available within forty-eight (48) hours for professionals and within thirty-six (36) hours of its availability for hospitals.

There may be limited reasons for a denial and a patient could request a review of the denial. Furthermore, an individual doesn't need to provide a reason for a request and if voluntarily offered, the reason can't be used as a determination for a denial. Finally, the covered entity can't deny access just because another entity like a business associate maintains the record.

The Department of Health and Human Services (HHS) has released a new frequently asked question webpage that goes into more details on an individual's right to access: http://www.hhs.gov/hipaa/for-professionals/privacy/guidance/access/index.html.

The HIPAA requirements have become the "de-facto" standard of care within some states. Organizations such as healthcare providers that fail to comply with HIPAA could face claims of negligence even though HIPAA does not directly provide a right of action. The opinion from the Connecticut Supreme Court in *Byrne v. Avery Center for Obstetrics and Gynecology* indicated that "HIPAA does not preempt the plaintiff's state common-law causes of action for negligence... implementing HIPAA may inform the applicable standard of care in certain circumstances" (Connecticut Supreme Court, 2016). In this case, a patient sued a healthcare provider over a breach of contract and negligent disclosure when the healthcare provider allowed an ex-boyfriend to review the patient's medical records in response to a subpoena involving a paternity lawsuit. The provider's HIPAA

Notice of Privacy Practices stated that it would not disclose patient information without the patient's authorization and the patient further requested that information not be shared with the ex-boyfriend. The case hinged on the duty of care that HIPAA requires for the protection of information.

Privacy isn't all about keeping unauthorized individuals from viewing or accessing personal information, albeit this is a part; true privacy comes from giving individuals control over their own information. The Obama Administration put forth a Consumer Privacy Bill of Rights back in 2012. As Daniel J. Weitzner, former U.S. deputy chief technology officer for Internet Policy in the White House, explains, "The critical transition that was made was this focus on individual rights. That was a significant shift that we made very intentionally" (Singer, 2016).

Excerpted from The Consumer Privacy Bill of Rights, it provides for the following:

- *Individual control*: Consumers have a right to exercise control over what personal data companies collect from them and how they use it.
- *Transparency*: Consumers have a right to easily understandable and accessible information about privacy and security practices.
- *Respect for context*: Consumers have a right to expect that companies will collect, use, and disclose personal data in ways that are consistent with the context in which consumers provide the data.
- *Security*: Consumers have a right to secure and responsible handling of personal data.
- *Access and accuracy*: Consumers have a right to access and correct personal data in usable formats, in a manner that is appropriate to the sensitivity of the data and the risk of adverse consequences to consumers if the data is inaccurate.
- *Focused collection*: Consumers have a right to reasonable limits on the personal data that companies collect and retain.
- *Accountability*: Consumers have a right to have personal data handled by companies with appropriate measures in place to assure they adhere to the Consumer Privacy Bill of Rights (The White House, 2016).

Although these tenets are well intended, not much has happened since they were introduced and consumer privacy advocacy groups are fighting an uphill challenge to get them enforceable. Congress has not passed baseline consumer privacy legislation and leaving it up to the industry by consensus has failed. As David Vladeck, a professor of Georgetown University Law Center, puts it, "If you want to protect consumers, you don't simply allow industry to decide what to do in a way in which they don't have any incentive to compromise" (Singer, 2016).

At odds is the way private companies collect, share, and use consumer data versus how companies utilize this data to innovate new products or services. As an example, when people search for information online, it creates a "data footprint." Regulators are concerned that this information could be utilized to label a consumer, which could lead to possible unfair treatment. Private companies may see this information as a way to create new applications, products, or services and companies, like data brokers, based their entire business model on capturing and analyzing these data "bread crumbs."

The Administration issued a Discussion Draft titled *Consumer Privacy Bill of Rights Act of 2015* (https://www.whitehouse.gov/sites/default/files/omb/legislative/letters/cpbr-act-of-2015-discussion-draft.pdf) to encourage law makers to pass needed legislation in the area of consumer privacy. Unfortunately, many critics believed "it nodded superficially to the idea of privacy rights, but ultimately ceded control over consumers' data to companies" (Singer, 2016). Consumer privacy advocacy groups aren't impressed by actions being taken at the Federal level, so many are turning to the States in hopes that they will pass legislation to protect consumers. The importance of having control over our own personal information can't be emphasized enough, especially in the age of the Internet.

Withholding Medical Information

Where else can be demonstrated the importance of privacy than within healthcare; from privacy comes trust. As we've mentioned, the healthcare industry is built on trust. You, as a patient, must trust your doctor to provide you adequate and satisfactory medical services. The relationship between you and your doctor, oftentimes, becomes very personal, very quickly. If you ever visited a doctor's office, I'm sure you probably heard these familiar words, "Please take your clothes off and put this robe on, the doctor will be in to examine you momentarily." Although withholding medical information from a doctor has occurred for a long time due to possible embarrassment or shame, with the dawn of the database, patients had another reason for not sharing vital information that could assist a medical professional in making the proper diagnosis of an illness.

With a historic number of data breaches occurring over the past in the healthcare industry, a question was posted to seven hundred fifty (750) American adults over the age of eighteen (18): *"Have you withheld information from your healthcare provider due to concerns about the security or privacy of your medical records"* (Cobb, 2016a). The results: more than one (1) in eight (8) (or 13.2%) responded that they did withhold information for fear over the security and privacy of their information. This number is higher than the previous numbers from a similar survey performed by the Office of the National Coordinator for Health Information Technology (ONC) between 2012 and 2014. In 2012, ONC indicated seven percent (7%) of respondents withheld information. It went up by one percent (1%) in 2013 to a total eight percent (8%) and then down to five percent (5%) of respondents in 2014 indicating concern over security or privacy made them withhold information (Vaishali Patel, 2016).

Although trending, per the ONC study, appears to indicate that concerns over privacy and security of patients' medical records are going down, with just a little over half of individuals nationwide indicating to be somewhat or very concerned in 2014, it will be very interesting to have ONC perform this study again due to all of the data breaches. With a new survey out, "it could be argued that the large medical data breaches of 2015 have doubled patient concerns" (Cobb, 2016a).

Privacy Platform

As I'm writing this book, we are in the midst of the primary election for the next President of the United States. It is interesting to see the different perspectives and important issues that are being presented to the candidates. With the increase of breaches, electronic fraud, identity theft, and the recent passing of Justice Antonin Scalia, it has become more apparent than ever before that privacy needs to be an important topic for discussion.

Let's look at the case of Josh Uretsky, former national data director for the Bernie Sanders 2016 presidential campaign. After inappropriately accessing data owned by the Hillary Clinton campaign, Uretsky was terminated from employment. Through a third-party vendor, the Democratic National Committee (DNC) maintains information on voters. The DNC allows campaigns to use this information for a fee and both campaigns for Clinton and Sanders pay for this service. At some point throughout the campaign, there was a flaw discovered in the separation of data between the campaigns. Uretsky claims he accessed the data only to demonstrate the extent of the issue; however, the DNC temporarily suspended access to the system for Sanders.

Just to put it into a frame of reference of how important this data is to the campaign, the Sanders campaign filed a Federal lawsuit against the DNC to restore access. In the complaint, the Sanders campaign references, "In a fundraising drive conducted between December 14, 2015 and December 16, 2015, the Campaign raised more than $2,400,000.00—or more than $800,000.00 per day. Most of this money came from individual donors identified through, *inter alia [among other things]*, the strategic use of Voter Data" (Bernie 2016, Inc., 2016).

Although the information contained in the database is primarily demographical information such as names, addresses, voter registration status, etc., the Clinton campaign apparently attached attributes to individual records at their own expense. This appeared to be the information that Uretsky accessed that led to his final dismissal of employment. What individuals may not realize is that it isn't necessarily your specific information that is of value as in this scenario, but the actionable items that are derived from this information such as your inclination to vote for a certain candidate or to donate money. Individuals are placed into groupings or classifications and this is the driving factor behind decisions.

Since Uretsky did not compromise the actual privacy of the individual, the incident didn't fall under any required breach notifications. As David Sheidlower, the chief information security officer (CISO) for a global media and advertising company, points out, "While it is a generally accepted principle of privacy among regulators that individuals should have the right to know what data is collected about them and be able to correct it, that right does not extend to the cohorts a data collector puts the individual in" (Sheidlower, 2016). Sheidlower explains an issue with regulations over privacy, "When identity is abstracted from privacy, data is no longer in the control of the subjects of the data" (Sheidlower, 2016). Sheidlower uses the U.S. "no-fly" list as an example. You may not know how or why your name got on this list and better yet, you may not know how to get your name removed once it is there.

For some of these reasons, the Electronic Privacy Information Center (EPIC) has established the DataProtection2016.org website to educate voters on the importance of privacy. As part of EPIC's Privacy Platform indicates, a privacy notice is no longer enough to protect an individual's right to privacy. The platform calls for a reduction of identity theft and financial fraud along with privacy safeguard enforcement. It also calls for limiting the collection of information, especially if companies aren't able to protect this information they collect. Furthermore, the platform suggests updating federal and state laws related to privacy and ending the mass surveillance performed by the police or the National Security Agency (NSA). Finally, data misuse should be investigated and there needs to be appropriate oversight of government agencies and organizations that are accountable for the protection of our privacy (Electronic Privacy Information Center, 2016).

Put a Tourniquet On: Stop the Bleeding

It can't be emphasized enough that it is not a question as to "if" a security incident is going to happen, but "when" a security incident will happen. The better question for organizations to ask is "*do we even know for certainty that we haven't been compromised already?*" The way we currently think about information security and privacy may be flawed and we need to rethink the ways that we handle our information. As Paul German, VP EMA, Certes Networks, states in his article *Security Breaches are Inevitable, So How are you Going to Contain them?*, "the reliance on traditional access control, threat detection and threat protection is clearly inadequate[;] organizations need to add another layer—breach containment" (German, 2016). We need to stop the bleeding.

If we take the assumption that we are going to be "hacked" and/ or the hacker is already in our network, the best course of action is to minimize the damage. We may have already built walls around the perimeter of our network through the use of firewalls, but as some organizations have discovered after falling victim to a breach, these boundary protection devices may not be enough. German proposes, "building (fire) doors between different parts of the infrastructure" (German, 2016). This may be easier said than done. The first area that most technical individuals will look at when proposing to segment their infrastructure is at the network layer. Unfortunately, changing access control lists or subnetting comes with risk by inadvertently opening possible avenues of attacks. As more and more companies leverage cloud environments, it becomes increasingly more difficult to maintain defense over the network layer as these safeguards fall outside of the scope of control of many companies.

German goes on to recommend, "Companies need to step back and look at this from a true business perspective and focus on users and applications" (German, 2016). He recommends the use of cryptographic segmentation controlling access to data by authorized individuals only. German further suggests that each cryptographic domain utilizes its own encryption key that will restrict an attacker from compromising an entire enterprise. Even if one of the domains were breached, the attacker would be isolated to that domain and not be able to access another domain. Response to a breach is more efficient in that a targeted approach could commence as opposed to an enterprise-wide system shut down.

I can't stress enough how important a chief information security officer (CISO) is to a company. Every company needs to have an individual that is well versed in security and privacy. Even the federal government has recognized the importance of a CISO by creating the post of the federal CISO as "the recognized federal expert and authority on policies, procedures, guidance, and technologies impacting the federal government's cybersecurity program" (Office of Management and Budget, 2016).

Unfortunately, many organizations, including the federal government, place the role of the CISO under the chief information officer (CIO) or the chief technology officer (CTO). The CISO can't effectively do his or her job from this position. There is a fundamental difference between the roles of the CIO/CTO and the CISO. Specifically, the CIO/CTO looks at an environment from a functional and operational perspective. The CISO looks at an environment from a security and privacy perspective. Although both views are important, oftentimes they are in conflict with each other.

To demonstrate these differences, let's take a look at the following scenario: the CIO/CTO is under pressure to get a new accounting system online by the chief financial officer (CFO). The CISO evaluates the system and determines that it contains several highly rated vulnerabilities that, if compromised, could lead to the breach of sensitive information. Mitigating these vulnerabilities takes some time and would put the project behind the scheduled "go live" date. The CISO wants to stop the implementation of this new system until the issues can be fixed, but the CIO/CTO is on a strict deadline to get the system into production. *What do you think is going to happen in this scenario when the CIO/CTO is the boss of the CISO?* The normal reality of the matter is that the system goes online with the vulnerabilities intact and it becomes the CISO's responsibility to attempt to fix them later on if he can.

The CISO needs to be on the same level as the CIO/CTO, and in fact, I argue that he or she should be slightly above when it comes to making the final determination of a system getting implemented or not based on security/privacy factors. The CISO should report directly to the CEO like all other senior executive staff and have a "dotted line" to the president or chairman of the board of directors. The CISO needs to have a seat at the executive decision-making table and should routinely report on security and privacy topics to the board of directors.

Companies can no longer ignore the reality over the importance of security and privacy. Companies that continue to downplay these risks will do so to their own detriment.

Shock to the Industry

Changes are always occurring in the healthcare industry. From the way care is provided to patient to the way providers get paid for the services they offer, healthcare remains an ever-evolving industry.

This is also evident when it comes to cybersecurity. With the growth in the amount of personal information collected and stored within healthcare, the industry faces more and more risks. These risks are also coming in different forms. No longer do healthcare organizations only need to worry about the lost laptop or the staff member that got too nosey in a medical record, but as Dan McWhorter, vice president of FireEye a threat intelligence company, pointed out during a presentation at the *HIMSS 2016 Conference Cybersecurity Symposium*, the healthcare sector needs to worry about attacks from nation actors, ransomware, and smart phones as well.

Attack trends are showing that larger health plans along with drug and research companies are being targeted by countries in Europe, Russia, and China. In the case of China, this stolen information doesn't appear to be for sale, but rather McWhorter believes the information is being utilized to advance China's own healthcare system. "China is under pressure to improve healthcare," McWhorter states, but for small U.S. startups, "Losing a little information could be losing it all" (McGee, 2016g).

Ransomware attacks are on the rise. In an effort to make some quick cash, these types of attacks will attempt to encrypt files and hold the information for ransom until a fee is paid for the key to unencrypt the files. Although this attack is generally opportunistic and may not target any one specific company, this malware is getting more sophisticated by destroying backups and attacking main databases.

Healthcare is being inundated with smart phones, applications, medical devices, and the Internet of Things. McWhorter warns, "New cell phones have all these new features ... with no security" (McGee, 2016g). These devices and applications are not undergoing the appropriate security vetting to validate that they are worthy to be utilized within a healthcare setting.

With the requirements placed on healthcare organizations to share information with each other and the move to interoperability come additional concerns: the matching of patient records. A person would think that this would be an easy task, but issues arise when nicknames are used instead of full names or maybe initials are used for middle names as opposed to the entire middle name. So, a combination of information must be utilized to obtain an appropriate match such as the name, date of birth, sex of the patient, and of course, Social Security number. Unfortunately, this still leads to issues since not all organizations are collecting this information the same way across the entire industry.

According to a 2014 Office of the National Coordinator for Health Information Technology report, healthcare organizations are having issues with their match rate. Take for instance an organization with a strong data quality program, Kaiser Permanente. The report indicates that they had a ninety percent (90%) success rate matching records over one of their regions; however, another region was at fifty percent (50%) even though the same electronic medical record solution was being utilized (Office of the National Coordinator, 2016). A survey conducted by the American Health Information Management Association (AHIMA), "revealed that over half of HIM [Health Information Management] professionals routinely work on mitigating possible patient record duplicates at their facility, and of those 72 percent work on mitigating duplicate records weekly" (AHIMA Staff, 2016).

This time spent to correct mismatch or duplicate records cost money. "According to the same ONC report, each case of misidentification at the Mayo Clinic costs at least $1200. Intermountain Healthcare spends between $4 million and $5 million per year on technologies and processes intended to ensure correct patient identification" (Grove, 2016). The operational costs to fix a duplicate record is $60 as calculated by Intermountain (Office of the National Coordinator, 2016). *What is the solution?*

National Patient Identifier

The College of Healthcare Information Management Executives (CHIME) in partnership with HeroX, a crowdsourcing innovation platform, along with support by other healthcare associations, has announced a year-long competition worth $1 million. The National Patient ID Challenge is "intended to incentivize the private sector to develop a patient identifying solution that would ensure '100 percent accuracy in identifying patients in the United States'" (Grove, 2016).

Revive Security Posture

Organizations across all industries, but especially in healthcare, need to do a better job at increasing their security posture. A good starting point for many of these organizations is implementing a security framework that can be followed. There are several different frameworks available, each with their pros and cons. For instance, as may be expected, eighty-two percent (82%) of federal IT professionals utilize the National Institute of Standards and Technology (NIST) frameworks (Jackson, 2016). These series of standard guidance are freely available and, according to a National Cybersecurity Institute study, are utilized by fifty-three percent (53.1%) of CISOs across multiple industries (Jackson, 2016). Other popular standards or frameworks are the Information Technology Infrastructure Library (ITIL), the International Organization for Standardization (ISO)/International Electrotechnical Commission (IEC) 27001:2005 27002:2005, the Payment Card Industry (PCI) Data Security Standards (DSS), the Control Objectives for Information and Related Technology (COBIT), and the Capability Maturity Model (CMM).

Although these frameworks will help steer a company in the right direction, it may not be enough. An organization ultimately needs to make security and privacy a high priority. They need to build a culture of security and privacy throughout the entire organization, from the top down, through every single business unit, service, or product. Security and privacy need to be baked into everything a company does, is doing, or will be doing in the future.

In most cases, the realization of the importance of security and privacy only appears after a short coming is discovered and is sometimes too little, too late. This short coming usually comes in the form of a breach or compromise. After a hefty fine from regulators, bad publicity, a law suit, or some other impact is felt by a company as a result of their indifference or ignorance to security and privacy does the reality of their situation set in. It is a lot like having a heart attack. Everything is going well and then all of a sudden, it happens. You are rushed to the hospital and if you are lucky, the doctors are able to save you. Unfortunately, some don't survive. This is usually a life changing event and just like most companies, you don't even know you are having an issue until it comes upon you and may be too late by the time it arrives.

I hate to describe the state of security and privacy in such grim detail, but the reality of the matter is that organizations are seldom prepared for when the "big one" hits. When it does happen, fingers start pointing and individuals duck for cover to avoid the fallout even though the symptoms may have been there for some time. A weak security and privacy posture is a systemic condition of an unhealthy business culture that needs to be treated and revived back to a healthy state.

Preventive Medicine

A lot can be learned by performing after action reviews of organizations that have been involved in a breach. What these organizations did, have done, or should have done to prevent and/or handle an incident can be very valuable to other organizations to improve their security postures. Let's go through some of the lessons learned by Anthem a year after being involved in a hack that affected nearly seventy-nine (79) million individuals. These include the following: social engineering education, monitoring for abnormal behaviors, updating anti-malware software, utilizing multifactor authentication, implementing data loss protection, assessing data collection/retention policies, and developing/testing incident response plans (McGee, 2016b).

Social Engineering

According to research performed by Trend Micro, ninety-one percent (91%) of targeted attacks started with spear phishing (Bagnall, 2016). By appearing to be a legitimate person or business, criminals attempt to fool users into clicking on links, downloading applications, or performing some act that may (and probably will) cause the victim some harm. In the not-so-distant past, these fake e-mails were easy to spot. They contained a lot of misspellings and grammatical errors. Unfortunately, there was still three percent (3%) of the population that would do what the e-mail asked them to do (Bagnall, 2016).

As Ken Bagnall, managing director of The Email Laundry, cautions, "The most successful phishing mails include little text because experience shows that people are more likely to trust messages if the content is short. The wording usually conveys a sense of urgency, which is designed to manipulate the recipient and compel them to act quickly" (Bagnall, 2016). Bagnall suggests continuous training be provided to users. For example, Bagnall recommends implementing phishing user training by sending users fake e-mails. If a user is tricked into clicking on a link within the e-mail, it will take the user to a security awareness training module that the user must complete. This is repeated continuously throughout the year and managers are able to obtain reports that keep them aware of the risks of these types of attack vectors throughout their organization. A good resource to learn more about social engineering techniques, tricks, resources, and education can be found at www.social-engineer.org .

Monitoring

The HIPAA Security Rules maintain three (3) related standards or implementation specifications that address monitoring. There is a standard requiring a covered entity or business associate to implement hardware, software, and/or procedural mechanisms that record and examine activity in information systems that contain or use electronic-protected health information (ePHI) [Audit Controls Standard: 45 CFR § 164.312(b)]. In basic terms, an organization needs to have solutions in place to record or have the ability to log activity on information systems.

When we look at controls or levels of protection, it may be easier to visualize them as layers or rings of protection. The first layer is the physical layer. This consists of safeguards around paper documents containing sensitive information, but it also consists of safeguarding the physical connection points that devices utilize to gain access to electronic or network resources. Some examples of physical controls include badge access on doors, surveillance cameras, physically locking ports, or disabling network jacks when not in use. Physical access can be monitored through visitor sign-ins, through badge access systems, or by monitoring surveillance cameras. Solutions can be implemented to alert when devices are physically connected to network ports.

The second layer of protection is the network layer. Only authorized devices should be able to access network resources. If a device is able to physically connect to a network port, it should be verified and then assigned an Internet Protocol (IP) address accordingly. Solutions such as Media Access Control (MAC) or Network Access Control (NAC) are examples. Every device connects to a network through a network interface. This could be through a hard wired connection or a wireless connection. In either case, the interface is assigned a unique identifier, usually by the manufacturer of the network interface device. Under Media Access Control (MAC), network interface devices are restricted access based upon their unique identifier. Only authorized identifiers may connect to network resources. Under Network Access Control (NAC), policies can be enforced on all endpoint devices. For instance, if a device attempts to connect to the network, not only can it be verified, but also ensure that antivirus is up-to-date, certain configurations are enforced on the endpoint, and the device can be assigned to specific network segments that the device is authorized to access. When it comes to monitoring, these solutions make it pretty simple to identify when devices are connected to the network.

The third layer of protection is the operating system or server layer. A majority of healthcare organizations utilize Microsoft's Active Directory Domain services. Under this type of network environment, users gain access to network services, but first must be authenticated against the Active Directory. This directory contains several resources, one of these being user and computer accounts. When a computer is connected to the domain and a user puts in their username and password, the credentials are sent to the Active Directory. If the user is on the "list" and has the correct password, they gain the access to the network resources that have been assigned to them. Current versions of operating systems have very robust monitoring and logging capabilities. Organizations are really only limited by the amount of space they reserve for logging depending on the activity being monitored. Some logging activity can generate a lot of logs, which in turn can require a lot of hard drive space to maintain. Although the HIPAA Security Rules are not specific when it comes to the details of the logging, there is one (1) implementation specification that addresses procedures for monitoring log-in attempts and reporting discrepancies [Log-in Monitoring (Addressable): 45 CFR § 164.308(a)(5)(ii)(C)].

The fourth layer of protection is the database layer. There are several common databases such as Microsoft's SQL, MySQL, or Oracle to name a few. All of these databases come with their own pros and cons, but each needs to be able to independently monitor their functions outside of any applications that may utilize them. Databases can be looked at like living organisms. They can grow in size very quickly and without proper care or attention, they can get very hard to maintain. It is important that organizations have the appropriate individuals with the requisite expertise in database management to assist in maintaining these systems. Databases should also be monitored for access and activity like other information systems.

The final layer of protection is the application layer. Application developers may utilize their own authentication mechanisms, or they may integrate with existing Active Directory resources through such protocols like the Lightweight Directory Access Protocol (LDAP). The HIPAA Security Rules require covered entities and business associates to implement procedures to regularly review records of information system activity, such as audit logs, access reports, and security incident tracking reports [Information System Activity Review (Required): 45 CFR § 164.308(a)(1)(ii)(D)]. Applications, especially those that maintain ePHI, should appropriately identify all users that access and the activities they perform on any record within the application.

Organizations should have procedures in place to regularly review these logs to identify suspicious activities, such as users looking into patient records that they have no reason to view, performing activity that is beyond their scope of responsibilities, and accessing the system outside of regular working hours. In large organizations, this review can be daunting, so organizations should look at solutions that can perform automatic reviews of all the logs and identify areas of concerns. When a certain threshold is met for a particular activity, the system should provide alerts that can be investigated further. An example of this might be a password type attack. If the logs show attempts by a user to enter their password too many times within a certain period of time, this could be an indication that someone may be attempting to guess or crack this credential. Alerts should be generated and further investigations should be conducted on this activity.

Anti-Malware

Malware is malicious software that is developed for the main purpose of compromising, damaging, or disrupting a computer. Malware comes in a lot of different versions, from the somewhat benign flavor that hijacks Internet sessions and presents a constant bombardment of advertising to the more recent (and more disruptive) ransomware. Some of the other more dangerous types are those that capture key strokes and search files for sensitive information like passwords, credit card information, or other information of value in the criminal underground.

Ransomware has become a major concern with a reported three hundred twenty-one (321) incidents alone reported in the second half of last year within federal agencies. According to the FBI's Internet Crime Complaint Center, in 2015 there were 7694 ransomware complaints received and an estimated \$57.6 million in losses (Chabrow, 2016b). These ransomware attacks are now hitting the healthcare sector. Hollywood Presbyterian Medical Center paid \$17,000 in ransom to unlock data and MedStar Health in the Maryland/Washington, DC area had to shut down systems to stop the spread of the malware. Alvarado Hospital Medical Center in San Diego, CA, was a third hospital owned by Prime Healthcare Systems affected by malware related to ransomware. The other two hospitals, Chino Valley Medical Center and Desert Valley Hospital, were able to recover without paying a ransom and with little disruption. Another hospital in Indiana, King's Daughters' Health, discovered a file for a single employee infected with ransomware and turned systems off to prevent any spread of the virus. The hospital is running on manual procedures until systems are verified safe and turned back on.

The increase in ransomware attacks even prompted the FBI to issue a podcast warning advising organizations to notify their local FBI office and not to pay the ransom (FBI, 2016b). Oliver Tavakoli, chief technology officer at Vectra Networks, a security firm, indicates that "All early versions of ransomware (CryptoLocker, CryptoWall, Locky) encrypted files, both local and on network share, and left computers operational. The newer versions, like Petya, encrypt the file system structures and render an entire machine unusable" (Kitten, 2016). The U.S. Department of Homeland Security also followed suit by issuing a warning on ransomware through the U.S. Computer Emergency Readiness Team (US-CERT). The advisory also warns "paying the ransom does not guarantee the encrypted files will be released; it only guarantees that the malicious actors receive the victim's money, and in some cases, their banking information" (US-CERT, 2016).

Although this software is always advancing and becoming more sophisticated, it is still a good security practice to install a reputable anti-malware solution. In fact, it is recommended to utilize multiple anti-malware solutions from different vendors as in the case of protecting systems from e-mail. First, an anti-malware solution should be implemented to filter and scan for malware attached to e-mails at the perimeter boundary. This solution could be installed at the e-mail gateway to check e-mail or some organizations may utilize a third party service to perform this first layer of inspection. This solution could also assist in blocking spam e-mail or unwanted e-mail advertising. Next, an anti-malware solution made by a different vendor should be installed on the e-mail server that again searches for malware attached to e-mail. Finally, all workstations and end-point devices should have install anti-malware that has a virus definition engine maintained by another vendor. In this scenario, e-mail would be checked three (3) times before the user opens and/or reads the content or any attachments.

Most anti-malware solutions still utilize virus definitions that match software with known bad signatures. Unfortunately, these malware applications can set up different variants automatically in an attempt to circumvent anti-malware protection. A few anti-malware vendors have introduced more behavioral analysis end-point protection by determining what is normal "safe" behavior and what activities that occur on the systems may indicate an infection has occurred. Gone are the days where anti-malware solutions were set up on schedules to scan entire computer systems, but rather more frequent "real-time" protection is taking place to alert users immediately upon a detected threat. Through an enterprise anti-malware solution, these detected threats are submitted to a centralized control server for immediate notification and response. New identified threats may be analyzed further and as necessary, these new malware signatures will be immediately updated to all systems throughout the enterprise.

Through this new total end-point protection process, anti-malware solutions have gotten better in detecting and responding to these threats; however, anti-malware vendors are always just one step behind attackers. Adding "white listing" functionality to your overall protection scheme can go a long way to make your systems more secure. As opposed to preventing known bad threats, white listing only allows known good services or applications to run on a system. It is much easier to determine what applications should run or are permitted to run on a system than to try and stop every possible bad variant of a malicious application. Limiting user rights on their computers will also help to protect against or minimize the damage caused by malware. Malware oftentimes attempts to run at an elevated privilege or system level. If a user were to be infected, but only has limited rights, the malware may not be able to completely compromise the system or be isolated to a limited area within the system. It will be much easier to contain an outbreak and eventually eradicate it.

Multi-Factor Authentication

Authentication is the process of validating an individual to ensure they "are" who they say they are when it comes to gaining access to a system. Commonly, this is done by the individual providing their username or identity along with a credential or password. This username/password credential is matched to a list of authorized users within a database. If the password is correct and matches the username within the database, it is assumed that the individual is the person they say they are. Of course, the assumption here is that only the appropriate person would know their own password. Sometimes, this isn't the case when it comes to individuals sharing passwords, an attacker compromising a password, social engineering—tricking the individual in giving up their password, or even a disgruntled or opportunistic employee selling a work password.

In a survey conducted by SailPoint, a user access managing software developing company, on one thousand (1000) people at companies with over one thousand (1000) employees, "one (1) in five (5) employees would be happy to sell their work passwords, some for just the price of a dinner" (Wong, 2016). U.S. workers appeared to be more willing than other employees from other countries; however, the average acceptable offer required by U.S. workers to sell their work password was over $50,000. More concerning was that two-thirds (2/3) of respondents indicated that for multiple applications, they utilize the same passwords "and a third of workers said they already shared their passwords with their colleagues" (Wong, 2016). As the founder of SailPoint, Kevin Cunningham warns, "It's imperative that employees understand the implications of how they adhere to [corporate security] policies. It only takes one entry point out of hundreds of millions in a single enterprise for a hacker to gain access and cause a lot of damage" (Wong, 2016).

To enhance the authentication process, the security industry has turned to multifactor authentication. There are basically three (3) tenets to authentication:

1. Utilizing something that you know (this is a username/password that we already discussed)
2. Utilizing something that you have (this can be a token or a badge)
3. Utilizing something that you "are" (like your fingerprint, facial recognition, iris scan, DNA, etc.)

In the case of multifactor authentication, an individual must utilize at least two (2) of the three (3) tenets described above. A really good example of multifactor authentication that is commonly utilized is the use of ATM or debit cards. For an individual to withdrawal money from these devices, they must have a card. The card is a physical token that has a magnetic strip or if you are lucky enough, will have a new built-in chip. Along with the card, the individual must know their personal identification number (PIN). The PIN is something that an individual should only know. The combination of these two (2) items, something that you have (the debit card) and something that you know (the PIN), provides a certain level of assurance to the bank that the person requesting money from their account is the person that owns the account or is authorized to make a withdrawal from that account.

As it is becoming the case that username and passwords are just not enough to provide the appropriate protection over sensitive systems or access to information, multifactor authentication is increasingly being implemented. In fact, some states like California are not mandating the use of multifactor authentication. "Organizations should not only use multi-factor authentication to protect critical systems and data, but should also make it available on consumer-facing online accounts that contain sensitive personal information. Such accounts include online shopping accounts, health care websites and patient portals, and web-based email accounts" (California's Attorney General, 2016).

Data Loss Protection

Organizations not only have to worry about external actors like hackers attempting to gain access to a network, but they have to worry about internal threats as well. According to "the cyberattacks recorded in 2014, 55 percent of attacks were carried out by those who had insider access to organizations' systems" (Thompson, 2016). Insiders such as your trusted employees, third party contractors, or other service providers open up a whole new area of risks since these individuals tend to have intimate knowledge of the network, systems, and protection that is in place. It is a lot easier to circumvent a control when you know what that control is.

These insider threat actors may be motivated by several different factors to cause harm to the organization. Such factors may include being disgruntled or angry over a raise or promotion an individual felt they were entitled to, the enticement of additional cash or opportunity at a competitor, or maybe the insider just wants revenge for something that was done to them and felt justice would be served by committing a certain act against the organization. In any event or whatever motivation an insider justifies their action, the insider threat is very real and an insider can do much more harm in most cases than an external party.

A perfect example of the damage that an insider can cause is the story behind Edward Snowden. This former Central Intelligence Agency (CIA) employee and government contractor gained global attention after leaking classified information about the surveillance programs of the National Security Agency's (NSA). Without going into a debate of whether or not Snowden was right or wrong in what he did or how he did it, the point of this discussion relates to the fact that he was able to obtain the information and ultimately walk out "the front door" with this information without anyone apparently noticing.

Organizations need to be aware of the activity that their employees and contractors are performing on their systems. They need to be alerted to suspicious activity including the exfiltration of sensitive information. The implementation of data loss protection (DLP) software is one solution that could be utilized in mitigating this threat. A DLP solution assists administrators in controlling how data may be transferred outside of an organization and to restrict sensitive information from leaving the organization. A DLP solution may work by examining all traffic leaving the internal secure network to ensure sensitive information is not contained within. This solution could also be utilized to restrict portable media devices like external hard drives or USB drives. A DLP solution could be implemented to restrict the use of these devices and alert administrators that these devices attempted to connect to the network.

Data Collection/Retention

Organizations need to be prepared for the amount of information they are going to create, receive, maintain, or transmit, especially in the healthcare sector. Not only will these healthcare organizations have ever-increasing electronic medical records solutions, but they will also face increases in data from other ancillary healthcare systems along with medical devices. These devices may only be capturing a small amount of data now like blood pressure, heart rate, steps, and etc., but this is just the start of the amount of information they will collect in the future. With the new ways in which healthcare providers will get reimbursed as it relates to outcomes, healthcare will start collecting more and more information as in the case of environmental, societal, or even genomic data.

Organizations need to develop plans for this influx of data. Healthcare entities need to ensure that this information is kept secured and private, but also need to ensure that the data is accurate. By ensuring that the data is trustworthy, important analytics can be performed on the data to produce actionable outcomes. "Once health organizations discover the nuggets of wisdom that are most useful, they should integrate these insights into their points of care" (Lynn, 2016a).

As we've already discussed, integration is becoming more and more crucial to the success of the entire healthcare system. The interoperability of various systems across healthcare has become a priority for many, including the regulators. "As the healthcare world evolves to include value-based care, ACOs [accountable care organizations], quality scoring and new reimbursement structures, the success of healthcare providers will depend on their ability to leverage health data effectively" (Lynn, 2016a).

It will also be important for healthcare organizations to know when "enough is enough." Having too much information can also be dangerous and raises their risks of a compromise. When fines and suits tend to revolve around the number of records that were compromised, it becomes apparent that limiting the amount of information collected may be a good thing. Unfortunately, organizations need to ensure they understand all of the retention requirements related to the data they handle. Establishing appropriate records retention policies and procedures is imperative along with ensuring that these processes are followed at all times. There are many different federal, state, or local regulations around certain information and it is a good idea to bring in experts that know the intricacies of these retention requirements. The first step is to know where the information is located or what information is being maintained. Then it becomes a matter of classifying this information and setting up procedures to handle this information in accordance to the organization's record retention policies.

Data Encryption

According to the Attorney General of California, "Organizations, particularly health care, should consistently use strong encryption to protect personal information on laptops and other portable devices, and should consider it for desktop computers" (California's Attorney General, 2016). Unfortunately, of the respondents to a survey performed by Sophos on seventeen hundred (1700) IT managers, only forty-four percent (44%) make extensive use of encryption and only forty-three percent (43%) utilize encryption to some degree (Sophos, 2016). The top three (3) reasons for not encrypting were lack of budget, concerns over issues with device performance if encrypted, and lack of knowledge around encryption technology. What is most concerning, especially for the healthcare industry, is the lack of encryption over mobile devices. Although PCs and servers come in at an encryption rate of sixty-six percent (66%) and seventy percent (70%), respectively, "only 29 percent of tables and smartphones are encrypted, and only 22 percent of wearable devices are encrypted" (Heath, 2016b).

In the second Mobile Threat Intelligence Report completed by Skycure, seventy percent (70%) of physicians rely on mobile devices and twenty-eight percent (28%) of them store patient data on these devices. To add to concerns, fourteen percent (14%) of those physicians that store patient data don't utilize passcodes to minimally protect the data on the devices. Furthermore, eleven percent (11%) of these physicians are utilizing outdated mobile operating system versions with known vulnerabilities. According to Adi Sharabani, Skycure's CEO, "smart devices are seen by the hacker community as the most vulnerable of gateways to sensitive data (HIPAA-protected patient data) for multiple reasons" (Zorz, 2016). Physicians are found texting patient data, utilizing picture messaging, and other mobile applications that may not be fully HIPAA compliant.

Encryption is nothing new and humans have been utilizing ways to keep messages secret for over thirty-five hundred (3500) years. Codes and ciphers were used to communicate military orders, trade secrets, and to keep information private. According to Gerhard Strasser, a professor emeritus and expert on the history of cryptology, the first documented use of encryption was discovered on a 1500 BC Mesopotamia cuneiform tablet. The Sumerians of Mesopotamia developed the writing system of cuneiform. "It is considered the most significant among the many cultural contributions of the Sumerians and the greatest among those of the Sumerian city of Uruk which advanced the writing of cuneiform. C. 3200 BCE" (Mark Graber, 2016). Strasser states the tablet contained, "an encrypted message in which craftsmen camouflaged the recipe for a pottery glaze that was a highly coveted item at the time" (Waddell, 2016). Strasser goes on to say that the message was encrypted utilizing a simple method of substitution: "One cuneiform symbol was used for another. That way, basically, the message got garbled" (Waddell, 2016). Although this method was pretty rudimentary, it was enough to keep the recipe private from those they didn't want to have it.

There are many examples of the use of encryption from the Romans, Greeks, and Hebrews. Even the atbash system was used in early Bibles where letters were transposed such as the last letter of the alphabet replacing the first and the second-to-last replacing the second and so on. Strasser explains that the *Kama Sutra*, in India, encouraged the practice of cryptography primarily between men and women. "It's the communication where men and women should have a language of their own, so that the neighbors could not understand" (Waddell, 2016).

One of the more interesting uses of cryptography was found in eighteenth-century France by the Count of Vergennes, the French foreign minister, utilizing coded messages in travel visas. This passport, of sorts, carried a frame around the name of the individual. The frame was uniquely drawn to provide a hidden code. When requesting such documents, an individual would be required to submit personal information about themselves or embassy employees would investigate them to gather this personal information. Based on this information, the individual would be analyzed and provided a frame or drawing around their name that depicted the individual's personality or status. For instance, if the individual was rich, the frame would have more circles drawn on it. The frame was printed on a card that also contained a number that was encoded with different meanings. The individual might have thought that they were just issued the 18,342 numbered card, but there was more to it. The card was carried by the individual and presented to the Count of Vergennes. Based on the analysis of the hidden codes, the Count would know all he needed about the dealings of the individual and whether or not he wanted the individual to stay longer in Paris to spend their wealth, if they were rich. It could have also alerted the Count to have police watch the individual more closely if the individual had a criminal past. "At its essence, that's the same idea that's still used in modern cryptography: When an electronic message is encrypted end-to-end, the messenger has no idea what the message says" (Waddell, 2016).

If you travel internationally, you may already have an e-Passport. In fact, "The United States requires that travelers entering the United States under the Visa Waiver Program have an e-Passport if their passport was issued on or after October 26, 2006" (Homeland Security, 2016).

The e-Passport contains an electronic chip that stores all the information that is printed on the passport like name, date of birth, or other biographic information. In addition, the e-Passport contains a biometric identifier. Biometric identifiers are distinct, physical characteristics of an individual to label or describe the individual. It could include such things as physical attributes, facial features, handprints, fingerprints, iris scans, voice identification, or other items. In fact, the Federal Bureau of Investigation appeared to have spent a billion dollars on enhancing their Next Generation Identification program in an effort to collect biometric identifiers on individuals (FBI, 2016a). If you have one of these e-Passports, don't worry, the e-Passport is designed with security features to prevent authorized access to the data stored on the chip and multiple layers of security to prevent duplication.

Not all encryption is the same and when encrypting sensitive information like ePHI, ensure the encryption meets the standards. Refer to the *Federal Information Processing Standard (FIPS) Publication 140-2: Security Requirements for Cryptographic Modules* or the *NIST Special Publication 800-175B: Guideline for Using Cryptographic Standards in the Federal Government: Cryptographic Mechanisms* for additional information on approved encryption technology.

Incident Response Plan

When operating a business, organizations should recognize the fact that bad things will happen from time to time. Organizations need to be able to handle these events in an efficient and effective way along with minimizing damages that could be caused when mayhem strikes. When it comes to cybersecurity incidents, an organization that is prepared ahead of time is better positioned to handle adverse events.

Throughout this section, we've taken a proactive perspective toward cybersecurity and although incident response activities usually occur as a reaction to something happening, the basis of this discussion is to have a plan to react to it in the first place. As Benjamin Franklin once said, "If you fail to plan, you are planning to fail." Your organization will be attacked, especially if you are working in the healthcare industry, no if's, and's, or but's about it. What you do to protect yourself by ensuring that you are aware of an incident occurring and how you react to this event will make all the difference.

For this reason, your organization needs to have monitoring, logging, and alerting implemented on your network and critical systems. Modern information systems, operating systems, and applications all have the capabilities of monitoring activities of the systems themselves and of the users that utilize these systems. Settings can be configured on these systems to log activities or events when they occur. Depending on the criticality of these systems, logging configurations can be set to the extreme covering every possible type of activity or they can be throttled back to only cover important events. Some of these important events could include when users log on to the system, when privileged activities occur like establishing new users or deleting accounts, or in the case of healthcare, when users view or access ePHI.

As you can imagine, the more users and activities that occur on these systems, the more events are created along with the increase in the size of the logs. This is where a security incident event management (SIEM) solution is vital to implement. This type of solution collects all of the logs from the different systems into a central repository. It is impossible for a person to search through all of the logs to detect anomalies or suspicious activities. This is where a SIEM solution is "worth its weight in gold" as the saying goes. The SIEM is capable of searching through a massive amount of logged events and activities to uncover patterns. By establishing certain normal behavior patterns, the SIEM is able to detect outlying activities that meet or exceed certain threshold settings. If certain criteria are met, an alert can be generated to inform system administrators that something is wrong and further investigation is required.

By collecting and examining logs from several different devices in one central repository, a complete picture of activity can be formed across the entire network. For instance, if a user is logging into one system on one side of a large facility at the same time that same user is appearing to log into another system on the opposite side of the facility, this could be an indication that the account is compromised. There is no physical way that an individual can be in two places at one time. The systems, individually, may permit multiple sessions to take place by one user, but without the ability to correlate the individual systems together and know the physical proximity of each, a compromise like this may not be detected without a SIEM solution in place.

Along with a SIEM solution, your organization needs to know what to do if they encounter a certain event. Complete books have been written about the proper handling of all types of events, but here is a summary of the CANCERR steps that should be followed in handling an incident:

1. **C**onfirm—Make a determination or confirmation that an incident really occurred. In some cases, there could be "false positives" created in logs or a system starts acting funny on its own, but it wasn't caused by an attack. It is imperative that a confirmation is made as to: *what type of event has taken place, what information was involved,* or *could this information be utilized to cause additional damage*? These are just a few of the questions that should be answered.

2. **A**nalyze—If an event is confirmed to be a security type of incident, an analysis must be made to determine the current or potential impact of the incident. The analysis should include the prioritization of the resources that are involved.

3. **N**otify—There are requirements for notification as it relates to an incident. Not only internal notifications need to be made to the appropriate personnel that need to be involved in incident response, but there are also regulatory requirements for notifications, in some cases, upon discovery of an incident. There are six (6) elements identified as the rationale for making certain notifications:
   a. Breach notification required by law
   b. Timeliness in making notifications
   c. Source of the breach
   d. Content of the information used or disclosed
   e. Means to providing notification
   f. Recipients required to be notified
   Specific to the Health Insurance Portability and Accountability Act of 1996 (HIPAA) Breach Notification requirements,

determinations will be made on the risk of harm taking into consideration the following factors:

a. Nature of the data elements that were breached

b. The number of individuals that are or could have been affected by the breach

c. The ability for the information to be accessed and utilized

d. The possibility that additional harm could occur from the breach

e. Mitigation factors

4. Contain—It is imperative that damage caused by an incident is kept to a minimum. In some cases, taking a system "off-line" may be the best solution to prevent further harm. In other cases, the system may now be considered an "active crime scene." As such, procedures to acquire, preserve, secure, and document the evidence of the incident may be appropriate. Additional expert resources may need to be called in to assist, such as law enforcement or digital forensic experts. Since it may not be feasible to anticipate every possible scenario, each incident will need to be evaluated individually.

5. Eradicate—After an incident gets under some sort of control, it may have been determined that a specific malware, hack, or other changes took place within the system. As such, the system needs to be cleaned up and malicious software eradicated.

6. Recover—In most cases, any affected systems should be restored from known good media or backups. Full tests should be run on the systems to ensure complete eradication has taken place before the systems are put back into production.

7. Review—Systems are put back on-line and everything seems to be back to normal; however, an after action review needs to be performed. This review, performed by all involved parties along with executive management, determines what activities went well and what items need to be improved. This is a time to reflect on what occurred and what needs to be done in the future to prevent a similar incident or to adjust responses to an incident.

Incident response planning is not solely left to an organization. Individuals should also be prepared to handle an incident involving the breach of their personal information. According to the Department of Justice, individuals can avoid falling victim to identity theft by remembering the word **ScAM**.

- **S**tingy—Don't give your personal information to strangers unless you trust them. Information should be provided only on a "need to know" basis.
- **A**sk—Review your credit report on a periodic basis.
- **M**aintain—Keep careful records of your accounts (Department of Justice, 2016).

If a breach occurs, the Attorney General for California recommends, "Organizations should encourage those affected to place a fraud alert on their credit files when Social Security numbers or driver's license numbers are breached" (California's Attorney General, 2016). The Identity Theft Resource Center located at www.idtheftcenter.org provides steps, resources, and other good information that individuals can use to minimize their impact to a breach of their personal information.

Vendor Management

Many healthcare organizations heavily rely on vendors or third-party service providers to assist in providing services that either the organization can't perform themselves maybe for lack of expertise or resource availability or the organization finds the service provider can do a better job for less. Regardless of the reason for using an outside service provider, the healthcare organization needs to take special care in selecting the provider, maintaining the provider relation throughout the service offering, and eventual termination of the service relationship. This is more important if a service provider is handling protected health information.

A business associate, by definition under 45 CFR §160.103, is a person (or company), which on behalf of a covered entity (or an organized healthcare arrangement in which the covered entity participates), creates, receives, maintains, or transmits protected health information for a regulated function or activity. Some examples of business associates include claims processing or administration, data analysis, processing or administration, utilization review, quality assurance, patient safety activities, billing, benefit management, practice management, and repricing. These business associates provide services to a covered entity in a capacity other than as a member of the workforce of such covered entity (or arrangement). Some other examples of business associates include legal, actuarial, accounting, consulting, data aggregation, management, administrative, accreditation, or financial services to or for a covered entity (or to or for an organized healthcare arrangement in which the covered entity participates) where the provision of the service involves the disclosure of protected health information from such covered entity (or arrangement). As a quick side note, disclosure means the release, transfer, provision of access to, or divulging in any manner of information outside the entity holding the information. In addition, a covered entity may be a business associate of another covered entity in some cases.

Furthermore, a business associate includes the following: a Health Information Organization, E-prescribing Gateway, or other person that provides data transmission services with respect to protected health information to a covered entity and that requires access on a routine basis to such protected health information; a person that offers a personal health record to one or more individuals on behalf of a covered entity; or a subcontractor that creates, receives, maintains, or transmits protected health information on behalf of the business associate.

When the Omnibus Rule became effective on March 26, 2013, business associates (and subcontractors of business associates) became directly liable to meet the requirements of the HIPAA Security Rules and applicable Privacy Rules. To further enforce this liability, satisfactory assurance of compliance must be obtained through a business associate/subcontractor agreement (or similar agreement that meets the requirements of a business associate agreement). Furthermore, the business associate agreement is necessary to ensure that the business associate (or subcontractor) is contractually required through a legally binding agreement to perform certain activities for which direct liability does (or does not) apply. This business associate agreement provides both parties to respectively clarify their responsibilities under the HIPAA Rules along with serving as notification to the business associate (or subcontractor) of their status under the HIPAA Rules so that these vendors or service providers are fully aware of their obligations and potential liabilities.

There are some exceptions to a business associate that includes the following: a healthcare provider, a plan sponsor, a government agency, or a covered entity that performs certain functions while participating in an organized healthcare arrangement. There is also a narrowly defined "conduit exception" that may apply to such service providers as an Internet Service Provider that just provides certain "conduits" for the transmission of data or mail service providers like Fedex and UPS.

This conduit exception, however, doesn't apply to service providers that "maintain" servers that store ePHI. The Department of HHS has made it clear that the test to determine if a provider is considered a business associate is the persistence of custody (and not the degree, if any, of access) they have over the servers. Even if it is the case that these service providers do not access the information, they are still considered business associates and must demonstrate their compliance to the applicable HIPAA administrative, physical, and technical safeguard requirements. The Office for Civil Rights (OCR) has "made it clear that cloud and colocation providers are business associates and subject to criminal and civil penalties if they are not compliant with the law" (Klein, 2016). In some of these cases, these hosting providers may only provide the three (3) P's: ping, power, and pipe; however, these components have a direct effect on the availability of ePHI stored within the systems housed at these facilities. Since information security relies on three (3) tenets: confidentiality, integrity, and availability in order to keep ePHI safe, this availability tenet may be directly affected by the controls in place that relate to maintenance of (or the persistence of custody over) ePHI.

It can't be stressed enough how important it is to have these business associate agreements in place. As a case in point, Triple-S Management Corporation (formerly American Health Medicare Inc.) settled multiple violations with the OCR for $3.5 million that included "Impermissible disclosure of its beneficiaries' PHI to an outside vendor with which it did not have an appropriate business associate agreement" (HHS Press Office, 2016). As attorney Owen Kurtin from Kurtin, PLLC Attorneys at Law, states, "It is a facial violation of HIPAA for a Covered Entity to transmit, and for a Business

Associate to receive, patient Protected Health Information without a written, compliant Business Associate Agreement in place" (Kurtin, 2016a). Without a business associate agreement in place, a covered entity and a business associate had no right to transmit and receive, respectively, any protected health information from the start.

A business associate agreement has certain requirements it must meet to be in compliance. A sample business associate agreement developed by the Department of HHS can be found here: http://www. hhs.gov/hipaa/for-professionals/covered-entities/sample-business-associate-agreement-provisions/index.html. In short, a business associate agreement must contain the following required elements:

- Implement administrative, physical, and technical safeguards that reasonably and appropriately protect the confidentiality, integrity, and availability of the ePHI that it creates, receives, maintains, or transmits on behalf of the covered entity.
- Ensure that any agent, including a subcontractor, to whom it provides such information agrees to implement reasonable and appropriate safeguards to protect it.
- Report to the covered entity any security incident of which it becomes aware.
- Authorize termination of the contract by the covered entity, if the covered entity determines that the business associate has violated a material term of the contract.

A couple other important, but optional items that I often recommend to clients to have within their business associate agreements is the right for a covered entity to audit their business associates. Having an agreement in place as required, in my opinion, is just a small part of an overall effective vendor management program. Organizations need to vet their vendors, ensure appropriate due diligence was performed in choosing the vendor, ensure the vendor is meeting its obligations throughout the term of the relationship, and if they don't, there needs to be remedies built in to correct the issues. Being able to audit the vendor to ensure that they are meeting obligations is an important part of the vendor due diligence process.

The other important item is to specifically address expected time frames. For instance, a covered entity is required to notify each individual whose unsecured protected health information has been, or is reasonably believed by the covered entity to have been accessed, acquired, used, or disclosed as a result of a breach without unreasonable delay and in no case later than sixty (60) calendar days after discovery of a breach [45 CFR § 164.404]. Furthermore, breaches are treated as discovered as of the first day on which such breach is known to the covered entity or should have known through reasonable diligence. A covered entity shall be deemed to have knowledge when a workforce member or *agent* of the covered entity (determined in accordance with the federal common law of agents) have known.

I bring this little caveat up as it relates to the included "agent" clause. Depending on how a business associate is defined (i.e. an agent or not) may impact the amount of time in making appropriate notifications. If a business associate is NOT an agent of a covered entity, they have up to sixty (60) days following the discovery of a breach to make notification to a covered entity. On the other hand, if a business associate is an agent of the covered entity "then the business associate's discovery of the breach will be imputed [done, caused, or possessed; attributed] to the covered entity for purposes of starting the sixty day clock on the covered entity's required breach notifications" (Smith, 2016). It is important to include the time permitted in making notifications and address if a business associate is an "agent" of a covered entity.

Determining if a business associate is an agent of a covered entity can be complicated and needs to be considered on a case-by-case basis. A determining factor to consider is the amount of control a covered entity has over a business associate when it comes to the services it provides. Other factors include how the relationship is received by another party or how a covered entity may control the results and the activities to obtain those results of a business associate. A good, albeit a little older, write-up of some common scenarios can be found here: https://aishealth.com/archive/hipaa1110-01.

For some of these reasons, I normally recommend to clients that a business associate should notify a covered entity within ten (10) to fifteen (15) days of discovery. This way, even if the business associate is an agent, the covered entity has another forty-five (45) to fifty (50) days to make their notification, which should be enough time to make the appropriate notifications accordingly. Covered entities should seek the advice of a qualified attorney in developing business associate agreements or other service provider type contracts.

Health Application Use

Mobile applications that track health-related information like heart rate, steps walked, or others that assist in the management of your health have become very popular over the last few years. We've discussed many benefits of these applications along with some of their drawbacks throughout this book, but I wanted to spend just a few moments to discuss a common question I get frequently regarding the application of HIPAA to the application developers of these applications: *Does HIPAA apply to information handled by these health applications and does the application developer need to comply with the HIPAA Rules?*

The Department of HHS developed a "white paper" on some of the more common scenarios and how HIPAA may apply. It can be found here: http://hipaaqsportal.hhs.gov/community-library/accounts/92/925889/OCR-health-app-developer-scenarios-2-2016.pdf.

As a reminder, covered entities such as health plans, healthcare clearinghouses, and healthcare providers must comply with HIPAA. As we discussed in the previous section, business associates are also required to comply with HIPAA. In the case of an application that is developed on behalf of a covered entity that creates, receives, maintains, or transmits protected health information, the application developer would be considered a business associate and must comply with applicable HIPAA rules. In addition, subcontractors of business associates must comply with HIPAA and are considered business associates themselves. Therefore, application developers that develop health applications on behalf of a subcontractor would be considered business associates as well and must comply with applicable HIPAA Rules.

As indicated, a key point to consider is if the health application is creating, receiving, maintaining, or transmitting protected health information on behalf of a covered entity or business associate. If so, the application developer is most likely a business associate. Other key factors to consider include what clients are being serviced by the application and how is funding obtained. *Was the application developer hired by a covered entity or business associate to produce the application and does the covered entity or business associate direct the health application as to the handling of the information?*

If, on the other hand, the application is offered directly to consumers and independently selected by consumers and not on behalf of a covered entity, the application developer is likely not subject to HIPAA. Other factors to consider are the control over decisions made about the data by the consumer and any relevant relationships with third parties. In any case the determination comes out regarding HIPAA, the privacy and security of the data is still important and care must be taken when collecting this information.

Standards/Certification/Accreditation

CIS Critical Security Controls

As previously mentioned, California has really led the way when it comes to protecting individuals' privacy and forcing organization to take security over the information they maintain seriously. In a recent turn of events, California's Attorney General released its *California Data Breach Report February 2016*. This report provided a lot of information on breaches that have affected residents of California over the past four (4) years. Along with this information, the report provides specific recommendations that organizations should take to protect their information.

Of these recommendations, the Attorney General calls for organizations to implement the twenty (20) controls managed by the Center for Internet Security (CIS), a nonprofit organization that promotes cybersecurity best practices. These controls were formerly known as the "SANS Top 20" and provide a prioritized list of controls that defines a minimum level of information security for organizations. Although these controls are not mandated by the Attorney General, the report indicates, "The failure to implement all the Controls [CIS Critical Security Controls] that apply to an organization's environment constitutes a lack of reasonable security" (California's Attorney General, 2016). The CIS Critical Security Controls for Effective Cyber Defense, Version 6.0, October 15, 2015 is available at www.cisecurity.org.

NIST CsF The National Institute of Standards and Technology (NIST), under Executive Order (EO) 13636, *Improving Critical Infrastructure Cybersecurity* issued in February 2013, was directed to develop a voluntary framework in order to reduce cyber risks for critical infrastructure systems. Since healthcare is considered a critical infrastructure industry, it would seem logical that the healthcare industry would adopt a framework to assist them in becoming more secure. Based on existing standards, guidelines, and practices that NIST has already created or worked on, the NIST Cyber Security Framework (CsF) was developed.

The NIST CsF's four (4) core elements: functions, categories, subcategories, and informative references. Functions are high-level activities. These functions include identification, protection, detection, response, and recovery. Categories subdivide the functions into groups of outcomes such as asset management, access control, and detection processes. The categories are further divided into subcategories that specify outcomes of technical and/or management activities. The last element, informative references, refers to other guidance such as other frameworks like the International Society of Automation (ISA) 62443, the International Organization for Standardization/ International Electrotechnical Commission (ISO/IEC) 27001:2013, and other NIST Special Publications such as NIST SP800-53 Revision 4, *Security and Privacy Controls for Federal Information Systems and Organizations*.

One of the important items to note in reference to the NIST CsF is it is *voluntary*. There is no governmental mandate or requirement that private sector industries utilize this guidance to protect their sensitive information; however, NIST CsF may become *the* standard. As attorney Shawn E. Tuma explains in his blog post as paraphrased here: the importance of cybersecurity compliance is being pushed by U.S. regulatory agencies and these agencies are relying on the NIST Cybersecurity Framework as the default standard. Since these regulatory agencies provide the guidance and influence the regulations or laws created, these laws are, in essence, created from the NIST Cybersecurity Framework. Tuma concludes, "The #1 reason why NIST Cybersecurity Framework is quickly becoming *the* standard that is being looked to (as opposed to, for example ISO 27001) for companies doing business in the United States is because that is what the regulatory agencies are looking to" (Tuma, 2016).

As a case in point, to further improve cybersecurity, President Barack Obama implemented the Cybersecurity National Action Plan (CNAP). From support by the NIST, the Commission on Enhancing National Cybersecurity will be developed. According to a White House statement, "The Commission is tasked with making detailed recommendations on actions that can be taken over the next decade to enhance cybersecurity awareness and protections throughout the private sector and at all levels of Government, to protect privacy, to maintain public safety and economic and national security, and to empower Americans to take better control of their digital security" (Carroll Publishing, 2016). CNAP also called for a Federal CISO, which is "the first time that there will be a dedicated senior official who is solely focused on developing, managing, and coordinating cybersecurity strategy, policy, and operations across the entire Federal domain" (FACT SHEET: Cybersecurity National Action Plan, 2016). In addition, the NIST's Cybersecurity Framework assisted in launching the National Cybersecurity Center of Excellence that "addresses businesses' most pressing cybersecurity problems with practical, standards-based solutions using commercially available technologies" (The National Cybersecurity Center of Excellence, 2016).

The NIST CsF was written to be general to cover all types of organizations and sizes. For this reason, organizations would need to adept the framework for their own specific use or needs depending on the type of environment and other regulatory requirements the organization may need to abide by. This is where specific certification programs for the healthcare industry become most beneficial.

HITRUST

Although there are several other security frameworks available, one of the more prescriptive control sets specifically addressing the needs of healthcare organizations was developed by the Health Information Trust Alliance (HITRUST). In collaboration with healthcare stakeholders, the HITRUST Common Security Framework (CSF) was created to be a certifiable framework for organizations handling sensitive information like personal health information. The HITRUST CSF normalized multiple frameworks, standards, and regulations relevant to healthcare into a comprehensive and flexible baseline of controls. The HITRUST CSF includes frameworks and regulations like ISO, NIST, PCI, HIPAA, COBIT, and state regulations like Texas and Massachusetts, just to name a few. In addition, HITRUST CSF has mappings to the NIST CsF. The HITRUST CSF is risk based allowing organizations to tailor the control set to different factors such as size, complexity, and other regulatory requirements. "By continuing to improve and update the CSF, the HITRUST CSF has become the most widely-adopted security framework in the U.S. healthcare industry" (HITRUST Alliance, 2016b).

To more efficiently manage vendors, major health insurance companies like Anthem, Health Care Services Corporation, Highmark, Humana, UnitedHealth Group, and others have made their support known to a certifiable standard that can assess an organization's security posture. In a press release dated June 29, 2015, these insurers will require over 7500 vendors to obtain the HITRUST CSF Certification over the next two (2) years. As the press release explains, these third-party organizations receive several requests to provide information to their customers related to their information security practices. In some cases, these requests take a lot of time and effort. The intent of the HITRUST CSF Certification would be to allow organizations to audit once and report to multiple clients their results. Since it is assumed that all organizations would recognize the rigor of the certification process, they would accept the certification as attestation to the security posture of that organization. Per the press release, "The CSF Assurance program is the first comprehensive and coordinated effort to address these challenges and to adopt, in a meaningful manner, a unified approach to third-party assurance" (HITRUST Alliance, 2016a).

As based on the response to the preamble of the Final Omnibus Rule of 2013 and since the Department of HHS "declines to establish or endorse a certification process for HIPAA compliance for business associates and subcontractors," it is refreshing to know that there are some within the healthcare industry that are trying to "police" themselves as opposed to regulators issuing mandates

(Department of Health and Human Services, 2013). I'm still under the opinion that regulators for the healthcare industry should mandate independent assessments just as being required for financial institutions like credit unions. Since enforcement activity is lacking, at least independent assessments would substantiate that some minimal level of security is in place for these healthcare organizations and provide some level of verification or validation that the healthcare organization has a baseline security posture. A certification process such as achieving HITRUST CSF Certification should be the "gold standard" that healthcare organizations strive to achieve.

Additional information about the HITRUST CSF Certification program can be found on their website at: https://hitrustalliance.net.

EHNAC

The Electronic Healthcare Network Accreditation Commission (EHNAC) is a nonprofit organization formed in 1993 to "promote accreditation in the healthcare industry to achieve quality and trust in healthcare information exchange through adoption and implementation of standards" (EHNAC, 2016a). EHNAC provides accreditation services to healthcare organizations such as Medical Billers/ Payers, Third-Party Administrators (TPAs), Electronic Health Networks (EHNs), Health Information Service Providers (HISPs), E-prescribing Networks, Managed Service Organizations (MSOs), Health Information Exchanges (HIEs), and other healthcare-related organizations.

EHNAC currently has nine (9) accreditation programs to include the following:

1. ACOAP: Accountable Care Organization Accreditation Program
2. DTAAP (HISP, CA, RA): Direct Trust Agent Accreditation Programs
3. ePAP: e-Prescribing Accreditation Programs
4. FSAP: Financial Services Accreditation Program
5. HIEAP: Health Information Exchange Accreditation Program

6. HNAP: Healthcare Network Accreditation Program
7. MSOAP: Management Service Organization Accreditation Program
8. OSAP: Outsourced Services Accreditation Program
9. PMSAP: Practice Management Systems Accreditation Program (EHNAC, 2016b)
(*Note*: There may be additional subcategories under individual accreditation programs for specific organizations.)

A few states even require EHNAC accreditation for organizations to operate in their respective states such as the following:

- Maryland Healthcare Access Commission (MHCC) requires EHN, e-Prescribing, and MSO.
- New Jersey requires EHN.
- Texas Health Services Authority requires HIE (EHNAC, 2016b).

EHNAC has taken security seriously and has taken steps to improve cybersecurity within the healthcare industry. In fact, EHNAC developed another accreditation designed for managing the trust between the registry credentials of health information exchange users known as the Data Registry Accreditation Program (DRAP). EHNAC has also signed a Memorandum of Understanding (MOU) with the National Health Information Sharing and Analysis Center (NH-ISAC) to improve cybersecurity measures in healthcare by collaborating "on initiatives supporting prevention and risk mitigation for HIPAA breaches, incidents and cybersecurity prevent, protection, response and recovery" (EHNAC, 2016c).

As NH-ISAC's President, Denise Anderson, states, "The healthcare sector is coming under increasing threat as can be seen in a number of incidents in the news. Bringing NH-ISAC's and EHNAC's expertise and communities together is a first step in helping to keep our members' operations resilient and safe as well as protected" (Snell, 2016b). EHNAC's Executive Director, Lee Barrett, agrees and adds, "With the dedicated focus of our collaborative teams, NH-ISAC and EHNAC look to make great strides in effective awareness and prevention tactics to minimize the crippling impact of these cybersecurity attacks" (Snell, 2016b).

Additional information about EHNAC's accreditation programs and criteria can be found on their website at: https://www.ehnac.org.

FHIR

As you are already aware, there is a ton of health information that is collected when a patient visits a healthcare provider and this information is now oftentimes incorporated into a digital medical record. To obtain the greatest benefit in analyzing this information, the Department of HHS is utilizing a framework developed by Health Level Seven International (HL7) known as the Fast Healthcare Interoperability Resources (FHIR), pronounced "fire." FHIR acts as both a standard and an architecture. Through the use of FHIR as a standard, important data elements are collected and structured in such a way that groupings can be formed from the information. The most common uses that represent eighty percent (80%) of clinical practices are contained within these data elements. FHIR, as an architecture, application programmable interfaces (API) are developed to get the information needed in a format that can be used. FHIR also takes into consideration privacy and security.

FHIR is flexible and modular breaking complicated health concepts into resources. These resources contain data, a description of the data, and extension for customization of specific use of the data. Resources can be built upon and can interact with each other. An advantage of utilizing FHIR is that it is free, scalable, and vendor neutral, allowing FHIR to assist in interoperability and innovation when it comes to developing healthcare-related applications.

Additional information about FHIR can be found here: http://www.hl7.org/implement/standards/fhir/.

Recovery

The Privacy Rights Clearinghouse provides a detailed fact sheet on actions that victims of identity theft can take as summarized in Table 7.1.

It is important to keep good records and documentation. This includes all steps you take, everyone you speak to in reference to your case (including dates and times along with detailed contact

Table 7.1 Checklist of Activities to Follow If You Are a Victim of Identity Theft

NUMBER	ACTIVITY OR ACTIONS	ADDITIONAL INFORMATION
1.	Place fraud alert with credit bureaus.	*Experian*: https://www.experian.com/fraud/center. html
		Equifax: https://www.alerts.equifax.com/ AutoFraud_Online/jsp/fraudAlert.jsp
		TransUnion: http://www.transunion.com/ fraud-victim-resource/place-fraud-alert
		Innovis: https://www.innovis.com/
2.	Obtain free credit reports and monitor activity.	If you received notification that your information was breached, in most cases, the company will offer free credit monitoring.
3.	Place a credit or security freeze with credit bureaus.	A freeze may be better than an alert in that companies can't access your credit information without your permission. If you were a victim of identity theft, in most states, this freeze is provided for free.
4.	If you have children, be cautious of their identity as well.	The Identity Theft Resource Center maintains a detailed fact sheet on child identity theft: http:// www.idtheftcenter.org/Fact-Sheets/fs-120.html
5.	Report identity theft to the Federal Trade Commission (FTC).	The FTC offers an online complaint form: http://www. ftc.gov/complaint
6.	Report identity theft to local police or sheriff's office.	Some law enforcement agencies may not know how to handle identity theft or may not want to take a report. The FTC offers a memo to law enforcement here: http://www.consumer.ftc.gov/sites/default/files/ articles/pdf/pdf-0088-ftc-memo-law-enforcement.pdf
		If incident involves the U.S. mail, contact the U.S. Postal Inspector; online complaints can be filed here: http://ehome.uspis.gov/fcsexternal/default.aspx
		If incident involves the use of a driver's license, contact your state's Department of Motor Vehicles.
		If a criminal is by chance arrested, contact your area's victim-witness assistance program to ensure that you have a change to be heard at legal proceedings.
7.	If you discover fraudulent accounts on your credit report, contact the creditors.	Request documentation that were provided to open the account. Sample letters are here: http://www. oag.ca.gov/idtheft/facts/guide-for-victims
		Provide them a fraud affidavit: http://www.consumer. ftc.gov/articles/pdf-0094-identity-theft-affidavit.pdf
		Provide them a copy of your government issued identification.
		Provide them a copy of police report.

(Continued)

Table 7.1 (*Continued*)   Checklist of Activities to Follow If You Are a Victim of Identity Theft

NUMBER	ACTIVITY OR ACTIONS	ADDITIONAL INFORMATION
8.	Inform your credit companies in writing immediately if you see any issues with existing accounts.	Request new cards and ensure passwords are secured on all accounts.
9.	If you receive calls from any debt collectors for unpaid balances on a fraudulent account, ensure that you advise them in writing that you are a victim of identity theft.	The Privacy Rights Clearinghouse has a detailed fact sheet to respond to debt collectors: https://www.privacyrights.org/node/417
10.	If incident involves stolen checks or bank accounts, contact bank to put a "stop payment" on the checks.	Have bank report issue to ChexSystems: https://www.consumerdebit.com Close existing and obtain new accounts. Although the U.S. Secret Service handles investigations of financial fraud, unless your case involves a large amount of money, they may not investigate. Check with your bank's/credit card's fraud department or law enforcement investigator to see if the Secret Service should get involved.
11.	If incident involves your ATM or debit cards, report the compromise immediately to your financial institution.	These types of cards fall under the Electronic Fund Transfer Act (EFTA) and even if you were a victim, you could be held liable for charges. FTC has put out a guide for further information here: http://www.consumer.ftc.gov/aarticles/0213-lost-or-stolen-credit-atm-and-debit-cards
12.	If incident involves brokerage accounts, notify your brokerage company.	Also notify the Securities and Exchange Commission and the Financial Industry Regulatory Association.
13.	If incident involves your Social Security number, contact the Social Security Administration (SSA).	Unfortunately, the SSA doesn't provide assistance with identity theft unless it involves benefit, employment, or welfare fraud. Only in serious cases would they issue another Social Security number. The SSA's online complaint form can be found here: http://oig.ssa.gov/report-fraud-waste-or-abuse/fraud-waste-and-abuse
14.	If incident involves a fraudulent tax return, contact the Internal Revenue Services (IRS).	For more information on the IRS Identity Protection Specialized Unit: https://www.irs.gov/Individuals/Identity-Protection To protect your tax records, you could file an IRS Identity Theft Affidavit (Form 14039): https://www.irs.gov/pub/irs-pdf/f14039.pdf

(Continued)

Table 7.1 (*Continued*) Checklist of Activities to Follow If You Are a Victim of Identity Theft

NUMBER	ACTIVITY OR ACTIONS	ADDITIONAL INFORMATION
15.	If incident involves your passport, contact the U.S. Department of State, Passport Services.	http://travel.state.gov/passport/lost/lost_848.html
16.	If incident involves a fraudulent phone/cell phone account, contact the carrier for additional information.	
17.	If incident involves a student loan, contact the school.	Report issue to the U.S. Department of Education: www.ed.gov/about/offices/list/oig/hotline.html?src=rt
18.	There are a lot of cases where family members perpetuate identity theft. *Why?* It is fairly easy for them to commit since they know a lot of personal information about you.	The Identity Theft Resource Center maintains a lot of valuable information regarding these types of incidents.
19.	Medical Identity Theft	The World Privacy Forum provides a lot of information on this and we'll discuss recommendations in further detail on Medical Identity Theft in another section of this book.
20.	If you are wrongfully accused of a crime due to identity theft, contact your local law enforcement and judicial system.	To find out how you might be able to restore your name, contact the Federal Bureau of Investigations (FBI) or the Department of Justice (DOJ).

Source: Privacy Rights Clearinghouse, Fact sheet 17a: Identity theft: What to do if it happens to you, Retrieved from Privacy Rights Clearinghouse, https://www.privacyrights.org/content/identity-theft-what-do-if-it-happens-you, February 7, 2016.

information), and all written evidence to support your situation. It is important to hold your ground against intimidating tactics, and being a victim of identity theft can be very stressful. Seek consultation, as needed, from your mental healthcare provider to cope with these issues. Finally, you can always seek legal assistance from an attorney that specializes in these types of crimes.

If you ever fall victim to medical identity theft, here are some specific things that the World Privacy Forum suggests you do (paraphrased as follows):

- Review your Explanation of Benefits statement: You may notice unexplained charges for services, office visits, or medical equipment that could indicate that your information has been used by another person.
- Obtain benefit listings: At least annually, ask your insurance provider to send you a list of all payments made on your behalf.
- Request to inspect or obtain a copy of your medical records from your healthcare provider: You have the right to review your own medical records; however, a provider may charge a reasonable fee for such copies. Since most providers now have electronic medical records, it is becoming easier to obtain the information you are requesting through these technology solutions.
- Ensure your medical records are up-to-date: If you find any discrepancies within your records, you should notify your provider and request an amendment to these records.
- Review an accounting of disclosures: A healthcare provider is required to account for information disclosed to others. Unfortunately, this disclosure may not account for items under treatment, payment, or other healthcare operations; however, some providers have the capability to maintain this information and may be able to provide it to you upon request. This accounting of disclosure may also be important to let you know which other providers may have wrong information about you so that you can ensure that this information is up-to-date with them. Providers have an obligation to notify others if original information shared with them is incorrect. You should follow up to ensure that amendments are appropriately made to your medical record by all providers that may have your records.
- Contact law enforcement: If you believe you are a victim of identity theft, it is a good idea to get this formally documented through a police report.
- Monitor your credit report: Even though medical identity theft may not necessarily be uncovered through financial reporting records, it is important to protect yourself from other possible financial fraud, especially if the criminals are utilizing your Social Security number and other personal information.

The World Privacy Forum provides other resources regarding medical ID theft here: https://www.worldprivacyforum.org/category/med-id-theft/.

If your organization falls victim to a security incident or even a breach, it is important to be prepared. Having a thorough incident response plan in place and testing this plan on a frequent basis to ensure it is up-to-date will go far in minimizing damage. Some incidents can get very complicated, very fast, so it is a good idea to have vetted outside sources only a phone call away to assist when needed. Many reputable and experienced companies provide incident response services that could be very beneficial to your organization when the situation arises.

In addition, there should be a lead assigned that will coordinate efforts and make decisions regarding the incident response activities. This individual should have the necessary authority to appropriately carry out the necessary actions involved in responding to an incident. Executive management needs to allow responsible parties of the incident response team to handle the situation. The team is not able to respond appropriately if executives want an update every five (5) minutes. The incident response team needs to be responsible to carry out the plan.

It is important to get your legal counsel involved as soon as possible. If internal legal counsel is not experienced in these matters, other legal expert advice should be obtained. Once legal is involved, some communications fall under client-attorney privileges and your counsel should be able to assist in coordination of disclosures to outside individuals. In addition, there are so many different privacy-related notification requirements, especially for organizations that work across state lines; these legal counsels should have expertise in these breach-related areas. Finally, there should be a formally documented communication plan in place prior to an incident and during an incident, good lines of communication must be maintained throughout both internal and external groups. An incident can be a high stress time and it is important that any misinformation is kept to a minimum.

Organizations need to appropriately understand the scope of the problem and attempt to understand the attack to ensure that all affected systems are evaluated. It is important that a root cause be determined, and it is verified that all systems are taken into consideration when recovering from an attack. It may be necessary to take actions to mitigate damages even though the full extent of the issue isn't clear at first. An incident may be fluid and changes occur frequently. Individuals need to be prepared to respond accordingly.

Finally, if the incident has been resolved, ensure that it has been completely resolved before any comments are made. There have been a few situations where organizations put out that a certain number of records have been breached only to find that more were compromised as further investigations were performed. It is important to have a plan in place to recover from an incident once the initial steps have taken place. Organizations that perform well throughout a breach are those that show concern for their clients. Setting up call centers to answer questions and keeping affected individuals notified through postings on an organization's website goes a long way in demonstrating this concern. Although not required, it has become common practice for organizations that have been breached to offer credit monitoring services to those individuals affected by the breach. Organizations should be prepared to assist individuals in the best way they can if these individuals fall victim to other crimes as a result of their breach.

Cybersecurity Insurance

As data breaches grow, liability over the cost of these compromises is being carried by the organizations that were responsible for the data that was breached. In the case of credit card compromises, the credit card processors and financial institutions that issued the payment cards were covering unauthorized transactions, but they are now pushing more costs onto the merchants that fell victim to a breach. These additional costs may come in the form of fines, replacement card costs, mandatory forensic analysis, and compliance reassessments. These extra costs average $36,000–$50,000 according to FirstData, a payment processor (FirstData, 2016).

"Under merchant payment processing agreements, payment processors can withhold money from merchants to reimburse banks for the costs of payment card fraud, and they can impose fees, fines, or penalties to cover other breach costs" (Pollack, 2016a). In fact, processors and card issuers are pushing merchants to utilize point of sale equipment that implement new EMV (Europay, Mastercard, and Visa standard, or better known as "chip" card readers) shifting liability to the merchants over counterfeit or stolen cards. Merchants argue that the costs to upgrade their systems may be cost prohibitive and may not be any more secure. In some cases, PINs are no longer required to be used when making a purchase with a chip card. Chips may make it harder to forge, but it doesn't necessarily ensure that an authorized person is utilizing the card. In addition, the chip doesn't prevent Internet fraud or the unauthorized use of a card when making online purchases.

Experts recommend that organizations should cover themselves by purchasing cyber insurance that will most likely cover them for initial costs, defense costs, and possibly liability settlement claims. "As things stand, fewer than half of organizations carry cyber insurance for breach events, and only about a third of organizations had enough coverage to completely cover post-breach costs, according to the report" (Chickowski, 2016a). In addition, organizations will want to ensure that these insurance policies will cover any contract liabilities or indemnities as may be addressed within the payment card/ merchant agreements.

Insurance companies do a pretty good job of covering initial costs, but when it comes to covering loss profits related to a breach, this is a little harder for insurance companies to calculate. Case in point that brings this discussion to the forefront relates to a lawsuit filed by Spec's Family Partners against Hanover Insurance Company asking the court to have the insurance company pay for legal fees involving their suit against a credit card processor involved in a breach (Martin, 2016). Due to increases in data breaches, insurance companies are excluding coverage for these related items under their general commercial liability policies and rewriting this coverage under a separate, more expensive policy.

Although courts have generally ruled that commercial general liability (CGL) policies don't necessarily cover the costs of data breaches, a federal appeals court of the U.S. Fourth Circuit Court of Appeals in Virginia ruled to the contrary. A class action lawsuit was filed in 2013 by patients of Glens Falls Hospital against Portal Healthcare Solutions, an electronic record-keeping service, regarding the publishing of their medical records online by Portal. Portal sued its insurance company, Travelers Indemnity Company of America, to cover the cost of the defense against the class action suit under their general liability coverage. The appellate court decided in favor of Portal indicating that the commercial general liability should cover this claim. This is a surprising turn of events for insurance companies as Robert Bregman, senior research analyst at the International Risk Management Institute, explains "CGL insurers don't really think that they should be on the hook for this type of claim. They see this as a cyber and privacy claim, not a general liability claim" (Barth, 2016). As a result, general liability policies will include many exclusions related to privacy and cybersecurity actions. These exclusions will be addressed in specific cyber insurance policies.

Insurers are setting the stage for a massive explosion within the cyber insurance market. Per PWC, the cyber insurance market is expected to reach $7.5 billion by 2020 (Chickowski, 2016b). As this newer market grows, insurance companies will get better in determining the risks of clients. In fact, RMS and AIR Worldwide, two companies that have done risk assessment and disaster modeling for the insurance industry, worked with eight (8) large insurers like Lloyd's of London along with the Center for Risk Studies at Cambridge University to develop a standard, the Cyber Exposure Data Schema, in an effort to share cyber risk data. Across the industry, this schema can be utilized to estimate losses, establish common definitions, and establish categories related to cyber risks.

It may take some time for this standard to mature, but it will provide opportunities throughout the market for carriers that initially were afraid to write policies, due to uncertainty of risks, to provide policies to a wider range of clients. Since insurers will require clients to perform an assessment prior to writing a policy, it may shed some light on information security practices within the organizations that need to be improved. In basic terms, if organizations want better rates for their cyber security policies, they'll need to meet certain requirements and enhance their security postures accordingly. Not only will insurance providers have experts on call to assist with post-breach activities such as forensic, legal, and recovery, but they'll also provide tools to assist their clients in identifying issues before something bad happens. These tools include incident response plans, guidance to establish policies, provide security training, and share information on new threats.

8

Summary

If you think technology can solve your security problems, then you don't understand the problems and you don't understand the technology.

—**Bruce Schneier,** *Secrets and Lies*

Message to the Board Room*

It is no surprise that cybersecurity has become a top-of-mind issue in many board rooms across healthcare providers large and small.

Beginning in 2015 with the staggering breach reported in February by Health Insurer *Anthem* that resulted in the loss of an estimated eighty (80) million customer records, it seems healthcare has become the "darling target" of the hacking community. Along with *Anthem*, organizations such as *Premera Blue Cross, Excellus Blue Cross,* as well as *UCLA Health System* and *CareFirst Blue Cross Blue Shield* were some of the larger breaches that added up to what was unquestionably one of the worst years for information security in healthcare.

Knowing and accepting that cybersecurity is a very real risk is the first step. In the last couple of years, many organizational boards have painfully learned that cybersecurity is no longer simply an arcane part of Information Technology but a significant risk management issue on par with patient safety and fraud prevention.

Unfortunately, just knowing something is an issue doesn't mean that everyone has the correct information and understands their role in their organization's cybersecurity program. To that end, this section lends some insights on what you, as a board member, can do to help mature your organization's cybersecurity program and provide meaningful guidance, support, and oversight.

---

* This section was provided with permission from contributing author Ramon Balut.

Steely-Eyed Missile Man

For most of the past twenty (20) years in my role as the chief information security officer (CISO) supporting a number of successful healthcare providers, I've attended more than a few board subcommittee meetings well prepared to discuss some aspect of cybersecurity. Unfortunately, I found that my place on the agenda simply didn't "make the cut" or if I was lucky, I had the final seven (7) minutes to discuss my topic while members began to pack up papers and materials in preparation for their next meeting.

Today, however, with significant losses from breaches no longer being "theoretical," but as real as floods, fires, or massive malpractice suits, I find myself discussing cybersecurity topics toward the top of the agenda or meetings will run long just to make sure this topic is discussed. That's good news, but let's make no mistake, there's a lot of ground to make up and fast.

For many organizations, the race is on and they are finding themselves years behind when it comes to securing their computing environment. Closing that gap will require making significant and sometimes difficult changes. These changes will require resources in the form of budgets, changes to the established culture, re-aligning priorities, and most of all...LEADERSHIP.

As a member of a board, that leadership must come from you. There will be no grassroots effort to improve security. No one is going to step up and say, "I'm willing to give up that new CAT scanner so we can have better security and implement two (2) factor authentication."

"Steely-eyed missile man" is considered the absolute highest compliment a person at NASA can receive. It means that you have the courage to make the tough call, go against what has become the established way of doing things, and stand your ground because you know you're right and lives depend on it.

Ladies and gentlemen, every day it seems we lose another battle in the effort to protect our data and systems. I'm an optimist and I believe we still can pull through, but if we don't get in the fight, if someone doesn't lead the charge, then soon, very soon, we will lose this war.

If the topic of cybersecurity is new to your board room, don't worry, you've got lots of company. For many, the challenge is in knowing where to begin. As a wise man once said, "Simple, you begin at the beginning." For most boards, this involves getting up to speed on the issues of cybersecurity, understanding what you need to know (and don't need to know), and understanding what your role as a leader requires.

Let's begin by focusing on what is probably the most common misconception when it comes to creating or maturing a security program. Simply put, it's the notion that if we become compliant with the requirements of regulations such as the Health Insurance Portability and Accountability Act (HIPAA) of 1996, we'll be secure.

"If we are compliant then we must be secure."

Unfortunately, reality has shown us this simply isn't true. Many organizations that have been breached would tell you, "Of course we're meeting compliance requirements," but in the end, while they may have been able to check a box that says they were doing something, in practice, that "something" fell far short of actually protecting the organization.

Understanding the difference between a security compliance and a security management program is key to successfully reducing organizational risk. It begins with the question, "Which risks are you trying to manage with a *compliance* program and which ones are you managing with your *security* program?"

As a security professional, I always like to consider the failure to comply with a specific regulatory or contractual set of requirements as its own unique risk. The act of "failing to comply" can definitely lead to painful consequences such as fines, increased scrutiny, and unplanned remediation costs.

A security compliance program is designed to help the organization ensure that it's meeting requirements as directed by regulatory or industry governing bodies. For most healthcare providers, this typically means regulations such as HIPAA and requirements such as those mandated by the Payment Card Industry (PCI).

Unfortunately, there are some shortfalls to the "compliance *equals* security" approach. These include:

1. Compliance requirements are often minimal and intended for a broad audience.

    Defining what "compliant" means can be difficult and too often because there are so many requirements to address and the task to comply can seem overwhelming; organizations can gravitate toward the lowest common denominator that will let them "check the box." Unfortunately, this often misses the mark on achieving *real* security.

A simple example might be meeting a requirement to authenticate a user before giving them access to a system. An organization may "check the box" by requiring the use of a user ID and password, but miss the security mark by allowing weak standards for what the password must be because people complained. In another example, not requiring a second factor for high-risk situations like remotely accessing the Electronic Medical Record because someone objected and said that, "it was a bother."

You may be "compliant" with that weak password or authentication, but you sure aren't "secure."

2. The drive to be compliant can quickly draw down already tight resources.

For most organizations, the individuals that are meeting with auditors and spending their time "dotting i's and crossing t's" are the same ones you depend on to perform the tasks of securing the organization.

In most healthcare organizations, a dedicated, well-trained, and appropriately staffed security team is "but a dream." Even if a dedicated security officer exists, they often find themselves not only trying to lead the band but playing every instrument in the orchestra as well.

Typically, the tasks required to perform the operational functions of security are carried out by already overworked network, server, and desktop personnel. Given that, an organization must be careful to consider that every hour spent by these people to participate in, performing audits, developing remediation plans, and reporting on such matters takes away from any actual security operations that may (or should) be occurring.

Having a security compliance program is important and there can be a beneficial relationship between security and compliance. Ultimately, it has been the need to meet regulatory and contractual requirements that has motivated many to have any form of security program at all. In short, without the regulatory "push," many organizations would be doing little or nothing about security.

Additionally, there is some overlap that contributes to actually creating a secure environment. Requirements can:

1. Set a baseline standard for a great many aspects of security if one doesn't exist
2. Serve as a starting point for an organization just beginning its security program
3. Provide something that can be measured, that is, a box that can be "checked" to demonstrate that the organization has done something to address the security requirement
4. Drive basic support from a budgetary perspective

At the end of the day, an organization must engage experienced individuals in assessing what truly puts the organization at risk and act on that, rather than hope that by doing everything a regulation requires, they will be secure. Each organization is unique in how it conducts business, what the culture of the organization will accept, and where it's going as a business.

Closing the gaps on the real threats as opposed to "checking all the boxes" is what will help prevent an organization from being the next *anthem no one wants to sing.*

Asking the Right Questions

So, if following the formula provided by a compliance mandate won't secure your organization, *what can you do to change the security posture in your organization in the real sense of the word?*

In 2014, *The Institute of Internal Auditors Research Foundation (IIARF)* and the *Information Systems Audit and Control Association (ISACA)* sponsored a research report written by Sajay Rai titled *CYBERSECURITY What the Board of Directors Needs to Ask.* This report deftly outlines both guiding principles and key questions that any board member should consider taking the time to review if they are looking to become more educated on their roles regarding cybersecurity.

As a "quick start," there are four (4) immediate action steps that can jump-start your engagement in managing cybersecurity risk:

1. Consider including a board director with specific security experience.

    While an in-depth technical knowledge of cybersecurity is not a requirement for all board members, organizations such as healthcare providers who are at a high risk for loss from cyberattack should strongly consider including a member who is well versed in the issues, technologies, and needs of a security program. A former CISO could bring valuable knowledge and insight to the table.

    If appropriate, this individual may even be the individual who can chair a subcommittee dedicated to cybersecurity if it's appropriate for the size and complexity of your organization.

2. Meet directly with your CISO.

    It is surprising how often a board will not go to its most valuable source of information when it comes to understanding its security environment, their own CISO.

    Your CISO is the individual in the organization who is best positioned to speak directly to the state of security and present security's strategic plan.

    If you don't have a CISO, then finding one who is versed in the technical aspects of security as well as having knowledge of the business aspects of healthcare is critical. It is then extremely important to position them such that they have the authority and resources commensurate with the responsibility you are placing on them.

3. Review the organization's latest risk assessment, commission one if it doesn't exist, and ensure it assesses your organization appropriately.

    A true risk assessment is invaluable and no security compliance or management program can be successful without it. The key takeaway is being sure that the assessment is not simply a compliance checklist. It must be an assessment tailored to your organization and how it conducts business. It must reflect the risks to your organization based on how you conduct business.

4. Adopt a cybersecurity framework.

Board members are used to managing risk, so general principles of risk management will certainly come to bear on the topic of cybersecurity. Beyond basic principles, however, there are several frameworks focused on cybersecurity that can help create, assess, and mature your program.

In particular, the National Institute of Standards and Technology (NIST) has developed a framework in response to President Obama's executive order 13636, which focused on improving cybersecurity around critical infrastructure—something healthcare is considered a part of.

While this framework is one of several available, its relationship to NIST positions those in the healthcare industry to more easily link their program back to standards that are well understood by the Department of Health and Human Services that provides oversight in regard to HIPAA regulations.

Securing the computing environment is challenging for any organization in any industry, but it is especially true in healthcare where years of comfortable inaction have left many scrambling to shore up old and inadequate defenses.

Objections that security is "too hard," "too inconvenient," "too costly," or "interferes with patient care" can no longer be considered sufficient argument to do nothing. That time has passed. We now live in an age where criminals have no hesitation in shutting down a hospital and endangering lives as demonstrated in the recent attack on *Hollywood Presbyterian Medical Center* where critical data was literally held for ransom. This is the new norm and as real as it gets.

To be successful in the fight for the confidentiality, integrity, and availability of data and systems, board members must become involved, educated, empower its leadership, insist that appropriate resources be brought to bear, and hold those in charge responsible.

*****

Message to Chief Executive Officers

As a chief executive officer (CEO) that is concerned about cyber threats and becoming a victim of a data breach, you are not alone.

Of eleven hundred (1100) senior executives of large companies around the world, including over one hundred (100) individuals from the U.S. government, ninety percent (90%) responded that their organizations are vulnerable to data threats, according to a report from 451 Research (Monegain, 2016). Many of these executives, and maybe you are one, feel that these risks are an IT or technology issue; however, this is generally not the case. Cyber threats and data breaches should be viewed as a business concern.

Good security should not be considered an expense, but rather an investment. Security folks are dedicated to protecting your company's brand and your company's "life blood," which is in many cases the data and intellectual property that your company has been built upon. As a CEO, you may be focused on achieving high profits for your investors and shareholders, but the reality is, as David Barton, chief information security officer at Websense, a security technology provider, puts it, "shareholder returns are directly tied to protecting the brand and managing the risk to the business" (Violino, 2016).

You may see security as a hindrance. The perception that security is inconvenient and will make doing your work harder needs to be changed. Sometimes this change can be difficult, but being aware of the risks that are present if the change doesn't occur should be a motivator in developing secure processes that are enforced throughout the organization. In my experience, I've found executives to be some of the most vulnerable individuals within an organization. Whenever security practices get in the way, you may make the command decision to "exempt" yourself from these practices. No one will question you and everyone wants to please you as their boss, *right*? You need to refrain from acting in this fashion. You should hold yourself accountable and set the example in following the security practices that you have probably approved in the first place. Dave Dalva, vice president at Stroz Friedberg, explains, "Security doesn't have to be an impediment to getting things done. It can enhance productivity at the same time as providing data protection" (Violino, 2016).

It may be hard to balance budgets in ever-changing environments, but security is important and must be given the appropriate priority. Technology changes very fast and new threats emerge daily. You must partner with security experts to manage these risks and determine what solutions will make the biggest impact on improving your overall security posture. You not only need to invest in technology, but also need to invest in people. The security industry is in desperate need of experts and the demand far outpaces the supply. These qualified individuals can demand higher compensation, but in many organizations the budgets for these security personnel are far under market levels. In turn, organizations that don't get adequate personnel to do the work or the jobs go unfilled cause other staff to get overworked, and eventually they will get burned out.

Successful CEOs understand all of the different factors at work. They provide the necessary support, both in finances and resources, to improve their security maturity levels. They get involved in making decisions and accept the responsibility that comes with these decisions. They take ownership over managing risks and lead by example. Finally, they never stop learning and accept the reality that security is important.

Message to the Legislators

Unfortunately, appropriate legislation around cybersecurity and privacy is behind technological advancements. Legislators are always playing "catch up" and the current laws are sometimes outdated by the time they get enacted. Enforcement of the laws may be hindered by the availability of resources to police the "Internet streets," and law enforcement may be ill equipped to take actions due to the lack of awareness, tools, or expertise to bring violators to justice. Although the intent of the laws may be straight forward, the regulations themselves may be complicated. Since the cybersecurity space that the laws apply to is fairly new, there may not be a lot of judicial backing or case law set causing more confusion as legislative intent and legal standing get "ironed out" in courts. With different political forces and pressures in play along with different interpretations from the bench in these matters, it doesn't take long for anyone to determine that we have a real mess on our hands.

Take for instance the discussion we've had on breach notifications. The intent of legislation is pretty easy; your information gets breached, you notify, *right*? Unfortunately, there are federal mandates that cover certain types of information and then, there are state laws that either make notification around breaches more stringent, such as notifying within a certain amount of time, or differing definition of terms, such as what information that was breached constitutes making a notification. Since most companies today provide services across state lines, they are now required to meet requirements of different states. As for this example, according to the Attorney General of California, "State policy makers should collaborate in seeking to harmonize state breach laws on some key dimensions. Such an effort could preserve innovation, maintain consumer protections, and retain jurisdictional expertise" (California's Attorney General, 2016).

Writing legislation over cybersecurity and privacy is no easy task. It takes a complete understanding of the environment along with input from key stakeholders and constituents at every level. Terms of the legislation need to be well defined and the intent of the law needs to be easily understood. It needs to stand up to judicial review and be relevant to the current state of affairs. As a legislator, you should seek out subject matter experts when drafting these types of bills. When it comes to technology, there could be a lot of nuances to consider that can make legislation unenforceable or ineffective to meet the intended needs.

You should never forget that you work for and at the will of the people. You have also sworn an oath to uphold and defend the Constitution of the United States. Although the Constitution may not specifically call out *Privacy*, our founding fathers knew that it was one of the most basic fundamental rights of a free society and didn't require further justification. Although there may be some that freely give away personal information about themselves to anyone that will listen, there still is a large majority of individuals that place a high value on privacy. We don't want the world to know what we are thinking or doing, and we sure don't want government to interfere in our personal lives. As an employee, *would it be right for you to keep tabs on your boss and track every action he or she takes throughout the day?* If you aren't getting paid specifically to keep tabs or it wasn't your job to do this, then the answer should be "No." Since the *people* are your boss, likewise, it isn't your place to keep track of us. If I'm not doing anything that will harm someone or is illegal, then frankly, it is none of your business what I say or do. I should be free to pursue my own happiness.

I'm a realist and as a former law enforcement officer, I understand the need to have certain laws in place to protect citizens. I know there are some bad people out there that want to do bad things, so I'm not opposed in taking actions in an attempt to prevent and/or bring individuals to justice for their actions. There has to be balance set between privacy and actions taken, for whatever reason, that does not violate this privacy. In addition, when this privacy is violated, individuals need the right to take a private cause of action to restore the balance. Government, especially, should not be implementing any laws that they, themselves, are not willing to comply with. As a legislator, it is your primary job to write laws; however, you should never feel that you are above abiding by these laws.

Message to Private Citizens

If you've lost confidence in companies and governments to do the "right thing" with your personal information along with keeping it private and secure online, you aren't alone. A survey conducted by the Centre for International Governance Innovation (CIGI) that included 24,143 Internet users from twenty-four (24) countries (to include the United States, United Kingdom, and Australia) between November 20, 2015 and December 4, 2015, "reveals that 83 percent of people around the world believe that there is a need for new rules about how companies and governments use personal data" (Ngo, 2016). A majority of people believe their Internet activity is being monitored and in some form or fashion censored. Even though concern over privacy rose, "only about a third believed that their own government is doing enough to keep their personal information safe from private companies, and vice versa" (Ngo, 2016).

One of the problems, however, is that there are many definitions of being private and what privacy means to different individuals. There is not a universally accepted definition of "privacy" and you will probably get many different answers if you ask someone, *"What is privacy?"* This was actually the basis of a photo series report by Ann Hermes conducted at South by Southwest Interactive, an annual film, interactive media, and music festival and conference held in Austin, TX. The full report can be found here at http://passcode.csmonitor.com/

definingprivacy, but some of the more general consensus around what privacy means are paraphrased here:

- Having control and being able to make decisions over your own information and your life.
- Being aware of what information about you is being shared and what effect it has on others.
- Having a safe and secure place to share thoughts, ideas, and discuss issues.
- Being fair and ensuring your information isn't used to harm you or discriminate against you for things you've done in the past.
- Privacy means everything; it is you, your identity, and how the world interprets or sees you; it should be respected.
- Privacy is something taken for granted, and some ask *whether or not we really have privacy in the age of technology?*

Ask yourself, *what does privacy mean to you?* Privacy can quickly get very complicated to explain and there can be multiple different levels along with perspectives that shape your own definition of privacy. *Are you willing to give up a little bit of your personal information for certain services or products? What value do you place on your private information? How much is privacy worth to you? What is going to happen to the information that you give out or how is this information going to be utilized?*

These and many other questions should be answered before you give out your personal information. Once your information is out, it is very hard to get it back. Each individual will have their own tolerance or acceptable level of privacy, that is, what information they are willing to share with others. You should ask yourself, *why is this company asking you to supply them with this information? Does the company really need this personal information such as your date of birth, Social Security number, or other private information to provide you the service or product?* If you don't feel comfortable giving this information, then don't. Put the company on task to explain to you *why they need it, what they are going to do with it, how is it going to be protected, and what rights you maintain over the information you share with them?*

This is especially true when you go to your doctor's office. Out of any industry that I'm aware of, you give more personal and private information to your doctor. Your medical service provider is required to give you a Notice of Privacy Practices. This notice details exactly what the provider is going to do with your information. If there is something you don't understand within the notice, you should ask your provider to explain it to you. You should feel comfortable about sharing the requested information and if you don't, then you should raise concern over it. If your concerns are not satisfied, you have the right not to share this information or request restrictions on the information you provide. Although there may be some consequences for not sharing certain information, you should understand what this might be and you should be allowed to make an educated decision on whether or not to share your personal information.

As an individual, you need to take control over your private information. You need to invoke your rights over privacy and put companies on notice that violating these rights will not be tolerated. The more individuals put companies on notice, the more these companies will bend to the will of their customers. Individuals must also remind the government that your information is private. Elected officials work at the will of the electorates. You should vote for individuals that will protect your rights, not those that are willing to pander to special interest groups or large corporations. As an individual, you can make a difference.

Throughout this book, I provided a lot of recommendations, guidance, and resources that can be utilized to protect yourself, your private information, and to assist you in recovering from events beyond your control. My last words of advice to you: *Be safe, private, and secure in all that you do.*

Final Thoughts

As I completed writing this book, I came to the realization that privacy is more important than security because, without the ability to be private in your own personal affairs, you are no longer secure. When businesses, the government, or even other people know *everything* about you—your actions, your thoughts, your feelings, your likes, your dislikes—you become a target. You can be manipulated and controlled. As I mentioned in the beginning of this book, it is all about gaining knowledge, which leads to obtaining power.

This is the power to control individuals, groups, governments, countries, and the world. You need to have both privacy and security to feel safe in this world along with taking back control of your life. Don't give into undue pressures since there is still a chance for privacy to survive.

References

201 CMR 17.00: Standards for the protection of personal information of residents of the commonwealth. (2016, February 21). Retrieved from Massachusetts Laws: http://www.mass.gov/ocabr/docs/idtheft/201cmr1700reg.pdf.

Abelson, M. G. (2016, February 02). Up to 1.1 million customers could be affected in data breach at Insurer CareFirst. Retrieved from *The New York Times*: http://www.nytimes.com/2015/05/21/business/carefirst-discloses-data-breach-up-to-1-1-million-customers-affected.html?_r=0.

AHIMA Staff. (2016, March 29). Survey: Patient matching problems routine in healthcare. Retrieved from *Journal of AHIMA*: http://journal.ahima.org/2016/01/06/survey-patient-matching-problems-routine-in-healthcare/.

American Medical Association. (2016, March 11). AMA launches Silicon Valley Integrated Innovation Company, Health2047. Retrieved from AMA Press Release: http://www.ama-assn.org/ama/pub/news/news/2016/2016-01-11-ama-launches-health2047.page.

American Telemedicine Association. (2016, January 28). What is telemedicine? Retrieved from American Telemedicine Association: http://www.americantelemed.org/about-telemedicine/what-is-telemedicine#.Vqo2xctIiRE.

Austin, J. (2016, January 28). 'I HACKED International Space Station' claims expert who said he could steer planes. Retrieved from Express: http://www.express.co.uk/news/nature/579295/I-HACKED-International-Space-Station-expert-said-could-steer-planes.

Bagnall, K. (2016, March 31). Teach someone to spot a phish and you'll secure them for a lifetime, advises Email Laundry's Bagnall. Retrieved from TechCentral.ie: http://www.techcentral.ie/teach-someone-to-spot-a-phish-and-youll-secure-them-for-a-lifetime-advises-email-laundrys-bagnall/.

Balkan, A. (2016, January 28). The Camera Panopticon. Retrieved from Ind.ie: https://ind.ie/the-camera-panopticon/.

Balko, R. (2016, March 13). Surprise! NSA data will soon routinely be used for domestic policing that has nothing to do with terrorism. Retrieved from *The Washington Post*: https://www.washingtonpost.com/news/the-watch/wp/2016/03/10/surprise-nsa-data-will-soon-routinely-be-used-for-domestic-policing-that-has-nothing-to-do-with-terrorism/.

Barth, B. (2016, April 21). Federal court bucks trend, rules general liability insurance covers data breach. Retrieved from *SC Magazine*: http://www.scmagazine.com/federal-court-bucks-trend-rules-general-liability-insurance-covers-data-breach/article/489320/.

Barwick, H. (2016, February 13). Report reveals scale of health record data breaches. *Computerworld*: http://www.computerworld.com.au/article/592148/report-reveals-scale-health-record-data-breaches/.

Baum, S. (2016, February 02). Is ProPublica's HIPAA violation search engine going to undermine confidence or create savvier patients? Retrieved from *MedCity News*: http://medcitynews.com/2015/12/patient-privacy/?utm_content=bufferbbe15&utm_medium=social&utm_source=linkedin.com&utm_campaign=buffer&rf=1.

BBC. (2016, May 09). Man jailed for failing to decrypt hard drives. Retrieved from *BBC News*: http://www.bbc.com/news/technology-36159146.

Bernie 2016, Inc. (2016, March 23). Bernie 2016 vs. DNC compliant. Retrieved from BernieSanders.com: https://berniesanders.com/wp-content/uploads/2015/12/Bernie2016vDNCComplaint.pdf.

Blue Coat. (2016, February 12). 1 in 10 broadly shared files in Cloud apps expose sensitive and regulated data, reveals new Elastica Cloud threat labs report from Blue Coat. Retrieved from Blue Coat: https://www.bluecoat.com/company/press-releases/1-10-broadly-shared-files-cloud-apps-expose-sensitive-and-regulated-data.

Brown, L. (2016, February 02). Lessons learned? A look back at five cybersecurity trends of 2015. Retrieved from *SC Magazine UK*: http://www.scmagazineuk.com/lessons-learned-a-look-back-at-five-cyber-security-trends-of-2015/article/461033/.

Brumfield, J. (2016, January 31). 90% of industries have patient data breaches, says Verizon 2015 Protected Health Information Data Breach Report. Retrieved from Verizon: http://news.verizonenterprise.com/2015/12/2015-protected-health-information-report/.

Burrus, D. (2016a, January 22). How fitness tracking could transform your healthcare. Retrieved from Daniel Burrus—LinkedIn: https://www.linkedin.com/pulse/how-fitness-tracking-could-transform-your-healthcare-daniel-burrus?trk=hp-feed-article-title-like.

Burrus, D. (2016b, January 21). The Internet of things is far bigger than anyone realizes. Retrieved from *Wired*: http://www.wired.com/insights/2014/11/the-internet-of-things-bigger/.

California Constitution—Cons. (2016, February 20). Article I Declaration of Rights [Section 1—Sec. 31]. Retrieved from California Legislative Information: http://leginfo.legislature.ca.gov/faces/codes_displaySection.xhtml?lawCode=CONS&sectionNum=SECTION%201.&article=I.

California Legislature. (2016, February 21). Civil Code Part 2.6 Confidentiality of Medical Information [56-56.37]. Retrieved from California Legislative Information: http://leginfo.legislature.ca.gov/faces/codes_displayText.xhtml?lawCode=CIV&division=1.&title=&part=2.6.&chapter=7.&article.

California Senate. (2016, February 20). SB-178 Privacy: Electronic communications: Search warrant. Retrieved from California Legislative Information: https://leginfo.legislature.ca.gov/faces/billNavClient.xhtml?bill_id=201520160SB178.

California's Attorney General. (2016, March 02). California data breach report February 2016. Retrieved from Office of Attorney General: https://oag.ca.gov/breachreport2016.

Carroll Publishing. (2016, April 13). Thomas Donilon appointed chairman, White House Commission on Enhancing National Cybersecurity. Retrieved from Carroll Publishing: https://www.carrollpublishing.com/whoentry.aspx?entry_number=121447.

Castelli, C. J. (2016, January 30). Researcher: DARPA effort will rate cybersecurity of software for public. Retrieved from Inside Cybersecurity: http://insidecybersecurity.com/share/3776.

CBS47 Fox30 Action News. (2016, February 09). Fitness trackers can be used against you in a court of law. Retrieved from *CBS47 Fox30 Action News*: http://www.actionnewsjax.com/news/fitness-trackers-can-be-used-against-you-in-a-court-of-law/66453302.

Chabrow, E. (2016a, April 15). House Panel OK's Email Privacy Act. Retrieved from CU Info Security: http://www.cuinfosecurity.com/house-panel-oks-email-privacy-act-a-9043.

Chabrow, E. (2016b, April 04). Ransomware: Attacks against government agencies widespread. Retrieved from GovInfo Security: http://www.govinfosecurity.com/ransomware-attacks-against-government-agencies-widespread-a-9005.

Chang, L. (2016, April 15). The U.S. Government is worse at cybersecurity than just about everyone else. Retrieved from Digital Trends: http://www.digitaltrends.com/computing/us-cybersecurity/?utm_source=socialm&utm_medium=twitter.

Chickowski, E. (2016a, April 21). Insurers getting smarter about assessing cyber insurance policy risks. Retrieved from Dark Reading: http://www.darkreading.com/analytics/insurers-getting-smarter-about-assessing-cyber-insurance-policy-risks/d/d-id/1324048.

Chickowski, E. (2016b, February 07). Post-breach costs and impact can last years. Retrieved from Dark Reading: http://www.darkreading.com/risk/post-breach-costs-and-impact-can-last-years/d/d-id/1324055.

Chickowski, E. (2016c, January 29). Schneier: Make wide-scale surveillance too expensive. Retrieved from Schneier on Security: https://www.schneier.com/news/archives/2013/11/schneier_make_wide-s.html.

CHIME. (2016, March 16). Letter to chair and ranking member of HELP Committee. Retrieved from Health IT Security: http://healthitsecurity.com/images/site/attachments/chimesenatehelpcomments.pdf.

Chou, D. (2016, March 12). The Amazon Echo—Bringing sci fi reality to healthcare. Retrieved from Hospital EMR and EHR: http://www.hospitalemrandehr.com/2016/02/16/the-amazon-echo-bringing-sci-fi-reality-to-healthcare/.

Chris Wixon, M. (2016, January 23). LinkedIn post. Retrieved from Electronic Health Record: Part 2: https://www.linkedin.com/pulse/electronic-health-record-part-2-chris-wixon-md.

Christensen, J. (2016, May 29). Medical errors may be third leading cause of death in the U.S. Retrieved from CNN: http://www.cnn.com/2016/05/03/health/medical-error-a-leading-cause-of-death/.

Claiming Human Rights. (2016, January 29). The Universal Declaration of Human Rights. Retrieved from Claiming Human Rights: http://www.claiminghumanrights.org/udhr_article_12.html.

Clarke, E. (2016, January 31). Hackers sell health insurance credentials, bank accounts, SSNs and counterfeit documents, for over $1,000 per Dossier. Retrieved from Dell SecureWorks: http://www.secureworks.com/resources/blog/general-hackers-sell-health-insurance-credentials-bank-accounts-ssns-and-counterfeit-documents/.

CMS. (2016, January 24). Data and program reports. Retrieved from CMS: https://www.cms.gov/Regulations-and-guidance/legislation/EHRIncentivePrograms/DataAndReports.html.

Cobb, S. (2016a, March 22). Healthcare data breaches lead patients to withhold information from doctors. Retrieved from We Live Security: http://www.welivesecurity.com/2016/02/18/security-privacy-patients-withholding/.

Cobb, S. (2016b, January 21). What does Fitbit hacking mean for wearables and IoT. Retrieved from We Live Security: http://www.welivesecurity.com/2016/01/12/fitbit-hacking-mean-wearables-iot/.

Collins, S. R. (2016, March 17). S. 2410. Retrieved from Congress: https://www.congress.gov/bill/114th-congress/senate-bill/2410/text.

Connecticut Supreme Court. (2016, March 16). *Emily Byrne v. Avery Center for Obstetrics and Gynecology, P.C.* Retrieved from State of Connecticut Judicial Branch: https://www.jud.ct.gov/external/supapp/Cases/AROcr/CR314/314CR78.pdf.

Cook, T. (2016, February 17). A message to our customers. Retrieved from Apple: http://www.apple.com/customer-letter/.

Creative Commons. (2016, January 29). Attribution 4.0 International (CC BY 4.0). Retrieved from Creative Commons: http://creativecommons.org/licenses/by/4.0/.

CSO Staff. (2016, February 12). CSO Online's 2016 data breach blotter. Retrieved from CSO Online: http://www.csoonline.com/article/3030735/security/cso-onlines-2016-data-breach-blotter.html?token=%23tk.CSONLE_nlt_cso_update_2016-02-11&idg_eid=6df4639b7a08b879102fa300fe06eea8&utm_source=Sailthru&utm_medium=email&utm_campaign=CSO%20Update%202016-02-11&u.

Data Protection—Consumer Groups. (2016, March 11). Broadband privacy letter to FCC January 20, 2016. Retrieved from *The Hill*: http://thehill.com/sites/default/files/broadband_privacy_letter_to_fcc_1.20.16_final.pdf.

Davis, J. (2016a, May 14). AHIMA: Patient matching problems plague healthcare, pose safety risk. Retrieved from Healthcare IT News: http://www.healthcareitnews.com/news/ahima-patient-matching-problems-plague-healthcare-pose-safety-risk.

Davis, J. (2016b, February 02). Despite breaches, patients trust healthcare with info, study tied to Data Privacy Day claims. Retrieved from Healthcare IT News: http://www.healthcareitnews.com/news/despite-breaches-patients-trust-healthcare-info-study-tied-data-privacy-day-claims.

Davis, J. (2016c, January 24). Patients struggle with sharing health information online, cite privacy concerns, breaches, Pew report says. Retrieved from Healthcare IT News: http://www.healthcareitnews.com/news/patients-struggle-sharing-health-information-online-cite-privacy-concerns-breaches-pew-report.

Davis Wright Tremaine LLP. (2016, April 14). Complaint for declaratory judgment. Retrieved from Davis Wright Tremaine LLP: https://assets.documentcloud.org/documents/2803275/Microsoft-challenges-constitutionality-of-gag.pdf.

Department of Health and Human Services. (2013). *Modifications to the HIPAA Privacy, Security, Enforcement, and Breach Notification Rules under the Health Information Technology for Economic and Clinical Health Act and the Genetic Information Nondiscrimination Act; Other Modifications to the HIPAA Rules.* Washington, DC: Department of Health and Human Services.

Department of Health and Human Services. (2016, February 09). Opioids: The prescription drug & heroin overdose epidemic. Retrieved from HHS.gov: http://www.hhs.gov/opioids/.

Department of Homeland Security. (2016, February 06). National Cybersecurity Protection System (NCPS). Retrieved from Homeland Security: http://www.dhs.gov/national-cybersecurity-protection-system-ncps.

Department of Justice. (2016, February 07). Identity theft. Retrieved from Department of Justice: http://www.justice.gov/criminal-fraud/identity-theft/identity-theft-and-identity-fraud.

Desalvo, A. S. (2016, January 30). EHR incentive programs: Where we go next. Retrieved from The CMS Blog: http://blog.cms.gov/2016/01/19/ehr-incentive-programs-where-we-go-next/.

Dhand, D. S. (2016, February 09). Health care is about relationships. Health IT fails to understand that. Retrieved from MedPageToday's KevinMD.com: http://www.kevinmd.com/blog/2016/01/health-care-relationships-health-fails-understand.html.

Dimick, C. (2016, February 16). Californian sentenced to prison for HIPAA violation. Retrieved from *Journal of AHIMA*: http://journal.ahima.org/2010/04/29/californian-sentenced-to-prison-for-hipaa-violation/.

Dräger. (2016, February 11). Technology for life. Retrieved from Dräger: http://www.draeger.com/sites/en_corp/Pages/about-draeger/technology-for-life.aspx.

Drinkwater, D. (2016, February 03). Does a data breach really affect your firm's reputation. Retrieved from Network World: http://www.networkworld.com/article/3019930/security/does-a-data-breach-really-affect-your-firm-s-reputation.html?token=%23tk.NWWNLE_nlt_networkworld_daily_news_alert_2016-01-07&idg_eid=8e883ce00dd91cc3ac7d464b86019bdf&utm_source=Sailthru&utm_medium=email.

Eckerson, O. L. (2016, March 06). Data breach lawsuits indicate a trouble trend for enterprises. Retrieved from Tech Target: http://searchsecurity. techtarget.com/news/4500273340/Data-breach-lawsuits-indicate-a-troubling-trend-for-enterprises.

EHNAC. (2016a, April 14). EHNAC accreditation programs. Retrieved from EHNAC Comprehensive Presentation: http://www.ehnac.org/ wp-content/uploads/2013/07/EHNAC-Comprehensive-040615.pdf.

EHNAC. (2016b, April 14). EHNAC and NH-ISAC align cybersecurity prevention efforts for healthcare. Retrieved from Nasdaq GlobeNewswire: http://globenewswire.com/news-release/2016/01/26/804668/0/en/ EHNAC-and-NH-ISAC-Align-Cybersecurity-Prevention-Efforts-for-Healthcare.html.

EHNAC. (2016c, April 14). EHNAC overview. Retrieved from EHNAC: https://www.ehnac.org/about/.

EHNAC. (2016d, April 14). Why companies pursue EHNAC accreditation. Retrieved from EHNAC Comprehensive Presentation: http://www. ehnac.org/wp-content/uploads/2013/07/EHNAC-Comprehensive-040615.pdf.

Electronic Health Records (EHR) Incentive Programs. (2016, January 24). Retrieved from Centers for Medicare & Medicaid Services: https://www.cms.gov/Regulations-and-Guidance/Legislation/ EHRIncentivePrograms/index.html?redirect=/EHRIncentivePrograms/ 01_Overview.asp.

Electronic Privacy Information Center. (2016, March 22). Privacy platform. Retrieved from Data Protection 2016: http://dataprotection2016.org/.

Elias, D. P. (2016, February 09). Medical stories and anecdotes: Memo to my successor. Retrieved from PeterEliasMD.com: http://petereliasmd.com/ index.php?module=news&type=user&func=display&sid=49.

Energy & Commerce Committee. (2016, January 24). 21st Century cures: What you need to know. Retrieved from Energy & Commerce Committee: http://energycommerce.house.gov/cures.

Esguerra, R. (2016, January 29). Google CEO Eric Schmidt dismisses the importance of privacy. Retrieved from Electronic Frontier Foundation: https://www.eff.org/deeplinks/2009/12/google-ceo-eric-schmidt-dismisses-privacy.

European Commission. (2016, February 04). EU Commission and United States agrees on a new framework for transatlantic data flows: EU-US Privacy Shield. Retrieved from European Commission: http://europa. eu/rapid/press-release_IP-16-216_en.htm.

explorys. (2016, January 22). Data is power in the New Healthcare Economy. Retrieved from explorys An IBM Company: https://www.explorys.com/.

FACT SHEET: Cybersecurity National Action Plan. (2016, April 13). Retrieved from The White House: https://www.whitehouse.gov/the-press-office/2016/02/09/fact-sheet-cybersecurity-national-action-plan.

FBI. (2016a, April 08). Exhibit 300: Capital asset summary. Retrieved from IT Dashboard—Investment: https://it-2013.itdashboard.gov/ investment/exhibit300/pdf/011-000003457.

FBI. (2016b, April 04). Ransomware on the rise. Retrieved from The Federal Bureau of Investigation: https://www.fbi.gov/news/podcasts/thisweek/ransomware-on-the-rise.mp3/view.

FCC and FTC. (2016, March 11). FCC-FTC consumer protection memorandum of understanding. Retrieved from FTC: https://www.ftc.gov/system/files/documents/cooperation_agreements/151116ftcfcc-mou.pdf.

FDA. (2016, January 25). FDA outlines cybersecurity recommendations for medical device manufacturers. Retrieved from FDA News Release: http://www.fda.gov/NewsEvents/Newsroom/PressAnnouncements/ucm481968.htm.

Federal Bureau of Investigations. (2016, January 31). Privacy Industry Notification (PIN#:140408-009). Retrieved from FBI: http://www.illuminweb.com/wp-content/uploads/ill-mo-uploads/103/2418/health-systems-cyber-intrusions.pdf.

Federal Communications Commission. (2016, May 27). Wireless phones and the national do-not-call list. Retrieved from FCC: https://www.fcc.gov/consumers/guides/wireless-phones-and-national-do-not-call-list.

Federal Trade Commission. (2016, March 05). Privacy & data security update (2015). Retrieved from Federal Trace Commission: https://www.ftc.gov/reports/privacy-data-security-update-2015.

Finkle, C. H. (2016, January 31). Your medical record is worth more to hackers than your credit card. Retrieved from Reuters: http://www.reuters.com/article/us-cybersecurity-hospitals-idUSKCN0HJ21I20140924.

FirstData. (2016, April 18). Small businesses: The cost of a data breach is higher than you think. Retrieved from FirstData: https://www.firstdata.com/downloads/thought-leadership/Small_Businesses_Cost_of_a_Data_Breach_Article.pdf.

Fitbit. (2016, January 21). *About Fitbit*. Retrieved from Fitbit: https://www.fitbit.com/about.

Fox-Brester, T. (2016, February 17). 300,000 American homes open to hacks of "unfixable" SimpliSafe alarm. Retrieved from *Forbes*: http://www.forbes.com/sites/thomasbrewster/2016/02/17/simplisafe-alarm-attacks/#3a97c62579a3.

Gardner, A. (2016, May 29). Surgery mix-ups surprisingly common. Retrieved from CNN: http://www.cnn.com/2010/HEALTH/10/18/health.surgery.mixups.common/.

Gellman, P. D. (2016, January 31). The scoring of America: How secret consumer scores threaten your privacy and your future. Retrieved from *World Privacy Forum*: http://www.worldprivacyforum.org/wp-content/uploads/2014/04/WPF_Scoring_of_America_April2014_fs.pdf.

German, P. (2016, March 28). Security breaches are inevitable, so how are you going to contain them? Retrieved from Information Security Buzz: http://www.informationsecuritybuzz.com/articles/security-breaches-are-inevitable-so-how-are-you-going-to-contain-them/.

Gill, T. (2016, February 13). 2016's top information security threats. Retrieved from ContinuityCentral.com: http://www.continuitycentral.com/index.php/news/technology/729-2016-s-top-information-security-threats.

Goldberg, R. (2016, May 16). Lack of trust in Internet privacy and security may deter economic and other online activities. Retrieved from U.S. Department of Commerce National Telecommunications & Information Administration: https://www.ntia.doc.gov/blog/2016/lack-trust-internet-privacy-and-security-may-deter-economic-and-other-online-activities.

Goldman, J. (2016, February 12). Over 113 million patient records were breached in 2015. Retrieved from eSecurity Planet: http://www.esecurityplanet.com/network-security/over-113-million-patient-records-were-breached-in-2015.html.

Goodin, D. (2016, February 03). Security firm sued for filing "woefully inadequate" forensics report. Retrieved from Ars Technica: http://arstechnica.com/security/2016/01/security-firm-sued-for-filing-woefully-inadequate-forensics-report/.

Google. (2016, January 29). Definition of doublethink. Retrieved from Google: https://www.google.com/#q=definition+of+double-think.

Gottlieb, D. F., Higgins, R. S., and Zacharias, E. G. (2016, March 16). OCR launches phase 2 HIPAA audit program with pre-audit screening surveys. Retrieved from McDermott Will & Emery: http://www.mwe.com/ocr-launches-phase-2-hipaa-audit-program-with-pre-audit-screening-surveys-05-18-2015/.

Groups, A. (2016, January 30). Broad coalition urges support for H.R. 4350, bipartisan legislation to repeal harmful cybersecurity provisions. Retrieved from RStreet: http://www.rstreet.org/wp-content/uploads/2016/01/Amash-letter-1_25.pdf.

Grove, T. (2016, March 29). Can a national patient identifier solve interoperability challenges? Retrieved from HIT Consultant: http://hitconsultant.net/2016/02/08/31764/.

Gruenfeld, L. (2016, February 09). The Internet of bad things: Why security will make or break the IoT. Retrieved from Support.com: http://www.support.com/the-internet-of-bad-things-why-security-will-make-or-break-the-iot/.

Gunderman, R. (2016, May 29). The drawbacks of data-driven medicine. Retrieved from *The Atlantic*: http://www.theatlantic.com/health/archive/2013/06/the-drawbacks-of-data-driven-medicine/276558/.

Gur-Arie, M. (2016, March 11). Meaningful use is dead. Long live something better! Retrieved from The Health Care Blog: http://thehealthcareblog.com/blog/2016/01/13/meaningful-use-is-dead-long-live-something-better/.

Hall, K. (2016a, May 14). Cybersecurity is slowing down my business, say majority of chief execs. Retrieved from The Register: http://www.theregister.co.uk/2016/02/17/cyber_security/.

Hall, S. B. (2016b, January 26). OIG cites security flaws in massive federal health insurance database. Retrieved from FierceHealthPayer: http://www.fiercehealthpayer.com/story/oig-cites-security-flaws-massive-federal-health-insurance-database/2015-09-25.

Hartzog, W. (2015, November 1). The scope and potential of FTC data protection (November 1, 2015). *83 George Washington Law Review* 83(6), 2230–2300.

Hautala, L. (2016, March 05). D'oh! FTC reveals attendees' email addresses before privacy conference. Retrieved from CNET: http://www.cnet.com/news/doh-ftc-reveals-attendees-email-addresses-before-privacy-conference/.

Health and Human Services. (2016a, March 24). Individuals' Right under HIPAA to Access their Health Information 45 CFR § 164.524. Retrieved from HHS: http://www.hhs.gov/hipaa/for-professionals/privacy/guidance/access/index.html.

Health and Human Services. (2016b, March 19). Statement of organization, functions, and delegations of authority; Office of the National Coordinator for Health Information Technology. Retrieved from *Federal Register*: https://www.federalregister.gov/articles/2014/06/03/2014-12981/statement-of-organization-functions-and-delegations-of-authority-office-of-the-national-coordinator.

Health2047. (2016, March 11). About. Retrieved from Health2047: https://www.health2047.com/about/.

HealthCatalyst. (2016, January 22). Healthcare analytics adoption model. Retrieved from HealthCatalyst: https://www.healthcatalyst.com/healthcare-analytics-adoption-model/.

HealthIT.gov. (2016, January 24). Meaningful use definition & objectives. Retrieved from HealthIT.gov: https://www.healthit.gov/providers-professionals/meaningful-use-definition-objectives.

Heath, S. (2016a, March 17). $7.5M healthcare data breach settlement for St. Joseph Health. Retrieved from Health IT Security: http://healthitsecurity.com/news/7.5m-healthcare-data-breach-settlement-for-st.-joseph-health.

Heath, S. (2016b, April 06). Too few organizations implement data encryption, survey says. Retrieved from Health IT Security: http://healthitsecurity.com/news/too-few-organizations-implement-data-encryption-survey-says.

HHS. (2016a, February 18). Administrative Law Judge rules in favor of OCR enforcement, requiring Lincare, Inc. to pay $239,800. Retrieved from HHS: http://www.hhs.gov/about/news/2016/02/03/administrative-law-judge-rules-favor-ocr-enforcement-requiring-lincare-inc-pay-penalties.html.

HHS. (2016b, February 14). Civil money penalty—Cignet health fined a $4.3M civil money penalty for HIPAA privacy rule violations. Retrieved from HHS: http://www.hhs.gov/hipaa/for-professionals/compliance-enforcement/examples/cignet-health/.

HHS Press Office. (2016, April 11). Triple-S Management Corporation settles HHS charges by agreeing to $3.5 million HIPAA settlement. Retrieved from HHS: http://www.hhs.gov/about/news/2015/11/30/triple-s-management-corporation-settles-hhs-charges.html#.

Higgins, K. J. (2016a, January 22). Employee data more exposed than customer data. Retrieved from Dark Reading: http://www.darkreading.com/endpoint/employee-data-more-exposed-than-customer-data/d/d-id/1323971.

Higgins, K. J. (2016b, February 13). Former director of NSA and CIA says US Cybersecurity Policy MIA. Retrieved from InformationWeek DarkReading: http://www.darkreading.com/attacks-breaches/former-director-of-nsa-and-cia-says-us-cybersecurity-policy-mia/d/d-id/1323888.

Hiser, D. C. (2016, February 14). HIPAA Compliance: Another year older, but hopefully not deeper in debt. Retrieved from Lexology: http://www.lexology.com/library/detail.aspx?g=929b0b7a-a5a3-42b9-b38e-dadb3a100222.

HITRUST Alliance. (2016a, March 03). CSF Assurance Program adoption key to more effective third-party risk management in the healthcare industry. Retrieved from HITRUST Alliance—Press Release: https://hitrustalliance.net/csf-assurance-program-adoption-key-to-effective-third-party-risk-management/?utm_medium=email&utm_campaign=Healthcare%20Organizations%20Expanding%20the%20Use%20of%20the%20HITRUST%20CSF%20to%20Reduce%20Third-Party%20Risk&utm_con.

HITRUST Alliance. (2016b, March 03). HITRUST CSF. Retrieved from HITRUST Alliance: https://hitrustalliance.net/hitrust-csf/.

Homeland Security. (2016, April 08). e-Passports. Retrieved from Department of Homeland Security: https://www.dhs.gov/e-passports.

Hsleh, P. (2016, May 29). Can you trust what's in your electronic medical record? Retrieved from *Forbes*: http://www.forbes.com/sites/paulhsieh/2014/02/24/electronic-medical-record/#3e0185a14680.

Hulme, G. V. (2016, January 21). The CSO IoT survival guide. Retrieved from CSO Online: http://www.csoonline.com/article/3019876/internet-of-things/the-cso-iot-survival-guide.html.

HuntScanlon. (2016, February 26). Cyber 20. Retrieved from Hunt Scanlon: http://huntscanlon.com/cyber-20/.

I Am The Cavalry. (2016a, January 30). "I Am The Cavalry" proposes Hippocratic oath for connected medical devices. Retrieved from I Am The Cavalry: https://www.iamthecavalry.org/wp-content/uploads/2016/01/Hippocratic-oath-press-release.pdf.

I Am The Cavalry. (2016b, January 30). Executive summary. Retrieved from I Am The Cavalry: https://www.iamthecavalry.org/about/overview/.

Ind.ie. (2016, January 29). Ethical design manifesto. Retrieved from Ind.ie: https://ind.ie/ethical-design/.

Information and Privacy Commissioner of Ontario. (2016, January 21). The 7 foundational principles. Retrieved from Privacy by Design: https://www.ipc.on.ca/images/Resources/7foundationalprinciples.pdf.

Internet Society. (2016, January 21). Brief history of the Internet—Internet timeline. Retrieved from Internet Society: http://www.internetsociety.org/internet/what-internet/history-internet/brief-history-internet#Origins.

IPC. (2016, January 21). Introduction to PbD. Retrieved from IPC—Office of the Information and Privacy Commissioner/Ontario: https://www.ipc.on.ca/english/privacy/introduction-to-pbd/.

ISACA. (2016, February 26). 2016 Cybersecurity skills gap. Retrieved from ISACA: https://image-store.slidesharecdn.com/24134834-c566-405a-ba02-8262d40e71ec-large.jpeg.

IT Governance. (2016, February 04). The EU General Data Protection Regulation (GDPR). Retrieved from IT Governance: http://www.itgovernance.co.uk/data-protection-dpa-and-eu-data-protection-regulation.aspx.

ITV. (2016, February 12). Third of cyber crime victims are under 18. Retrieved from ITV: http://www.itv.com/news/west/2016-02-09/third-of-cyber-crime-victims-are-under-18/.

Jackson, K. (2016, March 30). What has NIST done for me lately? By @ Kevin_Jackson | @CloudExpo #Cloud. Retrieved from Linux Containers: http://linux.sys-con.com/node/3619282.

Jayanthi, A. (2016, February 01). 10 latest data breaches. Retrieved from Becker's Health IT & CIO Review: http://www.beckershospitalreview.com/healthcare-information-technology/9-latest-data-breaches-1-25-16.html.

Jeremy, C. and Storm, D. (2016, January 28). AHRQ telehealth report says more research needed in urgent care, pediatrics, maternal medicine, and ACO's. Retrieved from Healthcare Executives Network: http://healthcareexecutivesnetwork.org/ahrq-telehealth-report-says-more-research-needed-in-urgent-care-pediatrics-maternal-medicine-and-acos/.

Johnson, A. (2016, January 21). The Internet is now officially too big as IP addresses run out. Retrieved from *NBC News*: http://www.nbcnews.com/news/us-news/internet-now-officially-too-big-ip-addresses-run-out-n386081.

Judicial Watch. (2016, January 26). Judicial Watch: New HHS documents reveal security concerns, Healthcare.gov had no "Authorization to Operate". Retrieved from Judicial Watch: http://www.judicialwatch.org/press-room/press-releases/judicial-watch-new-hhs-documents-reveal-security-concerns-healthcare-gov-had-no-authorization-to-operate/.

Khandelwal, S. (2016, May 02). U.S. Supreme Court allows the FBI to hack any computer in the world. Retrieved from *The Hacker News*: http://thehackernews.com/2016/04/fbi-hacking-power.html.

Khimji, I. (2016, February 09). Cybercrim is now more profitable than the drug trade. Retrieved from Tripwire: The State of Security: http://www.tripwire.com/state-of-security/regulatory-compliance/pci/cybercrime-is-now-more-profitable-than-the-drug-trade/.

Kitten, T. (2016, April 04). Ransomware epidemic prompts FBI guidance. Retrieved from Data Breach Today: http://www.databreachtoday.com/ransomware-epidemic-prompts-fbi-guidance-a-9008.

Klein, M. (2016, April 11). HIMSS 13: HHS final ruling changes the rules & roles for HIPAA hosting. Retrieved from Online Tech: http://resource.onlinetech.com/himss-13-hhs-final-ruling-changes-the-rules-roles-for-hipaa-hosting/.

Knibbs, K. (2016, February 06). Disneyland's local police force caught secretly using powerful phone spying tools. Retrieved from Gizmodo: http://gizmodo.com/disneylands-local-police-force-caught-secretly-using-po-1755671568.

Knopf, B. (2016, February 26). Five Star Rating (J. Trinckes, Interviewer).

Koppel, R. (2016, May 15). What do we know about medical errors associated with electronic medical records? Retrieved from The Health Care Blog: http://thehealthcareblog.com/blog/2016/01/11/what-do-we-know-about-medical-errors-associated-with-electronic-medical-records/.

Korolov, M. (2016a, February 02). Healthcare firms three times more likely to see data breaches. Retrieved from CSO Online: http://www.csoonline.com/article/2985401/cyber-attacks-espionage/healthcare-firms-three-times-more-likely-to-see-data-breaches.html.

Korolov, M. (2016b, February 01). One out of every three Americans was affected by a healthcare record breach last year. Retrieved from InfoWorld: http://www.infoworld.com/article/3026846/security/over-113-million-health-records-breached-in-2015-up-10-fold-from-2014.html.

Kranzberg, D. M. (2016, January 29). Kranzberg's six laws of technology, a metaphor, and a story. Retrieved from The Frailest Thing: http://thefrailestthing.com/2011/08/25/kranzbergs-six-laws-of-technology-a-metaphor-and-a-story/.

Krebs, B. (2016a, February 02). 06 China to blame in Anthem hack. Retrieved from Krebs on Security: http://krebsonsecurity.com/2015/02/china-to-blame-in-anthem-hack/.

Krebs, B. (2016b, January 21). Account takeovers fueling "warranty fraud". Retrieved from KrebsonSecurity: https://krebsonsecurity.com/2016/01/account-takeovers-fueling-warranty-fraud/.

Krebs, B. (2016c, February 08). FTC: Tax fraud behind 47% spike in ID theft. Retrieved from Krebs on Security: http://krebsonsecurity.com/2016/01/ftc-tax-fraud-behind-47-spike-in-id-theft/.

Kurtin, O. (2016a, April 11). HIPAA business associate agreement best practices: Update 2016. Retrieved from JDSupra Business Advisor: http://www.jdsupra.com/legalnews/hipaa-business-associate-agreement-best-49072/.

Kurtin, O. D. (2016b, February 28). HIPAA business associate agreement best practices: Update 2016. Retrieved from JDSupra Business Advisor: http://www.jdsupra.com/legalnews/hipaa-business-associate-agreement-best-49072/.

Legal Information Institute. (2016, February 17). 28 US Code § 1651—Writs. Retrieved from Cornell University of Law School: https://www.law.cornell.edu/uscode/text/28/1651.

Levin, J. (2016, March 13). Florida Sheriff Grady Judd threatens to lock up Apple CEO Tim Cook. Retrieved from TOTPI: http://www.totpi.com/florida-sheriff-grady-judd-threatens-lock-apple-ceo-tim-cook/.

Leyden, J. (2016, January 21). Wi-Fi standard could make Internet of Things things even easier ... for hackers. Retrieved from The Register: http://www.theregister.co.uk/2016/01/07/wifi_standard_802_11_ah_internet_things/?mt=1452443782970.

Litchman, J. (2016, March 17). The false promise of HIPAA for healthcare cybersecurity. Retrieved from Health IT Security: http://healthitsecurity.com/news/the-false-promise-of-hipaa-for-healthcare-cybersecurity.

Love, D. (2016, January 21). Hackers love the Internet of things because security doesn't sell toasters. Retrieved from Inverse: https://www.inverse.com/article/10049-hackers-love-the-internet-of-things-because-security-doesn-t-sell-toasters?utm_content=28237067&utm_medium=social&utm_source=twitter.

Lynn, J. (2016a, January 22). Health IT in 2016: Waves of data on the horizon. Retrieved from Iron Mountain: http://blogs.ironmountain.com/2016/industry/healthcare-information-management/health-it-in-2016/#.VpafB1b6Ia8.linkedin.

Lynn, J. (2016b, February 03). Healthcare data breach Deja Vu... more like Groundhog Day. Retrieved from EMR & HIPAA: http://www.emrandhipaa.com/emr-and-hipaa/2016/01/27/healthcare-data-breach-deja-vu-more-like-groundhog-day/.

Lynn, J. (2016c, February 27). The biggest challenge in healthcare: Excuses. Retrieved from EMR & HIPAA: http://www.emrandhipaa.com/emr-and-hipaa/2016/01/29/the-biggest-challenge-in-healthcare-excuses/.

Mark, J. J. (2016, April 07). Cuneiform definition. Retrieved from *Ancient History Encyclopedia*: http://www.ancient.eu/cuneiform/.

Mark Graber, D. S. (2016, May 15). Electronic health record-related events in medical malpractice claims. Retrieved from *Journal of Patient Safety*: http://pdfs.journals.lww.com/journalpatientsafety/9000/00000/Electronic_Health_Record_Related_Events_in_Medical.99624.pdf?token=method|ExpireAbsolute;source|Journals;ttl|1463323186055;payload|mY8D3u1TCCsNvP5E421JYK6N6XICDamxByyYpaNzk7FKjTaa1Yz22MivkHZqjGP.

Martin, J. (2016, April 21). Spec's lawsuit raises questions on how insurance companies should handle data breaches. Retrieved from *Houston Business Journal*: http://www.bizjournals.com/houston/news/2016/02/26/specs-lawsuit-raises-questions-on-how-insurance.html?ana=lnk.

Massachusetts Legislature. (2016, February 21). The 189th General Court of The Commonwealth of Massachusetts. Retrieved from Chapter 214, Section 1B: https://malegislature.gov/Laws/GeneralLaws/PartIII/TitleI/Chapter214/Section1B.

McCarthy, J. (2016a, February 28). International Space Station teaches healthcare about telemedicine. Retrieved from Healthcare IT News: http://www.healthcareitnews.com/news/international-space-station-teaches-healthcare-about-telemedicine.

McCarthy, K. (2016b, April 14). You won't believe this, but... nothing useful found on Farook iPhone. Retrieved from The Register: http://www.theregister.co.uk/2016/04/14/nothing_useful_on_farook_iphone/?utm_source=twitterfeed&utm_medium=twitter.

McGee, M. K. (2016a, May 15). A jump start for a national patient ID? Retrieved from HealthcareInfoSecurity: http://www.healthcareinfosecurity.com/jump-start-for-national-patient-id-a-8813.

McGee, M. K. (2016b, March 13). Anthem breach: Lessons one year later. Retrieved from HealthcareInfoSecurity: http://www.healthcareinfosecurity.com/anthem-breach-lessons-one-year-later-a-8897.

McGee, M. K. (2016c, January 25). Ensuring EHRs are secure: A new approach. Retrieved from HealthcareInfoSecurity: http://www.healthcareinfosecurity.com/blogs/ensuring-ehrs-are-secure-new-approach-p-2040.

McGee, M. K. (2016d, March 19). More funding for HIPAA audits? Retrieved from HealthcareInfoSecurity: http://www.healthcareinfosecurity.com/more-funding-for-hipaa-audits-a-8862.

McGee, M. K. (2016e, February 16). Prison term in HIPAA violation case. Retrieved from InfoRisk Today: http://www.inforisktoday.com/prison-term-in-hipaa-violation-case-a-7938/op-1.

McGee, M. K. (2016f, January 25). Privacy downside to proposed HIPAA changes. Retrieved from HealthcareInfoSecurity: http://www.health careinfosecurity.com/interviews/privacy-downside-to-proposed-hipaa-changes-i-3057.

McGee, M. K. (2016g, March 29). Rules of cybersecurity changing for healthcare sector. Retrieved from HealthcareInfoSecurity: http://www. healthcareinfosecurity.com/blogs/rules-cybersecurity-changing-for-healthcare-sector-p-2073.

McGee, M. K. (2016h, February 16). Sentencing in S.C. Medicaid breach case. Retrieved from HealthcareInfoSecurity: http://www.healthcareinfosecurity. com/sentencing-in-sc-medicaid-breach-case-a-7546.

Medical Identity Fraud Alliance (MIFA). (2016, February 09). Our mission, goals and vision. Retrieved from MIFA: http://medidfraud.org/about/.

Medical Practice Compliance Alert. (2016, February 11). Several HIPAA compliance trends likely to affect medical practices in 2016. Retrieved from Fox Rothschild LLP: http://www.foxrothschild.com/news/several-hipaa-compliance-trends-likely-to-affect-medical-practices-in-2016/.

Menke, M. (2016, March 13). Why EHR vendors are next healthcare data breach target. Retrieved from Health IT Security: http://healthitsecurity. com/news/why-ehr-vendors-are-next-healthcare-data-breach-target.

Metzger, K. C. (2016, March 01). HIPAA privacy: New landscape for civil enforcement under HITECH. Retrieved from Ice Miller Strategies LLC: http://www.icemiller.com/ice-on-fire-insights/publications/hipaa-privacy-new-landscape-for-civil-enforcement/.

Miliard, M. (2016a, March 12). Cybersecurity pro: Networked medical devices pose huge risks to patient safety. Retrieved from Healthcare IT News: http://www.healthcareitnews.com/news/cybersecurity-pro-networked-medical-devices-pose-huge-risks-patient-safety.

Miliard, M. (2016b, February 11). FDA exec on cybersecurity: Hospitals, healthcare providers under constant attack. Retrieved from Healthcare IT News: http://www.healthcareitnews.com/news/fda-exec-cybersecurity-hospitals-healthcare-providers-under-constant-attack.

Mole, B. (2016, January 27). In a brain, dissolvable electronics monitor health and then vanish. Retrieved from arstechnica: http:// arstechnica.com/science/2016/01/in-a-brain-dissolvable-electronics-monitor-health-then-vanish/?utm_campaign=Abundance+Insider+1%2F 21&utm_source=abundance+insider&utm_medium=abundance+insider&utm_ content=Networks%2FSensors&utm_term=Networks%2FSensor.

Monegain, B. (2016, April 25). IT execs face security vulnerabilities amid talent shortages and tight budgets. Retrieved from Healthcare IT News: http://www.healthcareitnews.com/news/us-federal-it-execs-face-security-vulnerabilities-amid-talent-shortages-and-tight-budgets.

Morgan, S. (2016, February 27). Top five U.S. defense contractors bungle commercial cybersecurity market opportunity. Retrieved from CSO Online: http://www.csoonline.com/article/3027383/security/top-five-u-s-defense-contractors-bungle-commercial-cybersecurity-market-opportunity.html.

Ms. Smith. (2016, January 25). Healthcare IT execs fear loss of life due to hacked medical devices or networks. Retrieved from Network World: http://www.networkworld.com/article/3024794/security/healthcare-it-execs-fear-loss-of-life-due-to-hacked-medical-devices-or-networks.html.

Muncaster, P. (2016, February 06). Audit finds massive holes in US government's Einstein Security System. Retrieved from *Infosecurity Magazine*: http://www.infosecurity-magazine.com/news/massive-holes-in-us-governments.

Musil, S. (2016, March 15). Home Depot offers $19M to settle customers' hacking lawsuit. Retrieved from CNet: http://www.cnet.com/news/home-depot-offers-19m-to-settle-customers-hacking-lawsuit/.

National Partnership for Women & Families. (2016, March 16). Letter to chairman and ranking member of Senate HELP Committee. Retrieved from Health IT Security: http://healthitsecurity.com/images/site/attachments/npwfsenatehelpcomments.pdf.

Nevada State Constitutional Convention. (2016, February 22). The Constitution of the State of Nevada. Retrieved from State of Nevada Legislature: https://www.leg.state.nv.us/const/nvconst.html#Art1.

Nevada State Legislatures. (2016a, February 22). Assembly Bill Number 179. Retrieved from Legislation of the State of Nevada: https://www.leg.state.nv.us/Session/78th2015/Bills/AB/AB179_EN.pdf.

Nevada State Legislatures. (2016b, February 22). Chapter 603A—Security of personal information. Retrieved from State of Nevada Legislation: https://www.leg.state.nv.us/NRS/NRS-603A.html.

Ngo, D. (2016, April 23). Global trust in the Internet is in decline, survey says. Retrieved from C Net: http://www.cnet.com/news/global-trust-on-the-internet-is-in-decline-survey-says/.

O'Connor, F. (2016a, February 09). NSA: Hackers use persistence, not zero days, to breach companies. Retrieved from Cybereason: http://www.cybereason.com/nsa-hackers-use-persistence-not-zero-days-to-breach-companies/.

O'Connor, F. (2016b, February 13). Samsung: Our smart TVs aren't eavesdropping on your conversations. Retrieved from PCWorld: http://www.pcworld.com/article/2882676/samsung-our-smart-tvs-arent-eavesdropping-on-your-conversations.html.

O'Reilly, M. (2016, March 15). Statement of Commissioner Michael O'Reilly on the release of the Broadband Consumer Privacy Proposal fact sheet and circulation of item. Retrieved from FCC: http://transition.fcc.gov/Daily_Releases/Daily_Business/2016/db0310/DOC-338166A1.pdf.

OCR. (2016a, March 17). $1.55 million settlement underscores the importance of executing HIPAA business associate agreements. Retrieved from HHS: http://www.hhs.gov/about/news/2016/03/16/155-million-settlement-underscores-importance-executing-hipaa-business-associate-agreements.html#.

OCR. (2016b, February 15). Complaints received by calendar year. Retrieved from HHS: http://www.hhs.gov/hipaa/for-professionals/compliance-enforcement/data/complaints-received-by-calendar-year/index.html.

OCR. (2016c, February 15). Enforcement highlights. Retrieved from OCR: http://www.hhs.gov/hipaa/for-professionals/compliance-enforcement/data/enforcement-highlights/index.html.

OCR. (2016d, February 15). Numbers at a glance. Retrieved from HHS: http://www.hhs.gov/hipaa/for-professionals/compliance-enforcement/data/numbers-glance/index.html.

Office of Inspector General. (2013). *The Office for Civil Rights Did Not Meet All Federal Requirements in Its Oversight and Enforcement of the Health Insurance Portability and Accountability Act Security Rule.* Washington, DC: OIG.

Office of Inspector General. (2016a, February 28). Civil monetary penalties and affirmative exclusions. Retrieved from Office of Inspector General— U.S. Department of Health & Human Services: http://oig.hhs.gov/fraud/enforcement/cmp/index.asp.

Office of Inspector General. (2016b). *Work Plan Fiscal Year 2016.* Washington, DC: U.S. Department of Health and Human Services.

Office of Inspector General: Report A-06-14-00067. (2015, January 26). The Centers for Medicare & Medicaid Services' implementation of security controls over the multidimensional insurance data analytics systems needs improvement. Washington, DC: Office of Inspector General. Retrieved from http://oig.hhs.gov/oas/reports/region6/61400067.pdf.

Office of Management and Budget. (2016, March 28). Federal Chief Information Security Officer. Retrieved from USA Jobs: https://www.usajobs.gov/GetJob/ViewDetails/428904900.

Office of the National Coordinator. (2016, March 29). Patient identification and matching final report. Retrieved from Health IT: https://www.healthit.gov/sites/default/files/patient_identification_matching_final_report.pdf.

Olenick, D. (2016, February 02). NCH Healthcare suffers data breach. Retrieved from *SC Magazine*: http://www.scmagazine.com/nch-healthcare-suffers-data-breach/article/469192/.

Open Minds. (2016a, February 06). Kentucky considering new telemedicine proposal to cover remote patient monitoring in 2016. Retrieved from Open Minds: https://www.openminds.com/market-intelligence/news/718019.htm/.

Open Minds. (2016b, February 06). Missouri considering two new telemedicine proposals to cover remote patient monitoring in 2016. Retrieved from Open Minds: https://www.openminds.com/market-intelligence/news/missouri-considering-two-new-telemedicine-proposals-to-cover-remote-patient-monitoring-in-2016.htm/.

Open Minds. (2016c, February 06). Remote patient monitoring to reach 1.8 million patients by 2017. Retrieved from Open Minds: https://www.openminds.com/market-intelligence/news/021113strat5.htm/.

OPM. (2016a, January 27). Cybersecurity Resource Center. Retrieved from OPM: https://www.opm.gov/cybersecurity/cybersecurity-incidents/.

OPM. (2016b, January 27). Our agency. Retrieved from OPM: https://www.opm.gov/about-us/.

Oregon Legislature. (2016, February 23). Senate Bill 601. Retrieved from Oregon State Legislation: https://olis.leg.state.or.us/liz/2015R1/Downloads/MeasureDocument/SB601/Enrolled.

Ornstein, C. (2016, February 15). Fines remain rare even as health data breaches multiply. Retrieved from ProPublica: http://www.propublica.org/article/fines-remain-rare-even-as-health-data-breaches-multiply.

Osborne, C. (2016, March 12). Cancer clinic warns 2.2 million patients of data breach. Retrieved from ZDNet: http://www.zdnet.com/article/cancer-clinic-warns-2-2-million-patients-of-data-breach/.

OWASP. (2016a, January 21). Welcome to OWASP—Main page. Retrieved from OWASP: https://www.owasp.org/index.php/Main_Page.

OWASP. (2016b, October 10). OWASP Proactive Controls—Top 10 Mapping 2016. Retrieved from https://www.owasp.org/index.php/OWASP_Proactive_Controls#tab=Top_10_Mapping_2016.

Painter, M. (2016, February 13). Cybersecurity predictions: Protecting your digital enterprise. Retrieved from FierceITSecurity: http://www.fierceitsecurity.com/story/cybersecurity-predictions-protecting-your-digital-enterprise/2015-12-31.

Palmer, D. (2016, February 09). Malicious insiders the fastest growing threat to cyber security, warns report. Retrieved from Computing: http://m.computing.co.uk/ctg/news/2442565/malicious-insiders-the-fastest-growing-threat-to-cyber-security-warns-report.

Patterson, A. (2016, February 08). The privacy security forum. Retrieved from *Boston Health Privacy Forum*: http://boston.healthprivacyforum.com/sites/boston.healthprivacyforum.com/files/09%20-%20D2%20-%20The%20High%20Price%20of%20Medical%20Identity%20Theft%20and%20Fraud.pdf.

Paul. (2016, February 02). Doctors still in the dark after electronics records hack exposes data on 4 million. Retrieved from The Security Ledger: https://securityledger.com/2015/07/doctors-still-in-the-dark-after-electronics-records-hack-exposes-data-on-4-million/.

Payne, M. (2016, March 12). Tell Mel: Radiology Regional breach involves 483,000. Retrieved from News-Press: http://www.news-press.com/story/news/2016/02/19/data-breach-radiology-regional-records-lost/80638602/?from=global&sessionKey=&autologin=.

Pennic, F. (2016, February 02). Report: Hackers caused 98% of healthcare data breaches in 2015. Retrieved from HIT Consultant: http://hitconsultant.net/2016/01/28/hackers-caused-98-of-healthcare-data-breaches/.

Peter Elias, M. (2016, February 09). How should errors in the patient medical record be addressed? Retrieved from The Health Care Blog: http://thehealthcareblog.com/blog/2015/12/30/how-should-errors-in-the-patient- medical-record-be-addressed/.

Peters, S. (2016a, February 04). EU, US agree on new data transfer pact, but will it hold? Retrieved from Information Week Darkreading: http://www.darkreading.com/cloud/eu-us-agree-on-new-data-transfer-pact-but-will-it-hold/d/d-id/1324150.

Peters, S. (2016b, February 04). No safe harbor is coming—CISA made sure of it. Retrieved from Information Week Dark Reading: http://www.darkreading.com/threat-intelligence/no-safe-harbor-is-coming—cisa-made-sure-of-it/d/d-id/1323930.

Peterson, A. (2016a, May 16). Why a staggering number of Americans have stopped using the Internet the way they used to. Retrieved from *The Washington Post*: https://www.washingtonpost.com/news/the-switch/wp/2016/05/13/new-government-data-shows-a-staggering-number-of-americans-have-stopped-basic-online-activities/.

Peterson, E. N. (2016b, February 07). Report: Cybercrime and espionage costs $445 billion annually. Retrieved from *The Washington Post*: https://www.washingtonpost.com/world/national-security/report-cybercrime-and-espionage-costs-445-billion-annually/2014/06/08/8995291c-ecce-11e3-9f5c-9075d5508f0a_story.html.

PHE. (2016, March 30). Health care industry cybersecurity task force. Retrieved from Public Health Emergency: http://www.phe.gov/preparedness/planning/CyberTF/Pages/default.aspx.

Philips. (2016a, February 11). Company profile. Retrieved from Philips: http://www.philips.co.uk/a-w/about-philips/company-profile.html.

Philips. (2016b, February 11). Philips responsible disclosure statement. Retrieved from Philips: http://www.philips.com/a-w/security/responsible-disclosure-statement.html.

Pollack, D. (2016a, April 18). It's a new day for payment card fraud liability. Retrieved from ID Experts: https://www2.idexpertscorp.com/blog/single/its-a-new-day-for-payment-card-fraud-liability.

Pollack, R. (2016b, January 24). Letter from the American Hospital Association to Chairman Upton and Ranking Member Pallone. Retrieved from American Hospital Association: http://www.aha.org/advocacy-issues/letter/2015/150710-let-pollack-upton-pallone.pdf.

Ponemon Institute. (2015a). *2015 Cost of Data Breach Study: Global Analysis*. Traverse City, MI: Ponemon Institute.

Ponemon Institute. (2015b). *Fifth Annual Study on Medical Identity Theft*. Traverse City, MI: Ponemon Institute.

Porup, J. (2016, January 30). "Internet of Things" security is hilariously broken and getting worse. Retrieved from Ars Technica: http://arstechnica.com/security/2016/01/how-to-search-the-internet-of-things-for-photos-of-sleeping-babies/.

Powderly, H. (2016, March 11). Andy Slavitt puts meaningful use on ice; Read his J.P. Morgan speech transcript. Retrieved from Healthcare IT News: http://www.healthcareitnews.com/news/andy-slavitt-puts-meaningful-use-ice-read-his-jp-morgan-speech-transcript.

PPAI Publications. (2016, March 19). FTC to study credit card industry data security auditing. Retrieved from PPAI Publications: http://pubs.ppai.org/2016/03/ftc-to-study-credit-card-industry-data-security-auditing/.

Privacy Rights Clearinghouse. (2016, February 07). Fact sheet 17a: Identity theft: What to do if it happens to you. Retrieved from Privacy Rights Clearinghouse: https://www.privacyrights.org/content/identity-theft-what-do-if-it-happens-you.

Ragan, S. (2016, February 16). Ransomware takes Hollywood hospital offline, $3.6M demanded by attackers. Retrieved from CSO Online: http://www.csoonline.com/article/3033160/security/ransomware-takes-hollywood-hospital-offline-36m-demanded-by-attackers.html?token=%23tk.CSONLE_nlt_cso_continuity_recovery_2016-02-15&idg_eid=6df4639b7a08b879102fa300fe06eea8&utm_source=Sailthru&utm_medium=.

Rappleye, E. (2016, February 13). Top 20 healthcare lobbyists by spending. Retrieved from Becker's Hospital CFO: http://www.beckershospitalreview.com/finance/top-20-healthcare-lobbyists-by-spending.html.

Rash, W. (2016a, March 12). Big data analysis makes breaches a greater threat to cyber-security. Retrieved from *eWeek*: http://www.eweek.com/security/big-data-analysis-makes-breaches-a-greater-threat-to-cyber-security.html.

Rash, W. (2016b, March 15). FCC attempts new power grab with privacy regulation proposal. Retrieved from *eWeek*: http://www.eweek.com/cloud/fcc-attempts-new-power-grab-with-privacy-regulation-proposal-2.html.

Raths, D. (2016, May 27). Sixth Annual Ponemon Survey: Criminal attacks cause 50% of breaches. Retrieved from Healthcare Informatics: http://www.healthcare-informatics.com/article/sixth-annual-ponemon-survey-criminal-attacks-cause-50-breaches?utm_source=feedburner&utm_medium=feed&utm_campaign=Feed%3A+healthcare-informatics+%28Healthcare+Informatics%29.

Reuters. (2016, January 27). Big pharma's bet on big data creates opportunities and risks. Retrieved from *The New York Times*: http://www.nytimes.com/reuters/2016/01/26/technology/26reuters-pharmaceuticals-data.html?_r=2.

Robert, S. and Mueller, I. (2016, February 07). *Speeches: RSA Cyber Security Conference*, March 1, 2012. Retrieved from FBI: https://www.fbi.gov/news/speeches/combating-threats-in-the-cyber-world-outsmarting-terrorists-hackers-and-spies.

Roberts, P. (2016, March 15). Judge in anthem case rules that breach harmed patients. Retrieved from *Digital Guardian*: https://digitalguardian.com/blog/judge-anthem-case-rules-breach-harmed-patients.

Robertson, M. R. (2016, January 25). It's way too easy to hack the hospital. Retrieved from *Bloomberg Business*: http://www.bloomberg.com/features/2015-hospital-hack/.

Rys, R. (2016, June 07). The imposter in the ER. Retrieved from *NBC News*: http://www.nbcnews.com/id/23392229%20-%20.V0rfnsv2aRF#.V1dBDpXrvZ4.

Ryssdal, K. (2016, March 12). The new frontier of voter tracking. Retrieved from Marketplace: http://www.marketplace.org/2016/02/10/business/new-frontier-voter-tracking.

Samsung. (2016, February 13). Samsung privacy policy—SmartTV supplement. Retrieved from Samsung: http://www.samsung.com/sg/info/privacy/smarttv.html.

Samuels, J. (2016, January 25). Obama administration modifies HIPAA to strengthen the firearm background check system. Retrieved from HHS.gov: http://www.hhs.gov/blog/2016/01/04/obama-administration-modifies-hipaa.html.

SC Magazine UK. (2016, February 02). 2015 was data protection awareness year. Retrieved from *SC Magazine UK*: http://www.scmagazineuk.com/2015-was-data-protection-awareness-year/article/469165/.

Scanlon, S. A. (2016, February 26). The hunt for cyber security leadership intensifies. Retrieved from LinkedIn: https://www.linkedin.com/pulse/hunt-cyber-security-leadership-intensifies-scott-a-scanlon.

Schneier, B. (2016, March 12). Data is a toxic asset. Retrieved from Schneier on Security: https://www.schneier.com/blog/archives/2016/03/data_is_a_toxic.html?utm_source=twitterfeed&utm_medium=twitter.

Seals, T. (2016, February 01). Large-scale hacks cause 98% of leaked healthcare records. Retrieved from *Info Security Magazine*: http://www.infosecurity-magazine.com/news/largescale-hacks-leaked-healthcare/.

Share Your Story—Medical Errors. (2016, May 29). Retrieved from Safe Patient Project: http://safepatientproject.org/sys-medical_errors.html.

Sheidlower, D. (2016, March 23). The Sanders-Clinton data brouhaha: It is not about privacy and all about identity. Retrieved from Security Current: http://www.securitycurrent.com/en/ciso_journal/ac_ciso_journal/the-sanders-clinton-data-brouhaha-it-is-not-about-privacy-and-all-about-identity#%2EVpRXVdpbNgc%2Elinkedin.

Shin, L. (2016, June 07). What's behind the dramatic rise in medical identity theft? Retrieved from *Fortune*: http://fortune.com/2014/10/19/medical-identity-theft/.

Sidel, R. (2016, March 13). Study finds majority of U.S. companies unprepared for cyber attacks. Retrieved from *The Wall Street Journal*: http://blogs.wsj.com/moneybeat/2016/02/25/study-finds-majority-of-u-s-companies-unprepared-for-cyber-attack/.

Singer, N. (2016, March 25). Why a push for online privacy is bogged down in Washington. Retrieved from *The New York Times*: http://www.nytimes.com/2016/02/29/technology/obamas-effort-on-consumer-privacy-falls-short-critics-say.html?_r=1.

Siwicki, B. (2016, January 21). 8 out of 10 mobile health apps open to HIPAA violations, hacking, data theft. Retrieved from Healthcare IT News: http://www.healthcareitnews.com/news/8-out-10-mobile-health-apps-open-hipaa-violations-hacking-data-theft.

Slavin, L. (2016, March 12). Premier Healthcare notifying 200,000 patients after laptop with PHI stolen from office. Retrieved from Office of Inadequate Security: http://www.databreaches.net/premier-healthcare-notifying-200000-patients-after-laptop-with-phi-stolen-from-office/.

Slavitt, T. (2014, January 24). Andy Slavitt puts meaningful use on ice; Read his J.P. Morgan speech transcript. Retrieved from Healthcare IT News: http://www.healthcareitnews.com/news/andy-slavitt-puts-meaningful-use-ice-read-his-jp-morgan-speech-transcript.

Smith, R. C. (2016, April 11). Final HIPAA Rule will regulate business associates, change HIPAA breach notification obligations. Retrieved from Dorsey: https://www.dorsey.com/newsresources/publications/2013/01/final-hipaa-rule-will-regulate-business-associat__.

Snell, E. (2016a, January 24). Health data sharing bill passes house in 344-77 vote. Retrieved from Health IT Security: http://healthitsecurity.com/news/health-data-sharing-bill-passes-house-in-344-70-vote.

Snell, E. (2016b, April 04). Healthcare cybersecurity pushed in EHNAC, NH-ISAC agreement. Retrieved from Health IT Security: http://healthitsecurity.com/news/healthcare-cybersecurity-pushed-in-ehnac-nh-isac-agreement.

Snell, E. (2016c, January 24). How health data sharing relates to healthcare privacy. Retrieved from Health IT Security: http://healthitsecurity.com/news/how-health-data-sharing-relates-to-healthcare-privacy.

Snell, E. (2016d, March 16). How recent Senate HELP bills affect healthcare data security. Retrieved from Health IT Security: http://healthitsecurity.com/news/how-recent-senate-help-bills-affect-healthcare-data-security.

Snell, E. (2016e, March 13). Ponemon: Healthcare cyber attack averages one per month. Retrieved from Health IT Security: http://healthitsecurity.com/news/ponemon-healthcare-cyber-attack-averages-one-per-month.

Snell, E. (2016f, February 12). What are top HIPAA compliance concerns, obstacles? Retrieved from Health IT Security: http://healthitsecurity.com/news/what-are-top-hipaa-compliance-concerns-obstacles.

Snell, E. (2016g, February 12). Why healthcare data security is no longer "just an IT issue". Retrieved from Health IT Security: http://healthitsecurity.com/news/why-healthcare-data-security-is-no-longer-just-an-it-issue.

Snider, S. (2016, February 12). HIPAA breaches—Explosive growth, but fundamentals still matter. Retrieved from Linkedin: https://www.linkedin.com/pulse/hipaa-breaches-explosive-growth-fundamentals-still-matter-snider.

Solove, D. J. (2002). Digital dossiers and the dissipation of fourth amendment privacy. *Southern California Law Review* Volume 75 (1083), 1084–1167.

Solove, D. (2016a, March 19). The 5 things every privacy lawyer needs to know about the FTC: An interview with Chris Hoofnagle. Retrieved from LinkedIn Post: https://www.linkedin.com/pulse/5-things-every-privacy-lawyer-needs-know-ftc-interview-daniel-solove.

Solove, D. (2016b, March 21). The Hulk Hogan Gawker sex video case, free speech, and the verdict's impact. Retrieved from LinkedIn: https://www.linkedin.com/pulse/hulk-hogan-gawker-sex-video-case-free-speech-verdicts-daniel-solove.

Solove, D. (2016c, February 17). Without Scalia, will there be a 4th Amendment revolution? Retrieved from LinkedIn: https://www.linkedin.com/pulse/without-scalia-4th-amendment-revolution-daniel-solove.

Solove, D. J. (2016d, March 21). The Gawker-Hulk Hogan case shows not all truth has the same value. Retrieved from *The New York Times*: http://www. nytimes.com/roomfordebate/2016/03/18/should-the-gawker-hulk-hogan-jurors-decide-whats-newsworthy/the-gawker-hulk-hogan-case-shows-not-all-truth-has-the-same-value.

Sophos. (2016, April 06). The state of encryption today. Retrieved from Sophos: https://secure2.sophos.com/en-us/medialibrary/Gated%20Assets/white%20papers/the-state-of-encryption-today-wpna.pdf.

State of Florida. (2016, January 29). Constitution of the State of Florida. Retrieved from State of Florida: http://www.leg.state.fl.us/statutes/index.cfm?submenu=3#A1S23.

Stempel, J. (2016, March 05). FTC has power to policy cyber security: Appeals court. Retrieved from Reuters: http://www.reuters.com/article/us-wyndham-ftc-cybersecurity-idUSKCN0QT1UP20150824.

Storhm, C. (2016, March 12). Your smartphone knows who you are and what you're doing. Retrieved from Bloomberg Business: http://www.bloomberg.com/news/articles/2016-02-29/your-smartphone-knows-who-you-are-and-what-you-re-doing.

Taylor, H. (2016, February 09). An inside look at what's driving the hacking economy. Retrieved from CNBC: http://www.cnbc.com/2016/02/05/an-inside-look-at-whats-driving-the-hacking-economy.html.

Texas State Legislature. (2016, February 25). Health and Safety Code: Title 2, Subtitle 1, Chapter 181 Medical Records Privacy. Retrieved from Texas State Regulations: http://www.statutes.legis.state.tx.us/Docs/HS/htm/HS.181.htm#181.001.

Thalen, M. (2016, February 06). Hackers allegedly hijack drone after massive breach at NASA. Retrieved from Infowars: http://www.infowars.com/hackers-allegedly-hijack-drone-after-massive-breach-at-nasa/.

The Advisory Board Company. (2016, May 15). Misidentifying patients is an $8 billion problem—and the government can't fix it. Retrieved from The Advisory Board Company: https://www.advisory.com/daily-briefing/2016/02/02/misidentifying-patients-is-an-8-billion-problem.

The American Legion. (2014, January 25). Legion to White House: "Gun order must protect vets seeking treatment". Retrieved from *The American Legion*: http://www.legion.org/pressrelease/230792/legion-white-house-%E2%80%98gun-order-must-protect-vets-seeking-treatment%E2%80%99.

The Daily Dot. (2016, April 15). Burr-Feinstein encryption bill. Retrieved from Scribd: https://www.scribd.com/doc/308408743/Burr-Feinstein-Encryption-Bill.

The Economist. (2016, February 08). Health-care fraud: The $272 billion swindle. Retrieved from *The Economist*: http://www.economist.com/news/united-states/21603078-why-thieves-love-americas-health-care-system-272-billion-swindle.

The Glider: A Universal Hacker Emblem. (2016, June 07). Retrieved from http://www.catb.org/hacker-emblem/.

The National Cybersecurity Center of Excellence. (2016, April 13). About the center. Retrieved from The National Cybersecurity Center for Excellence: https://nccoe.nist.gov/about_the_center.

The White House. (2016, March 25). Consumer data privacy in a networked world: A framework for protecting privacy and promoting innovation in the global digital economy. Retrieved from White House: https://www.whitehouse.gov/sites/default/files/privacy-final.pdf.

Thompson, C. (2016, April 03). Don't let the fox guard the henhouse: Protect your sensitive data from the insider threat. Retrieved from Security Intelligence: https://securityintelligence.com/dont-let-the-fox-guard-the-henhouse-protect-your-sensitive-data-from-the-insider-threat/.

Thycotic. (2015). *Black Hat 2015: Hacker Survey Report*. Thycotic.

Thycotic. (2016, February 01). Hackers confirm an alarming lack of protection for privileged accounts. Retrieved from Thycotic: https://thycotic.com/resources/black-hat-2015-survey/.

Tuma, S. E. (2016, April 13). The #1 reason NIST cybersecurity framework is becoming the standard. Retrieved from Cybersecurity Business Law: https://shawnetuma.com/2016/02/13/the-1-reason-nist-cybersecurity-framework-is-the-standard-of-care/.

U.S. Department of Health & Human Services. (2016, February 28). Business associate contracts. Retrieved from HHS.gov: http://www.hhs.gov/hipaa/for-professionals/covered-entities/sample-business-associate-agreement-provisions/index.html.

US-CERT. (2016, April 05). Alert (TA16-091A)—Ransomware and recent variants. Retrieved from US-CERT—Department of Homeland Security: https://www.us-cert.gov/ncas/alerts/TA16-091A.

Vaishali Patel, P. H. (2016, March 22). Trends in individuals' perceptions regarding privacy and security of medical records and exchange in health information: 2012–2014. Retrieved from Health IT: https://www.healthit.gov/sites/default/files/briefs/privacy-and-security-trends-data-brief-21616.pdf.

Vargas, J. A. (2016, January 29). The face of Facebook. Retrieved from *The New Yorker*: http://www.newyorker.com/magazine/2010/09/20/the-face-of-facebook.

Veracode. (2016, January 25). State of application security in healthcare. Retrieved from Veracode: https://info.veracode.com/whitepaper-state-of-web-and-mobile-application-security-in-healthcare.html.

Vinton, K. (2016, February 02). Premera Blue Cross breach may have exposed 11 million customers' medical and financial data. Retrieved from *Forbes*: http://www.forbes.com/sites/katevinton/2015/03/17/11-million-customers-medical-and-financial-data-may-have-been-exposed-in-premera-blue-cross-breach/#106624d2143c.

Violino, B. (2016, April 26). Overcoming stubborn execs for security sake. Retrieved from CSO Online: http://www.csoonline.com/article/3019794/data-protection/overcoming-stubborn-execs-for-security-sake.html#tk.twt_cso.

Volkow, D. N. (2016, February 09). From the director: Prescription drug abuse. Retrieved from National Institute on Drug Abuse: http://www.drugabuse.gov/publications/research-reports/prescription-drugs/director.

Waddell, K. (2016, April 07). The long and winding history of encryption. Retrieved from *The Atlantic*: http://www.theatlantic.com/technology/archive/2016/01/the-long-and-winding-history-of-encryption/423726/.

Waldman, C. O. (2016, February 15). Few consequences for health privacy law's repeat offenders. Retrieved from ProPublica: http://www.propublica.org/article/few-consequences-for-health-privacy-law-repeat-offenders.

Weisman, S. (2016, February 06). What the IRS isn't telling you about identity theft. Retrieved from *USA Today*: http://www.usatoday.com/story/money/columnist/2016/01/30/what-irs-isnt-telling-you-identity-theft/79306984/.

Wheeler, T. (2016, March 15). Chairman wheeler's proposal to give broadband consumers increased choice, transparency & security with respect to their data. Retrieved from FCC: http://transition.fcc.gov/Daily_Releases/Daily_Business/2016/db0310/DOC-338159A1.pdf.

Wikipedia. (2016a, January 29). Boiling frog. Retrieved from Wikipedia: https://en.wikipedia.org/wiki/Boiling_frog.

Wikipedia. (2016b, February 13). Constructive ambiguity. Retrieved from Wikipedia: https://en.wikipedia.org/wiki/Constructive_ambiguity.

Wilber, D. Q. (2016, March 14). Imprisoned identity-fraud kingpin shares secrets of his scams. Retrieved from Bloomberg Politics: http://www.bloomberg.com/politics/articles/2016-03-07/imprisoned-identity-fraud-kingpin-shares-secrets-of-his-scams.

Winton, M. H. (2016, May 02). The government wants your fingerprint to unlock your phone. Should that be allowed? Retrieved from *Los Angeles Times*: http://www.latimes.com/local/california/la-me-iphones-fingerprints-20160430-story.html.

Wolin, R. M. (2016, May 27). Debt collector for affiliated physician group can rely on patient contact consent obtained by hospital. Retrieved from BakerHostetler—Health Law Update: http://www.healthlawupdate.com/2016/03/debt-collector-for-affiliated-physician-group-can-rely-on-patient-contact-consent-obtained-by-hospital/.

Wong, J. I. (2016, March 31). One in five employees would sell their work passwords, some for less than $100. Retrieved from Quartz: http://qz.com/649996/one-in-five-employees-would-sell-their-work-passwords-some-for-less-than-100/.

Wyden, R. (2016, May 02). Wyden: Congress must reject sprawling expansion of government surveillance. Retrieved from Ron Wyden Senator for Oregon: https://www.wyden.senate.gov/news/press-releases/wyden-congress-must-reject-sprawling-expansion-of-government-surveillance.

Yoder, E. (2016, January 31). Pentagon to take over control of background investigation information. Retrieved from *The Washington Post*: https://www.washingtonpost.com/news/federal-eye/wp/2016/01/22/pentagon-to-take-over-control-of-background-investigation-information/.

Zeidel, K. M. (2016, March 11). Massachusetts Court: Patients have standing to sue for data breach based on data exposure alone. Retrieved from Privacy & Security Matters: https://www.privacyandsecuritymatters.com/2016/01/massachusetts-court-patients-have-standing-to-sue-for-data-breach-based-on-data-exposure-alone/.

Zetter, K. (2016a, February 20). California now has the nation's best digital privacy law. Retrieved from *Wired*: http://www.wired.com/2015/10/california-now-nations-best-digital-privacy-law/.

Zetter, K. (2016b, February 09). NSA hacker chief explains how to keep him out of your system. Retrieved from *Wired*: http://www.wired.com/2016/01/nsa-hacker-chief-explains-how-to-keep-him-out-of-your-system/.

Zieger, A. (2016, February 06). Security concerns threaten mobile health app deployment. Retrieved from EMR and HIPAA: http://www.emrandhipaa.com/katherine/2016/01/26/security-concerns-threaten-mobile-health-app-deployment/.

Zorz, Z. (2016, April 08). Healthcare industry has an alarming mobile security gap. Retrieved from Help Net Security: https://www.helpnetsecurity.com/2016/04/07/healthcare-industry-mobile-security-gap/.

Index

Printed and bound by CPI Group (UK) Ltd, Croydon, CR0 4YY

23/10/2024

01777961-0001